Security, Development, and Violence in Afghanistan

Security, Development, and Violence in Afghanistan provides a unique insight into the lived realities of the international intervention in Afghanistan and highlights the diversity, relationships, and interdependence of various groups including both external actors and Afghan communities. Analysis of the international intervention in Afghanistan following the post 9/11 invasion in 2001, one of the largest and most expensive in history, tends to focus on the perspective of organisational dynamics and policies or external actors. Drawing on the author's five years of experience living, researching and working in Afghanistan, this book uses ethnographic methodologies to explore the micro-level interactions between different actors, showing how communities, local leaders, aid workers, UN officials, military and others navigated shifting security, development, and conflict dynamics.

Starting with a contextual introduction to the intervention and the key debates surrounding it, this book goes on to explore the stories of security, development, and violence as constructed through official policy discourse, and then through the lived experiences of interveners and local actors. The book weaves a compelling narrative which links local and global issues and focuses on the everyday practices, relationships and acts of resistance which take place in two provinces of Afghanistan. Finally, the author highlights what this book's findings mean both for what we know about Afghanistan and for how we understand international interventions and the everyday dynamics between actors who live and work in spaces of conflict.

Security, Development, and Violence in Afghanistan: Everyday Stories of Intervention will be of considerable interest to scholars and professionals with an interest in Afghanistan, aid work, humanitarian intervention, development studies, and peace and conflict studies.

Althea-Maria Rivas is a Lecturer at the School of African and Oriental Studies (SOAS), University of London in Development Studies. Her work focuses on the politics of violence, humanitarian intervention, post-conflict reconstruction, and transitional justice. Her academic work is complemented by 12 years of professional experience in diplomacy, development, gender relations, and equality and humanitarian action in Central Asia and East and West Africa.

Routledge Explorations in Development Studies

This Development Studies series features innovative and original research at the regional and global scale. It promotes interdisciplinary scholarly works drawing on a wide spectrum of subject areas, in particular politics, health, economics, rural and urban studies, sociology, environment, anthropology, and conflict studies.

Topics of particular interest are globalisation; emerging powers; children and youth; cities; education; media and communication; technology development; and climate change.

In terms of theory and method, rather than basing itself on any orthodoxy, the series draws broadly on the tool kit of the social sciences in general, emphasising comparison, the analysis of the structure and processes, and the application of qualitative and quantitative methods.

Practices of Citizenship in East Africa
Perspectives from Philosophical Pragmatism
Edited by Katariina Holma and Tiina Kontinen

Political Financing in Developing Countries
A Case from Ghana
Joseph Luna

Dilemmas of Regional and Local Development
Edited by Jerzy Bański

Security, Development and Violence in Afghanistan
Everyday Stories of Intervention
Althea-Maria Rivas

Economic Development in Ghana and Malaysia
A Comparative Analysis
Samuel K. Andoh, Bernice J. deGannes Scott, and Grace Ofori-Abebrese

Security, Development, and Violence in Afghanistan

Everyday Stories of Intervention

Althea-Maria Rivas

Routledge
Taylor & Francis Group
LONDON AND NEW YORK

First published 2020
by Routledge
4 Park Square, Milton Park, Abingdon, Oxon OX14 4RN
605 Third Avenue, New York, NY 10017

First issued in paperback 2023

Routledge is an imprint of the Taylor & Francis Group, an informa business

British Library Cataloguing-in-Publication Data
A catalogue record for this book is available from the British Library

Library of Congress Cataloging-in-Publication Data
Names: Rivas, Althea-Maria, author.
Title: Security, development and violence in Afghanistan : everyday stories of intervention / Althea-Maria Rivas.
Description: New York: Routledge, 2020. | Series: Routledge explorations in development studies | Includes bibliographical references and index.
|Identifiers: LCCN 2019056538 (print) | LCCN 2019056539 (ebook) | ISBN 9781138234642 (hardback) | ISBN 9781315306438 (ebook)
Subjects: LCSH: Internal security–Afghanistan. | Postwar reconstruction–Afghanistan. | Economic development–Afghanistan. | Terrorism–Afghanistan–Prevention. Classification: LCC HV8242.6.A3 R58 2020 (print) | LCC HV8242.6.A3 (ebook) | DDC 363.3209581–dc23
LC record available at https://lccn.loc.gov/2019056538
LC ebook record available at https://lccn.loc.gov/2019056539

ISBN: 978-1-03-256995-6 (pbk)
ISBN: 978-1-138-23464-2 (hbk)
ISBN: 978-1-315-30643-8 (ebk)

DOI: 10.4324/9781315306438

Typeset in Times New Roman
by Wearset Ltd, Boldon, Tyne and Wear

Publisher's Note
The publisher has gone to great lengths to ensure the quality of this reprint but points out that some imperfections in the original copies may be apparent.

Always for Kathleen and Alriguez

Contents

Illustrations

Figure

Tables

Acknowledgements

The writing of this book has taken several years since the findings from the research project were first compiled into a doctoral thesis. The journey was enabled through the support and encouragement of many people. I would like to thank all of the people who shared their perspectives and stories with me, and who gave freely of their time. Their candour and cooperation allowed me to gain great insights into the questions that I was exploring, their everyday realities, and my own experiences. This research could not have taken place without the assistance of the organisations in Afghanistan who hosted me during my time there. I am indebted to my research team Wais, Abdul, and Naila, whose friendship, reflections, and humour were invaluable throughout my time in Afghanistan. I would like to thank my family and friends who assisted, advised, and supported this project intellectually and emotionally. In particular, I would like to express my enormous gratitude to Divya Toila-Kelley for her encouragement to get this *done*, and to Falana Huggins, Caroline Falaiye, Sui-Mee Chan, Natasha Gordon-Chipembre, and Nadya Ali who were never too busy to review a chapter, provide honest feedback and make me laugh, and for their excellent proofreading skills. Special thanks go to Roger Saul for his constant reassurance, friendship, and intellectual engagement over the last two decades and to Ruth Saul for always being a bright light and a source of warmth and encouragement. Finally, to Kathleen, Rodriguez, and Alriguez Rivas, thank you for everything.

Abbreviations

3D	Development, Diplomacy, and Defense
ACAP	Afghanistan Civilian Assistance Programme
ACBAR	Agency Coordinating Body for Afghan Relief and Development
ACSFO	Afghanistan Civil Society Forum Organization
AOG	Anti-Government Groups
ANA	Afghan National Army
ANDS	Afghan National Development Strategy
ANP	Afghan National Police
APB	Afghanistan Programming Body
ARD	Association for Rural Development
AREU	Afghanistan Research and Evaluation Unit
ASG	Afghanistan Support Group
AWN	Afghan Women's Network
CIA	Central Intelligence Agency
CDC	Community Development Council
CDP	Community Development Plan
CDP-K	Community Development Program – Kabul
CMWG	Civil–Military Working Group
CoP	Chief of Party
CRS	Catholic Relief Services
DA	District Administrator
DAI	Development Alternatives International
DCoP	Deputy Chief of Police
DDA	District Development Assembly
DDR	Demobilisation, Disarmament and Reintegration
DFID	Department for International Development
DPKO	Department of Peacekeeping Operations
DSRSG	Deputy Special Representative of the Secretary General
ESC	Executive Steering Committee
FOB	Forward Operating Bases
GoIRA	Government of the Islamic Republic of Afghanistan
GWOT	Global War on Terror
HC	Humanitarian Coordinator

ICC	International Criminal Court
IDA	International Development Association
IOM	International Organisation for Migration
IPA	International Peace Academy
IRD	International Reconstruction and Development
ISAF	International Security Assistance Force
JICA	Japan International Cooperation Agency
LAS	Land Allocation Schemes
LGC	Local Governance and Community Development
MoD	Ministry of Defense
MoE	Ministry of Education
MoF	Ministry of Finance
MoFA	Ministry of Foreign Affairs
MRR	Ministry of Refugees and Reparations
MRRD	Ministry of Rural Rehabilitation and Development
NATO	North Atlantic Treaty Organisation
NGO	Non-Governmental Organisation
NRC	Norwegian Refugee Committee
NSP	National Solidarity Program
OCHA	Office for the Coordination of Humanitarian Affairs
ODA	Official Development Assistance
OEF	Operation Enduring Freedom
PDC	Provincial Development Committee
PRA	Participatory Rural Appraisal
PRT	Provincial Reconstruction Team
PSC	Private Security Companies
QIP	Quick Impact Projects
R2P	Responsibility to Protect
RC	Resident Coordinator
SCR	Senior Civilian Representative
SFA	Strategic Framework for Afghanistan
SRSG	Special Representative of the Secretary General
SWABAC	South-West Afghanistan Balochistan Association for Co-ordination
SSR	Security Sector Reform
TCN	Third Country Nationals
UK	United Kingdom
UN	United Nations
UNAMA	United Nations Assistance Mission in Afghanistan
UNOCA	United Nations Operations Centre in Afghanistan
UNCT	United Nations Country Team
UNDP	United Nations Development Programme
UNICEF	United Nations Children's Fund
UNOCHA	United Nations Office for the Co-ordination of Humanitarian Affairs

UNOPS	United Nations Office for Project Services
US	United States of America
WFP	World Food Programme
WWII	World War II

Introduction

The intervention in Afghanistan has not gone well. While opinions regarding the reasons for the violence and chaos that has taken hold of Afghanistan since the beginning of the US-led intervention in October 2001 may vary, one would be hard-pressed to find advocates willing to claim its success. No stranger to occupation, violence, and international experimentation, the country has been for many years, the object of securitisation and development attempts by an apparatus of foreign nations, international organisations, and aid agencies. Since 2001, these attempts have accelerated, intensified, and become the focus of worldwide attention. Indeed, in the post 9/11 era Afghanistan has been a testing ground for different approaches and strategies of an intervention, rooted in the logics of the liberal peace, which consistently invokes the maxim, 'There will be no development without security and no security without development' (UN Secretary General Office [UNSG], 2005, Annex para. 2). Events in the 1990s and 2000s led to a re-conceptualisation of the two concepts as inextricably linked and henceforth, the evocation of a 'security–development nexus' that has gained increased interest in policy and academic literature. Despite widespread critique of the practices of international intervention, the validation of the liberal peace paradigm, and the security-development nexus which underpins it persist in policy circles. The post-9/11 experiment in Afghanistan, however, has raised important questions about the relationship between development and conflict, and the consequences of intervention for *the interveners* and *the intervened* that this volume will explore. Based on fieldwork undertaken there and in North America and Europe, it revisits Afghanistan in the four-year period between 2010 and 2013, and aims to unravel the contradictions of the intervention. A nuanced, intimate and yet troubling picture of security, development, and violence in Afghanistan emerges through the seemingly ordinary, mundane, and interconnected everyday practices, relationships and emotions presented in this book. These stories provide important insights into the lived experience of intervention and the ways in which global politics are played out in everyday spaces.

Thinking about development, security, and intervention

A rethink about development and security took place in the wider context of the growth and acceptance of the *liberal peace paradigm* as the dominant organising principle for Western foreign policy and peacebuilding interventions. The linkage of security and development, however, is not new. For example, both were central themes in projects of foreign intervention and expansion and were central to colonial expansion, and as a rationale for the Marshall Plan and during the Cold War (Hearath, 2009). The radicalisation of development and the re-problematisation of security (Duffield, 2001), in the post-Cold War era, however, led to their explicit and urgent linkage, and represented a shift in international discourse and practice. No longer parallel pursuits, the now 'inextricably linked concepts' (UNSG, 2005) are commonly referred to as the *security–development nexus*, which suggests that development is the foundation of security, and security the precondition for development. There is little debate about the centrality of the nexus in international policy (UNSG, 2004, 2005; OECD, 2010, 2018; World Bank, 2011, 2018; European Commission, 2017). The blurring and convergence of development and security brought together previously distinctive policy areas, sets of actors, and organisations in efforts to build peace, in *so-called fragile states* (Call, 2008) located mainly in the Global South, through social, political, and economic transformation. Indeed, the security–development nexus is at the root of the liberal peace paradigm, which forms the guiding framework for external engagement in post-conflict reconstruction and internationally supported peacebuilding interventions.

Development as a concept was initially given meaning through particular geographical imaginaries. The mapping of the world in the name of development was very much influenced by the 'scramble for Africa', the trans-Atlantic slave trade and other colonial enterprises in the 18th and 19th centuries. Scholars, amongst others, have documented the history of development thought and practice in the colonial period, and its literal translation into development theory in a post-colonial world (Leys, 1996; Cooper, 2005; Kothari, 2005). During the 19th century similar ideals were contained in the French policy of constructive exploitation[1] (Hoodge and Hodl, 2014) and the British Empire's constructive imperialism policy[2] (Green, 1999). Such policies suggested a softer form of imperialism where extraction occurred alongside more altruistic-themed social programming. The constructed divisions that justified the colonial project were reproduced in development discourse, as the populations in the Global South (constructed as primitive and backwards), were mapped on to the new development-speak, and became the underdeveloped and the poor.

In the 1940s, however, 'development' emerged as a specific international project, focusing on the condition of poverty mainly in the colonial and post-colonial worlds. Early initiatives centred on the idea of progress, and were based on modernisation theories which framed development as a distinctly linear evolutionary process (Lewis, 1954; Rostow, 1960). In the 1960s and 1970s, state-led economic growth and development theories grew in popularity. Powerful critiques of the linear and market-based approaches to development had emerged in the 1950s, 1960s, and 1970s from dependency (Singer, [1950] 1975; Prescibch, 1950; Rodney, 1972; Frank, 1996, 1977), and world systems theorists (Wallerstein, 1974; Amin *et al.*, 1982). Despite this, the prominence of market-led approaches grew and were realised in the structural adjustment policies of the 1970s and 1980s. These trickle-down economic theories, however, met rising opposition in both the developed and developing world in the 1980s, the devastating effects of structural adjustment, which drove many countries deeper into debt and poverty, became apparent. This impasse gave rise to both a search for development alternatives and a rejection of the development project as a whole.

Scholars and policymakers proposed different ways of understanding and assessing development in the Global South, including human-centred development (United Nations Development Program [UNDP], 1990), and rights-based development (UN, 1997; Sen, 1999), and participatory development (Chambers, 1994). The new approaches attempted to redefine development objectives and practices and focused on alternative agents of development such as non-governmental organisations (NGOs) and communities, rather than states and large international organisations. The language of development expanded to include concepts such as freedom, capabilities, and self-reliance. Post-development, post-colonial, and decolonial scholars, however, argued that it was not possible to simply reform a project that was borne from colonialism and rooted in global inequalities (Nandy, 1989; Escobar, 1995, 2000; Rahemana and Bawtree, 1997; Sachs, 1992, Mohanty, 1984). Therefore, the only option was a rejection of development, the development industry, and its practices. The new post-Cold War strategies, still used by development agencies today, were essentially rooted in the same knowledge–power dynamics of early development initiatives which operated on a vision that the underdeveloped Global South was dependent upon resources and solutions held by the Global North, which also represented the standard upon which the 'poor and backwards' should model themselves.

In the 1990s, *human security* emerged on the development scene. The human security agenda was in part an attempt by development actors at the end of the Cold War, to shift resources that had previously been dedicated to the military to the development sector, suggesting that greater investment in the development sector would reduce conflict (MacFarlene and Khong, 2006, pp. 171–172). The UNDP (1994) describes human security as: 'safety from chronic threats such as hunger, disease and repression, and protection from sudden and hurtful disruptions in the patterns of daily life – whether in homes, in jobs, or in communities' (pp. 20–23). The UN version of human security included two components: freedom from want, which envisions security as a human entitlement tied to the concepts of human development and human rights; and freedom from fear, including direct violence and armed conflict emerged (UNDP, 1994). Through this broad lens, human development concerns and entitlements were re-framed as indispensable for the security of the individual and conflicts were themselves argued as having huge costs in terms of missed development opportunities and causing low indexes of human development. A series of international reports and academic articles in the 1990s and 2000s discussed the indivisibility of security, economic development, and human freedom (UNDP, 1994, 2004;

UNSG, 2005; Jolly and Ray, 2007). Consequently, poverty was removed from its prime position in the development discourse as the expanded notion of development needed to address insecurity and state fragility to promote human security. While international aid has always been linked to Western foreign policy, as international agencies and INGOs pursued human security, the prioritising of foreign policy agendas became more explicit and legitimised and the development agendas of partner governments, and other national and local organisations began to move even further from consideration that had already been the case (Beall, Goodfellow, and Putzel, 2006).

In the late 1990s, as the first decade after the Cold War was coming to a close policymakers and scholars alike were debating what they perceived to be the changing character of organised violence and war. Intra-state rather than inter-state conflicts became the dominant security challenge of the time. Various terms emerged which attempted to describe the 21st-century conflicts including – wars of the third kind, post-modern wars, privatised wars, and networked wars (Holsti, 1996; Hables, 1997; Duffield, 2002). Important amongst them, was the concept of *new wars* (Kaldor, 1999; Munkler, 2004). The new wars – often located in areas labelled by international organisations and donor governments as *fragile or failed* which remains a contentious term (Call, 2008) – were argued to involve 'different logics (methods, goals, actors and forms of financing) than the wars of the 20th century' (Kaldor, 2013, pp. 3–6). They were increasingly violent, targeted the civilian populations, and blurred the lines between and 'non-state, public and private, external and internal … and even war and peace' (p. 2). Though heavily contested (see Kalyvas, 2001; Berdal, 2003; Newman, 2004) the new wars concept has maintained reverence in policy and academic circles.

Traditionally security was understood as being state-centric and focused externally on issues such as military threat and territorial integrity (Waltz, 1979). The perceived shift from inter to intra-state war contributed to a new post-Cold War security agenda in which states maintained their importance but the way scholars and policymakers began to think about the actors and the issues discussed under the umbrella of security changed. The resultant security agenda included new referent objects of analysis that were non-state entities, such as transnational networks, communities and individuals, and securitised issues that had not previously been considered under the domain of security (Buzan, Wæver, and de Wilde, 1998). The new non-traditional security threats included immigration and border security, cybersecurity, and terrorism, but also environmental decline, natural disasters, poverty, diseases, and resource scarcity (Andersen, 2012). Consequently, underdevelopment, sickness, and disaster were now discussed not only as threats to the state itself, but to individual and international security.

The shifts in the development and security communities at the end of the Cold War contributed to two troubling trends which linked security and development in more explicit ways. The *securitisation of development* placed security concerns at the centre of the development initiatives rather than the individual and the *developmentalisation of security* increasingly framed development concerns in the language of security. Within development circles individual well-being was increasingly tied to international security, as *doing development* become part of preventing and *resolving conflict and achieving security*. An expanding Western development agenda began to gradually place more attention on state-building, seen as a principal development concern that was equally, if not more, important than other issues, and development organisations began to coherently integrate conflict resolution and post-conflict reconstruction, security sector reform reforms, and good governance into programming (DANIDA, 2004; DFID, 2005; OECD, 2007b, 2008). Conversely, security actors began engaging in areas previously seen as falling under the domain of the UN and aid agencies to address the new security challenges and using development assistance as a tool for conflict prevention. A common example of this trend is the incorporation of infrastructure development, livelihoods training, and even gender equality as part of military campaigns to win hearts and minds in Iraq and Afghanistan.

After 9/11, the failed states discourse gained renewed prominence as Afghanistan's harbouring of al-Qaeda was constructed as a prime example of the potential danger of state failure. In their prescriptive book the current Afghan President Ashraf Ghani and Lockhart (2008) argued,

> that 9/11 and the subsequent attacks showed, people in prosperous states can no longer take the security of their daily lives for granted. This problem – the failed state – is at the heart of a worldwide systemic crisis that constitutes the most serious challenge to global stability in the new millennium
>
> (p. 4)

The so-called failed state described both the 'main security challenge of our time' (Gates, 2010) and 'the toughest development challenge of our era' (Zoellick, 2008), became a rallying point for the impetus to embark on liberal peacebuilding interventions.

The liberal peace logic suggests that certain types of societies that adopt certain norms and institutions will be more peaceful internally and in their relations with other states. Peace in this view is predicated on the adoption of social, economic, and political norms and institutions that conform to a mixture of liberal and neo-liberal international expectations. In particular, democratic and market-driven institutions are seen as mutually reinforcing basic foundations for peaceful societies (Paris, 2010; Fukuyama, 2004). *Liberal peacebuilding* aims to expand Western-centred market-based democratic zones of peace through a range of diverse policies, structures, programmes, and practices in areas such as democracy promotion, the rule of law and good governance, promotion of human rights, economic reform, and privatisation. The reconceptualisation of security and development, at the heart of the liberal peacebuilding agenda, necessitates the transformation of so-called fragile states to fit into liberal norms and expectations (Zaum, 2012). The need and urgency for an international response was heightened by the construction of underdevelopment and (in)security as global problems. Intervention, therefore, was constructed in international policy as beneficial to both the local populations and foreign nations representing the best way forward for producing relevant and coherent policies, and as necessary for addressing the issues facing fragile states and ensuring human and global security (Picciotto, 2004; OECD, 2007a, 2010). This logic was an important part of the justification for the large-scale international interventions, which took different forms, that were launched in the late 1990s and early 2000s in Bosnia and Kosovo, East Timor, Haiti, and Iraq and Afghanistan.

The key components of this post-Cold War intervention toolbox are carried out around the world by foreign governments, international organisations, multilateral donors, and an array of non-state actors. Intervention or international intervention, in this book, refers to the full spectrum of international responses which include a military, aid, humanitarian, peacebuilding, social development, governance, and public sector reform initiatives policies and programming to so-called complex crisis or emergencies, in which there are multiple causes, narratives and past and present trajectories often but not always located in the Global South (Smirl, 2015). An anticipated critique, particularly for humanitarian scholars, might be the need for more specification of the concept as intervention itself can take different forms and is often used interchangeably with terms such as invasion. Important debates have taken place which have attempted to categorise external involvement in so-called *fragile states* according to the different types of actors or agendas involved, military vs. humanitarian, development vs. humanitarian, or peacebuilding vs. state-building (Goodhand and Sedra, 2013; Donini, 2011). Indeed, the resistance and denial of this persistent reality amongst interveners is a key theme in the book. In practice, however, and specifically in the context of post 9/11 Afghanistan, these are spaces where multiple actors and agendas meet and are intimately connected in a complex web that they themselves find difficult to comprehend. To separate agencies or groups neatly into silos would do a disservice to the realities which I observed during the research for this volume and the perspectives shared with me, in particular by the local district residents.

The underlying logic of the liberal peace model suggests that the achievement of peace is predicated upon societal re-engineering. Therefore, the argument follows that the social, political, and economic environment of countries in the Global South are in and of themselves the root cause of the seemingly unbreakable cycles of violence and poverty. Furthermore, justification for intervention is accelerated by arguing that the local ‘problems’ in these ‘unkept’ nations are global threats (Duffield, 2010) and that if they cannot be civilised, which is never really possible within the (neo)colonial mindset (Bhabha, 1994), they must be contained. Ultimately, continued investment in security–development nexus logic provides a justification for the liberal intervention experiment in so-called failed states, arguing that through these means, local and global security and development will be ensured. These international efforts, however, have rarely resulted in increased stability or peace (Richmond, 2011). As security and development are constructs and cannot be removed from the global matrices of power in which they are defined and then enacted.

Given the shifts in the international security and development agendas, wide acceptance of liberal peace model, the growth in the number of international interventions since the 1990s and the impact of 9/11 it is not difficult to see why there have been calls for a better understanding of security and development. Attempts to redefine and broaden the definitions of security and development and their resultant relationship, however, have not necessarily been based on an increased understanding of the multiple realities on the ground, or theoretical advancements in this area. In particular, the devasting effects of international intervention in Iraq and Afghanistan have happened alongside growing critiques by scholars of liberal peacebuilding missions.

There is a significant body of literature which interrogates the related and underlying issues, and the logic and contradictions regarding the ways that security and development have been operationalised, linked, and conceptualised, within international discourse and practice on liberal peace interventions. Scholars have pondered timing and effectiveness of intervention planning and structures, (Fitz-Gerald, 2004; Tschigiri, 2009; Paris, 2010) the top-down approach of intervention (Beall, Goodfellow, and Putzel, 2006), the co-option of human security (Stewart, 2004), and the lack of research and evidence (Uvin, 2002; IPA, 2006). Others, adopting a more critical approach, have attempted to map out different typologies of security and development (Stren and Öjendal, 2010), raised questions about sovereignty and the legitimacy of peacebuilding and the promotion of liberal norms (Heathershaw, 2009; Lemay-Hébert, 2013); questioned whether peacebuilding efforts are liberal at all (Selby, 2013; Autesserre, 2014), analysed the intersection of peacebuilding and political economy (Pugh, 2011; Goodhand, 2006) defined intervention as global liberal governance seeking to control the uninsured lives of populations in the Global South (Duffield, 2007) critiqued the security–development nexus as an anti-foreign policy (Chandler, 2007) and interpreted peacebuilding as being driven by a colonial rationality (Jabri, 2013). While criticism of these frameworks and their related practices have been extensive, less attention has been given to uncovering different ways of conceptualising and thinking about security and development in the context of intervention and to understanding the everyday lived experiences, of external actors and local populations, of international interventions in which seek to securitise and develop conflict-affected spaces. An even smaller body of work has explored this topic adopting an analytical focus on the everyday realities of peacebuilding and intervention and using methodologies which involve direct engagement with those that live within situations of intervention.

This book contributes to this small body of literature through an examination of the everyday lived experience of international intervention. Using ethnographic methodologies, it explores everyday practices, relationships, and acts of resistance, to shed light on what the merging of development and security, sitting at the heart of the liberal peacebuilding project, has meant for the people who live and work in Afghanistan, both the interveners and Afghans themselves. The analysis here suggests that research into the everyday realities of areas affected by conflict, violence, and intervention can be an important explanatory tool that highlights the connections between local and global issues.

The everyday

The everyday is a notion which eludes consensus but generally invokes images of the banal routines and activities of life. Academic forays into the everyday suggested that great insights into the human condition and global politics could be found, not only through interrogation of the spectacular or explanations rooted in analysis of grand political and economic structures, but rather in work that sought to understand the '(un)mediated' everyday praxis of the lived human experience (Hall *et al.*, [1980] 2005; Lefebvre, 2004). Researchers have used the everyday lens to examine a vast range of topics from urban spaces and popular culture (de Certeau, 1984; Lefebvre, 2004; Hall and Jefferson, [1975] 2006; Mbembe and Nutall, 2004; Braesler and Tweedie, 2010), crime and punishment (Foucault, 1980), and social activism (Smith, 1987; Deegan, 2001). Analysis of everyday life examines the mundane and ordinary practices that are often overlooked but hold important clues about the structuring and the regulation of human life, social interaction, and the potential for agency and resistance. Thus, there is a complex interplay between everyday life and larger political, economic, and social processes and structures. As such the everyday is not a utopian or neutral space but rather is construed as a site of domination, struggle, and resistance. An examination of everyday practices provides insight into the practical ways human beings deal with the experience of domination in everyday life. These practices are performed, socially recognisable, patterned, demonstrate skill, and link the discursive and material worlds (Alder and Poulit, 2011, pp. 6–8). Therefore, practices are continuous and familiar as well as dynamic and transformative, and cannot be separated from the relationships, context, and histories which they are connected to. These mechanisms, and informalities allow for certain schemes to be put into practice and serve to imbue human life with meaning (Scott, 1998). As humans struggle with matrices of power that permeate everyday life acts of resistance emerge.

A principal technique of the powerful is to penetrate the everyday through the provision of resources, which meet needs that are often defined by dominant forces but come to be accepted by others as necessary for their survival. As their needs are met, individuals may begin to perceive the governing forces as emancipatory agents, while also becoming dependent upon them. However, people are not completely unaware of these mechanisms. Ortner (2005, p. 34) drawing on Giddens, suggests that people are always at least partially 'knowing subjects', with a degree of reflexivity which allows them to have 'some penetration' into the ways in which they are formed by their circumstances. This awareness does not replace but exists alongside the instances where the actors may be unaware of the specific underlying logics their everyday practices (Bourdieu, 1990 cited in Ortner, 2005). Consequently, through these less visible strategies of power, a sinkhole begins to form between the needs proposed by those in power and the everyday, immediate experiences of the individual and the collective (Deleuze and Guattari, 2008). Indeed the obsession with everyday survival and peace may lead to more violence through the dispossession of the material, social, and cultural resources that are constitutive of communities and individuals in the first place (Taylor, 1991). This is a familiar trope in the context of colonialism and capitalism but is also apparent in development initiatives, peacebuilding projects, and interventions wherein the violent consequences of attempting to re-order a society are discounted and framed as altruistic endeavours for the community benefit.

These processes above are global, historical, and international but are realised through the direct, lived experiences of local populations and external actors. Therefore, interrogation into the everyday provides a powerful lens for anyone seeking to understand the patterns of historical domination and the realities of international intervention in Afghanistan. The history of intervention in the country is one where hegemonic actors have justified their violence and social re-engineering attempts as necessary for local and global survival and security. As a result, local populations and interveners must constantly make choices regarding what they will give up to survive and to achieve constructed notions of development, peace, and security. Interrogation of the everyday is not, however, a study in human complacency as the techniques of the powerful also give rise to resistance.

Everyday acts of resistance are powerful mechanisms through which ordinary activities can be manipulated and imbued with political meaning to contest domination. In de Certeau's theorisation about everyday resistance two concepts are central. 'Strategies' – the domain of the powerful – are used to establish a panoptic position over the 'other' and aim to subjugate and control the individual and the collective. 'Tactics' – the purview of the non-powerful – are flexible and subtle practices in which individuals attempt to carve out spaces for themselves and create alternative visions which contest institutions of power. In very different ways, work by Foucault (1977, 1980) and by Scott (1985, 1990) which argued for an elaboration of the operation of power in the everyday opened up the possibilities of how resistance could be understood. Scott (1985) drawing upon his work on slave and peasant rebellions argued that by only focusing on organised events or collective action scholars were omitting to recognise more subtle, common, and powerful forms of everyday resistance, such as non-compliance, or using prescribed roles and language to contest power through rumours, songs, or metaphors (p. 137). Therefore, just as the powerful employ hidden forms of power, the less powerful groups can hide their strategies of resistance from dominant forces. Heller (1985) suggests that everyday activities like cooking produce self-contentment that is unrealised through engagement with the larger system that provides governance and control. This allows transcendence of individual alienation and connections can then be formed that lay the foundation for hope, creativity (Lefebvre, 2002), and change (Vanegeim, 1967). Accordingly, the everyday is a space where plurality and otherness can be located and different forms of power and agency can be expressed (Lefebvre, 2002; Smith, 1987). Therefore, studying the everyday, even in the context of a violent intervention, can illuminate different methods of resistance, affective rituals, and attempts at contestation that are central to the survival of individuals and the maintenance of community life.

Resistance, however, can produce varied effects when different power relations are involved. In a detailed discussion of the relationship between resistance, agency, and subjectivity, Ortner (2005) critiqued what she saw as a post-modern tendency (see Foucault, 1980) emerging in ethnographic work on resistance. She argued that 'the powerless' or 'subaltern' (Spivak, 1985) were presented in scholarship as if their only significant act was resistance. Consequently, in their enthusiasm to find resistance and disrupt power researchers had stripped actors of their complexity, failed to consider the internal political workings of different groups, and omitted important considerations such as the motivations and desires which lead to acts of resistance (Mitchell, 2007). Interestingly, similar critiques have been made of contemporary peace and conflict scholarship that uses the everyday lens to examine post-conflict and peacebuilding interventions which I discuss below. Therefore, investigations of everyday resistance and practices must also consider how agency, the desire or intention to engage, in acts of resistance is influenced by different subjectivities, the complex political, cultural, and historical orientations that are generated through people's engagement to the world (Ortner, 2005, p. 34). Accordingly, the everyday is a site of resistance, but also the location of uneven and differentiated power relations, and a realm of political conflict that is variable and dynamic. This articulation is particularly important in deconstructing the everyday practices, relationships, and acts of resistance amongst and between external actors and local populations in the context of large-scale interventions wherein different matrices of power connect diverse organisations, groups, and individuals in a violent context with constantly shifting political dynamics.

The everyday and intervention

Several disciplines have taken up the study of the everyday in relation to peace, conflict, and development. Anthropology and geography are home to the bulk of academic literature in this area. In both disciplines, scholars have employed ethnographic methods to examine everyday experiences of conflict and violence (see Richards, 1996; Nordstrom, 1997; Billaud, 2015) and local and community experiences of post-conflict transition and peace (see Moser and McIlwaine, 2004; Leopold, 2005; Das and Cavell, 2007) across different contexts. In the field of development studies everyday ethnographies of aid have focused on practices of international organisations and NGOs (Feurgeson, 1990; Mosse and Lewis, 2005; Mckinnon, 2011; Mosse, 2013) and more recently, on the lives of aid workers (Fechter, 2012, 2017). For the most part, however, the discipline has closely followed industry practice and traditionally focused on economic and community development. Conflict, violence, and peace, with some key exceptions (see Marriage, 2006; Polman, 2010), have not yet become central concerns to the discipline in the same manner as topics like rural development, gender, and poverty (Gorman, 2011). Consequently, outside of anthropology and geography, much of the literature on everyday conflict, peacebuilding, and intervention is found in the field of peace and conflict studies.

More recently, critical peace and conflict scholars, some of whom are in the field of international relations, have begun to use the everyday as an analytical framework to understand and highlight the failures of liberal peacebuilding projects. A growing number of researchers associated with the 'local turn' (see MacGinty, 2010) in peace and conflict studies, have adopted an everyday lens to the study of peacebuilding, and conflict. Exponents of the local turn critique the dominant logics of liberal peace projects and turn their attention to the local dimensions of peacebuilding including local agency, resistance, and practices. Important contributions to scholarship have been made by these scholars on local peace traditions and hybridity (Richmond, 2009, 2017; MacGinty and Sanghera, 2012; MacGinty and Richmond, 2013; Jarstad and Belloni, 2012; MacGinty, 2008, 2010; Richmond and Mitchell, 2011), affective peace practices (Mitchell and Kelley, 2011), and borderlands (Adamson, 2016). Outside of the local turn perspective, peace and conflict studies scholars using different theoretical approaches have used an everyday lens to examine the built environment of post-conflict reconstruction projects (Smirl, 2015); to explore peace education initiatives (Urmitapa, Kashimana, and Walkling, 2016), to decolonise intervention (Sabaratnam, 2017) and to highlighted the gaps between policy discourse and programme outcomes and the means through which external actors use their power to and capitalise on community vulnerability (De Waal, 2015; Autessere, 2010, 2014).

These accounts have made important contributions to the debates on international peacebuilding practices, post-conflict reconstruction, humanitarian aid, and locally embedded and driven peacebuilding processes. At times, however, there has been a tendency towards analytical choices which reify divisions between and attach generalised characteristics to certain groups. Consequently, research may either reinforce notions of the 'local' as a site of authenticity and as a result, inadvertently exclude, silence, and even deny alternative narratives out of a longing for an idealised version of a peaceful society (Hughes, Öjendal, and Schierenbeck, 2015; Nadarajah and Rampton, 2015; Paffenholz, 2015) or fuse external actors into generalised groups, thereby perhaps overestimating their power or underestimating their vulnerabilities (Randazzo, 2016; Lilja and Höglund, 2018). Thus, within the growing body of literature on everyday peace, conflict, and intervention, there is space to develop a more nuanced understanding of the actors involved and the circulation of power in situations of conflict and intervention drawing on empirical research. This book aims to contribute to the body of work by examining the paradoxes and contradictions of the everyday while recognising the diversity of actors and the intimate interplay of different practices, subjectivities, and acts of resistance.

In conceptualising the everyday in this book, I draw from the work of scholars in the section above, and in particular important research conducted by Mitchell (2011). Therefore, the everyday in this book can be described as

> the sets of experiences, practices, emotions and interpretations through which people engage with the daily challenges of occupying, preserving, and altering [the dynamic spaces] in which individuals and groups create and sustain their collective lives.
>
> (p. 1624)

In unpacking the definition, it is important to highlight three key themes which are central to my analysis of the everyday in this study of security, development and violence in the everyday of the intervention in Afghanistan and also speak to the contributions of this book.

First, the everyday is a dynamic and unpredictable space. As such, this study did not seek to isolate scenes of violence or acts of resistance. In fact, the fluidity and erratic nature of the environment would obstruct any such aspirations. Rather, I sought to understand the productive capacity of uncertainty in conflict and intervention. According to de Certeau (1984), unpredictability undermines strategies but is a tactical ally. Throughout the book the strategies of those fuelling the intervention not only produce devasting effects in some of the local districts but also undermine the attempts at control put in place and at times disrupt the powerful themselves. The dynamic nature of everyday was also reflected in situations in the districts where violence intersected with practices which build a sense of community. This argument is not meant to diminish the destructive impact of the direct violence of military occupation, and civilian causalities or the echoes of empire that characterise international intervention, which are recurrent themes in this book. Recognition of the uncertainty of the everyday allowed for a deeper understanding of violence, and resistance and the interplay of strategies between different actors.

Second, the everyday is a space where power circulates in differentiated ways amongst diverse individuals and communities who are, explicitly and indirectly, connected through their practices, experiences, and relationships. Another important contribution of this research is found in its efforts to complicate the local–international binary while remaining attentive to the pluralities of power and practice that emerge in these settings. The everyday political, social, and embodied realities of international intervention described in this book are explained through diverse and connected subject lenses. My analysis highlights the perspectives and practices of local community residents and officials, which have indeed been less central to most scholarship on intervention, as fundamental to the research. There are, however, limitations to problematising intervention from a standpoint that solely centres on either Western institutions and actors or static ideas of *the local*. As such the book examines but also goes beyond common dichotomies used in the study of intervention such as intervener-intervened, civilian-military, and humanitarian-development and highlights the range of identities, positionalities, and sub-communities within these groups. In addition, important perspectives are shared by subjects rarely included in research on intervention, such as regional aid workers, private civilian contractors from the Global South, and national security forces.

Deconstruction of the mosaic of different actors allows for a nuanced analysis of power relations. A complex matrix of relationships emerges in the book between individuals, communities, and organisations that influence perceptions, inform identities, and create hierarchies. In addition, individuals share the common experiences and spaces such as the dinner at a guesthouse, or coordination meetings at the office building. Even in these closed environments, however, different sets of practices take place and different realities emerge. Unpacking the gamut of positionalities within and between groups was central to the dislocation of a range of stereotypes, attributed to both the intervened and the interveners, understanding the connected nature of subjectivities, and the developing of a deeper understanding of how power circulates and different worlds collide in Afghanistan.

Lastly, the everyday here concerns physical activities, like walking and sharing a meal, but also the affective expressions and cognitive processes and that take place on an individual and community level. Relatedly, one of the important contributions of this book is its exploration of affect in the context of intervention. Throughout the book, emotions play a major role in the lived experiences of the interveners and local population. The examination of instances of emotional release was central to developing an understanding the impact of violence on individuals, the interactions between people, and the choices they made, and also the consequences for some interveners of implementing programmes that they do not believe in. Indeed, the mechanisms through which fear, frustration, friendship, and familial bonds are expressed in the narratives explored here become important in understanding how people negotiate the structures of intervention and the formation of community. The everyday space of intervention that this volume presents is one in which emotions frequently seek to conceal the messiness of practice, and the damaging consequences of violence and inequality, and sometimes work to explain the paths of resistance, collective action and the moments of silence.

The places and people

The field research for this book took place mainly in Afghanistan, but also in North America and Europe between 2009 and 2013. Conducting research in multiple sites allows the exploration of people, connections, and relationships across geographical, geopolitical, and cultural spaces and perspectives as the researcher moves through spatially dispersed locations (Falzon, 2016). Primary empirical research was carried out in Europe and North America during 2009 and 2010, and in Afghanistan from October 2010 until November 2011, with follow-ups in 2012, and 2013. The majority of the research in Afghanistan was done over a period of 14 months in two provinces: Kabul and Nangarhar. An in-depth analysis was carried out in one district of each province: Qarabagh District in Kabul province and Behsud District in Nangarhar Province. A district is a large place and it would have been impossible to speak to people in each village. Qarabagh alone has over 100 villages. In Qarabagh, I spent most of my time in its seven largest villages and two informal returnee settlements and in Behsud six large villages/areas became field sites. A detailed descriptions of each district are provided in Chapters 4 and 5.

This volume presents the reflections, interviews, and experiences shared with me by the people I encountered while conducting fieldwork, both the interveners and the intervened. Interveners are those with no familial or cultural ties to Afghanistan, whose principal motive for coming to the country was to support aspects of the externally driven intervention project. The intervened are Afghan citizens and residents who lived in Afghanistan at the time of the study. The terms local and external are contested in scholarship, but are used here for the ease of the reader, and to reflect the narratives and comments of the people I encountered and spoke to. For example, in the districts external actors are interveners, however, at certain times the term is used to refer to Afghans who live outside of the district and sometimes even outside of the village or area. Therefore, both of these terms must be read in the context in which they are written as their meaning shifts depending on space and time. Narratives were shared by politicians and senior public servants, local NGO, and INGO staff; representatives from the district government and leadership bodies; members of community groups, women's groups, and youth organisations; community leaders, health and education professionals; district residents such as business owners, farmers, taxi drivers, wives, and mothers, and students; officials from UN agencies, other international organisations, NATO military officers and civilian staff; diplomats, employees from private sector companies, development corporations, and Private Security Companies. As these subjects negotiate the world around them, they encounter breaks between the constructed ideas of who they are, who the other is, and the realities of everyday life. Many of the stories in this book elucidate these fractures, competing perspectives, and relationships as they were negotiated, ignored or resisted.

The frame

Throughout this book, I use the concept of 'stories' to organise my findings. A central component of the research process was trying to uncover the complexities of intervention in Afghanistan through narratives of the work and lives of individuals as told through their own subjectivities. Far from undertaking an 'objective' fact-finding mission, the task here was to understand how people made sense of the world around them, recognising that conflict involves a 'war of meanings' as much as it is about power (Frerks, 2013, p. 2). Story research originates in the humanities but has been used in the social sciences more recently, often employed as a research tool (Barry and Elmes, 1997, p. 3). The term 'stories' does not diminish the seriousness or validity of the perspectives shared and data collected through other research methods, but rather highlights the constructed, interconnected nature of the information shared, and the means through which knowledge is produced and translated. I did not use the story as a tool in the form of a pre-determined filter through which people had to communicate their thoughts; rather, 'the story' became part of the framework through which the narratives shared could be understood. Narratives are not disconnected from reality but rather historically, contextually, and temporally bound to the world around them, allowing us to gain access to the complexity of human interactions (Maynes, Pierce, and Laslett, 2008). Therefore, the stories in the book are a collection of narratives and reflections, but also emerge from everyday practices in their historical, social, political-economic, and cultural contexts. The stories here do not represent 'the Afghan voice' or 'the intervener voice'. Indeed, it would be difficult for one authentic voice to encapsulate any community. I also do not claim to represent the entirety of perspectives and experiences of all Afghans or external officials. As the stories in this book seek to demonstrate, however, Afghans and interveners, maintain diverse perspectives on the intervention, diverging views of other actors, and adopt a mixture of tactics through which they seek to navigate their environment and control their everyday realities.

The approach

This volume is an ethnographic study of the everyday of intervention. It contributes to a growing interdisciplinary body of work broadly described as 'ethnographic peace research' (Millar, 2014, 2018), characterised as research taking place in spaces affected by conflict and/or violence involving long-term engagement with the context and people, thick description, a commitment to understand how and why, in addition to simply what one is observing, reflexivity, and a diversity of data collection methods. My research was multi-sited, qualitative, and engaged. I employed mixed qualitative tools, including interviews (87), discussions groups (37), workshops (5) to focus on everyday interactions, connections, and relationships over 14 months in Afghanistan, drew upon my previous four years of knowledge and experiences in the country, and used observation of and participation in the location as part of my research methods. It is, however, important to discuss a two caveats in regard to my use of 'ethnography', namely, the historical and contemporary relationship between ethnography, colonialism, and war, and the growing use of ethnography by critical peace and conflict studies scholars.

First, ethnography has a contentious past within colonialism and was often used as tool of the colonial state to generate the very type of knowledge that post-colonial and decolonial scholars attempt to dismantle. During the colonial period, academics observed local people as objects of study and their data was often used to justify the dehumanisation and subjugation of non-European populations (Lewis, 1973). During the 20th century, colonial powers sometimes employed ethnographers, directly or indirectly, as agents of the state or the military (Van Bremen and Shimizu, 1999; Boas, 1919). In the 21st century, social scientists have become an integral part of the Global War on Terror and the occupying international military structures in Afghanistan and Iraq. This recent trend has been met with extensive critique (Price, 2011, 2014; Gonzalez, 2012) but also calls for further engagement with the military by scholars (Albro, 2014; Fluehr-Lobban, 2008). For example, the Human Terrain Systems (HTS), established in 2005 in Iraq and Afghanistan, are three- to five-person civilian units, which include research managers and academics, that are embedded into military commands. The HTS, designed with the involvement of anthropologists, are viewed as soft power for counterinsurgency campaigns (Lucas, 2009). In Afghanistan, the HTS are widespread. These military knowledge-production machines aim to create 'conflict ethnographies' (Kilcullen, 2006), which can be used by military officials to devise strategies to *win hearts and minds* (Lucas, 2009). Therefore, from the outset, it is important to distance myself from research which aims to study local populations to advance Western intervention and counterinsurgency.

Second, the ontological and epistemological challenges made by the local (Mitchell and Kelly, 2011; MacGinty and Richmond, 2013; MacGinty, 2014) and cultural turns (Bräuchler, 2015, 2018) and decolonial scholarship (Sabaratnam, 2013) in peace and conflict studies have raised methodological questions about how to research and engage with local actors and cultures. Consequently, a growing number of researchers have begun incorporating ethnographic methods into their work (Millar, 2018, p. 1). Interest in using ethnography to investigate local and the everyday, however, has tended to lag behind the critical reflection that has taken place in disciplines like anthropology, where debates on positionality, representation, politics, and ethics have produced different ethnographic variants including committed (Costa Vargas, 2004). political (Auyero, 2006; Gutmann, 2005), engaged (Scheper-Hughes, 1995; Casas-Cortés, Osterweil, and Powell, 2013), and post-colonial/decolonial ethnography (Gonzalez, 2003; Manning, 2018). As many critical peace and conflict studies scholars come from disciplines without a tradition of qualitative fieldwork, continued rigorous debate about what ethnography means in the context of peace and conflict studies is necessary (Vrasti, 2008; Rantacore, 2010). Scholars have been cautioned regarding making claims to ethnography because of their problematic interpretation and employment of methods seen to be central to ethnographic endeavours (Millar, 2018). Critiques have emerged regarding undervaluing the role of long-term engagement fieldwork and participant observation (Vrasti, 2008), and the dismissal of collaborative knowledge production (Lottholtz, 2018). I took the above concerns seriously when embarking on this study. In fact, one of the contributions of this book is its exploration of the research process not as a peripheral issue but rather as an integral part of the study, including the analysis and the production of knowledge that comes from this book.

The tools

The common usage of quantitative research methods in post-conflict zones is, according to Auyero and Mahler (2011), a reflection of 'the hegemony of the codeable over the messy' (p. 218). This was certainly the case in Afghanistan, where there was a clear preference, by donor governments at least, for reports laced with charts and numbers rather than case studies and narratives. Ironically, this push for supposedly 'hard data' created a cottage industry of local data collectors, who focused on the task at hand, filling out surveys and producing statistics for international reports. Where the numbers from and what it represented seemed to be of less concern to the research economy that demanded them. My statistical foray is limited to referencing quantitative data on aid disbursement, population demographics, and violent events in Afghanistan collected from various sources, some of which cannot be named explicitly for reasons of confidentiality. I wanted to ensure that the people I spoke to would have the opportunity to share their experiences with me in the way they understood them to be, and that their stories would not be lost in statistical analysis. Accordingly, I relied on interviews, discussion groups, workshops, and engaged participation and observation and informal conversations.

The interviews in Europe and North America were carried out solely by myself, while in Afghanistan I conducted many of the interviews independently, but also worked with research partners in Qarabagh and Behsud Districts. The team was composed of myself, Naila, and Wais,[3] who were local researchers, and Abdul a logistics specialist. The interviews took place in different countries and were also held in a variety of locations: official offices, restaurants, private homes, government offices, military bases, hospitals, and shops. The discussion groups were held with members of parliament (MPs) and civil society organisations (CSOs) and district residents. The workshops in Europe and the US were held with civilian and military officials, and academics and in Afghanistan with Afghan staff members of both local and international INGOs.

My engagement with the context was multi-layered. I attended NGO meetings, and several stakeholder meetings between the government, donors, aid, and military actors. I also worked with an Afghan research organisation that specialised in conflict analysis and at a local university. My daily activities were part of the different worlds that existed within the context. I lived in an Afghan neighbourhood, went to local shops, had dinners, coffees and lunches with friends, and colleagues in international restaurants and local cafés, went to government offices and embassies for administration, and to pay bills and local and international health centres when I was ill. Finally, many personal and informal conversations held over the years of the research, and particularly during the months spent in Afghanistan, informed this book. These experiences and conversations provided different vantage points from which to understand the communication patterns, frustrations, and interactions amongst different individuals, groups, and organisations as my own subjectivity became intertwined with theirs.

Translation and positionality

Afghanistan has two dominant languages, Dari and Pashto. I spoke decent Dari and many of the concepts I discussed with communities were able to be directly translated. Meaning, however, is also located in the context in which one speaks about something; the stories they use to explain their thoughts and the associations they make between ideas and actors. At times, particularly in Behsud, where Pashto is commonly spoken, I had to rely heavily on my research partners. Therefore, discussions about meaning with other researchers and the people I spoke to form an important part of my research process. Inevitably, however, some of the meaning of those conversations conducted will have been lost in translation and understanding and acknowledging those limitations are also an important part of the research process. Throughout this book, however, I have tried to present the findings in a manner that remains true to what I learned from the people I spoke to, and the dynamics of the environment that I observed and engaged with. Ultimately, those conversations are both temporally and spatially bound, but are given meaning through the experience of those that are involved.

This project involved a reflection, not just of the time I spent specifically working on this research study, but of my previous decade long experience as an aid worker. I had travelled back and forth to Afghanistan since 2005 and spent four years working there in international organisations and NGOs. Eventually, I came to feel that I occupied a middle ground between insider and outsider (Corbin Dwyer and Buckle, 2009; Berger, 2013). Being able to draw upon connections I had previously made in Afghanistan significantly helped in arranging interviews. My professional background was viewed in a positive light by many and provided a point of entry to some groups, particularly aid workers, sometimes described as ‘a closed tribe’ (Smirl, 2015). It was clear, however, that as a researcher and no longer a colleague, the dynamics of these relationships and the lens through which I was viewing the situation were altered, since I was no longer a member of that ‘tribe’. Nevertheless, an important part of the research process was recalling how I felt during those years and what beliefs and experiences had motivated me.

As a foreigner in Afghanistan, whether as a researcher, member of an international organisation, or whatever role I occupied, I was viewed as an outsider and as part of an architecture that occupied their space, and therefore there was some caution in approaching conversations with me. Therefore, it was important to have discussions on the aims and objectives of the research whereby the wider power dynamics of intervention and conflict were acknowledged with local communities and with the interveners spoken to. Power relations were apparent in all of the relationships and spaces I entered. These dynamics played out in different ways according to the spaces and actors involved and were racialised, gendered, and reflected local and global hierarchies of power and inequality.

Trust, consent, and safety

A certain amount of trust was already in place at the outset of the project because I had been based with the organisation a few months before starting interviews in the districts, and Wais and I had got to know each other in this context. This trust evolved over the months of working together and through the conversations we had, both formal and informal, while travelling to the districts and in the debriefing sessions afterwards. Naila and I had known each other for several years, so there was already a bond of trust, and a professional relationship had been well-established. The local research organisation I was based with had been working with leaders from the districts surrounding where the field research was conducted for many years. They not only introduced me to important research participants, but also vouched for me to a certain extent, which enabled people to be at ease when speaking to me, even when the topics were of a sensitive nature. Ultimately, I was asking people to trust me and share their thoughts and emotions within an environment that was often subject to violence, vulnerability, and chaos. The relationships and the bonds of trust were imperative, not only to facilitate interviews but also as foundations upon which I could begin to understand the data itself.

The process of gaining consent was complex and multi-layered in the urban centres and the districts, and, at times, a hierarchy of gatekeepers had to be negotiated. At the district level, the research team had to speak to government officials before entering the villages. At the community level, elders and *shura* members had to be spoken to before organising the focus groups. Between the aid, military, and government actors there was an internal process of consent-giving (the details of which were not disclosed to me), that took place before an interview was granted. Once permission was received from the gatekeeper, the path was open to speak to anyone at the next level down. In most cases, people were very willing to talk; however, in some cases, they were not, or after a few minutes they preferred not to continue.

There is a growing body of literature on doing research in areas affected by violence and conflict, which I will not survey here (See Rivas and Browne, 2018; Mazurana, Jacobsen, and Lacey, 2013; Nordstrom and Robbens, 1996); however, it is important to say a few words about the negotiation of the overall unstable and constantly shifting parameters of the conflict within Afghanistan. My previous experience served as a guide and helped me to negotiate the environment and security concerns. More importantly, however, I relied on the knowledge and advice of the local staff and an organisation that provided security assistance to NGOs. Too often, Western researchers dismiss security warnings, attempting to challenge what they see as an overly cautious Western narrative about the danger of the context. This reflects a deep misunderstanding of the environment, and a disregard of the consequences for those around them if something were to happen, and perhaps a fascination with being in a violent place yet having both the privilege and entitled belief that they are beyond the violence itself.

The topic of this study was sensitive. I was not bringing resources into the community that could disrupt the social systems; rather, my main concerns focused on ensuring that those I spoke to and the process of the research did not disturb the lives of those that participated in the project. It was very likely that after my first few days in the district, local leaders would have provided feedback to district officials regarding the research activities and topics discussed. Therefore, ensuring the confidentiality of the perspectives shared with me was essential and being consistent in my presentation reduced but did not eliminate any suspicions that I had intentionally misrepresented myself or the research. Relatedly, all of the interviews, focus group feedback, and conversations have been coded and anonymised, any names used in the book are pseudonyms unless otherwise requested and project and organisation titles have been changed where necessary.[4]

It is not common for books on intervention or aid work in peace and conflict studies to include a detailed section on research process, unless methodology is the main topic under investigation. Using a critical framework, however, requires more than a brief overview of theory and tools; it also requires reflexivity in academic praxis (Rivas, 2018). So, it was imperative to begin by talking about how I approached the study and located myself within the context. Accordingly, I have tried to lay out the way I entered the field in iterative and slow steps. The research process is a story in and of itself, as are the mechanisms through which my own subjectivity became intertwined with the subjects of this research. As Laurie *et al.* (1999) explain 'the uncertain nature of our knowledge and our ambiguities are … research moments' (p. 65). As I began to understand more about the subjects of the research and how to negotiate the context, I also began to understand more about myself as a researcher; this reflection might be useful to other researchers or practitioners in the field, not in their specifics, but as an example of self-awareness in-field and self-criticality, which are essential to the development of an 'ethnographic imagination' (Mills, 1959; Willis, 2000).

The structure

After this brief introduction, Chapter 1 presents the policy stories and explores the various ways in which Afghanistan has been used as a testing ground for international experiments on how to manage conflict, underdevelopment, and supposedly 'unruly' populations. The chapter highlights the continuity between pre- and post-9/11 international policy discourse on Afghanistan, particularly in terms of the linkages made between security and development, the role of foreign governments and international organisations, and the institutional arrangements and structures established in support of the intervention. The shifting international narratives have characterised the intervention between 2002 and 2012 as the international security transition and aid transformation agendas were set in place. Drawing upon key policy documents, official statements, organisational mandates, interviews, speeches, national government policy, and international reports, from the US, other intervening nations, the UN, and the Afghan government, the chapter seeks to tease out the contradictions and colonial logics reflected in the different iterations of international attempts to intervene, securitise and develop Afghanistan.

Chapter 2 focuses on the interveners' stories. With Kabul as its main backdrop, this chapter examines how NATO soldiers, aid workers, UN officials, diplomatic representatives, private contractors, and other external actors came to know Afghanistan and Afghans. Drawing upon interviews and conversations, the chapter briefly maps out the 'interveners' and then locates their experiences in context. In particular, the chapter examines how interveners negotiate the space of intervention, communicate diverse understandings of security and development, and accept and contest the social reproduction of institutional frameworks and policy guidance on the intervention. In this chapter, the pervasiveness of empire and eurocentrism as a part of intervention come into focus, not as a meta-discourse or set of practices, but as a belief system which closely informs how many intervening subjects construct the other and, consequently, themselves. Therefore, the chapter raises important questions about the relationship between knowledge and power in the context of intervention; mainly, how do we know the interveners and how do the interveners come to know Afghanistan and the intervention project they participate in?

Chapter 3 presents civil–military stories. This chapter explores the coordination efforts, disputes and tensions that characterised interactions between and amongst civilian and military organisations and individuals. It pays special attention to the dynamics within the Provincial Reconstruction Teams (PRTs) and the integrated UN mission, but also investigates the impact of these arrangements on civilians outside of these structures, such as INGO staff. It provides insight into the boundaries and hierarchies that emerged and were sometimes fashioned against the borders of integrated structures themselves, between and amongst groups.

Chapters 5 and 6 tell the stories of two districts, Qarabagh and Behsud. These chapters aim to unravel the material and discursive realities of security and development in Qarabagh and Behsud, through an exploration of the commentary, relationships, and practices that existed amongst the people, Afghan district residents, and interveners, that lived and worked in the districts. However, each chapter begins by exploring how local Afghan residents think about security and development, and experience intervention. A main theme in both chapters is the complex dynamics not only between residents and international aid workers, UN staff, and military officials, but also amongst the district inhabitants themselves. At the heart of the discussion in each chapter is the complex situation that occurs when different realities intersect, whereby actors may be looking at the same situation but ultimately seeing security and development through a different lens within the same time-space. These complicated dynamics were recognised by many of the actors within the districts, whether local or external. However, the ways in which they chose to respond to this complexity differed. Finally, violence, in the last two chapters in particular, but also in much of the book, is a major theme. A short concluding chapter brings together the main contributions of the book and outlines the cross-cutting themes.

Notes

1 Constructive exploitation replaced expansion and plunder as official French colonial policy in the 1890s.
2 Constructive imperialism was a response to the decline of the empire, which envisioned building one progressive, united empire.
3 The names of my research team have been anonymised.
4 In the book all instances where the project tiles have been changed are indicated by a referent endnote.

References

Adamson, J. 2016. Encounter with a Mexican jaguar: Nature, NAFTA, militarization, and ranching in the U.S.–Mexico borderlands. In Sadowski-Smith, C. (ed.) *Globalization on the Line: Culture, Capital, and Citizenship at U.S. Borders*. London: Palgrave Macmillan, pp. 221–240

Adler, E. and Pouliot, V. 2011. International practices. *International Theory*, 3 (1), 1–36.

Albro, R. 2014. *Cultural Awareness in the Military: Developments and Implications for Future Humanitarian Cooperation*. Basingstoke: Palgrave Macmillan.

Amin, S., Arrighi, G., Frank, A. G., and Wallerstein, I. 1982. *Dynamics of Global Crisis*. London: Macmillan Press.

Andersen, L. 2012. The liberal dilemmas of a people-centred approach to state-building. *Conflict, Security & Development*, 12 (2), 103–121.

Autesserre, S. V. 2010. *The Trouble with the Congo: Local Violence and the Failure of International Peacebuilding*. New York, NY: Cambridge University Press.

Autesserre, S. V. 2014. *Peaceland: Conflict Resolution and the Everyday Politics of International Intervention*. Cambridge: Cambridge University Press.

Auyero, J. 2006. Introductory note to politics under the microscope: Special issue on political ethnography I. *Qualitative Sociology*, 29, 257–259.

Auyero, J. and Mahler, M. 2011. Invisible connections and the making of collective violence. In: Duenas, G. P. and Rueda, M. (eds.) *Meanings of Violence in Contemporary Latin America*. Basingstoke: Palgrave Macmillan, 197–222.

Barry, D. and Elmes, M. 1997. Strategy retold: Toward a narrative view of strategic discourse. *The Academy of Management Review*, 22, 429–452.

Beall, J., Goodfellow, T., and Putzel, J. 2006. On the discourse of terrorism, security and development. *Journal of International Development*, 18, 1–67.

Berdal, M. 2003. How 'New' are 'New Wars'? Global economic change and the study of Civil War. *Global Governance*, 9 (4), 477–502.

Berger, R. 2013. Now I see it, now I don't: Researcher's position and reflexivity in qualitative research. *Qualitative Research*, 15 (2), 219–234.

Bhabha, H. 1994. *The Location of Culture*. New York, NY: Routledge.

Billaud, J. 2015. *Kabul Carnival: Gender Politics in Postwar Afghanistan*. Philadelphia, PA: University of Pennsylvania Press.

Boas, F. 1919. Scientists as Spies, *The Nation*, 20 December 1919, New York, NY. Printed in *Anthropology Today*, 2005, 21 (3), 27.

Braesler, Y. and Tweedie, J. (eds.) 2010. *Cinema at the City's Edge: Film and Urban Networks in East Asia*. Hong Kong: Hong Kong University.

Bräuchler, B. 2018. The cultural turn in peace research: prospects and challenges. *Peacebuilding* 6(1): 17–33.

Bräuchler, B. 2015. *The Cultural Dimension of Peace: Decentralization and Reconciliation in Indonesia*. London: Palgrave Macmillan.

Buzan, B., Wæver, O., and de Wilde, J. 1998. *Security: A New Framework for Analysis*. Boulder, CO: Lynne Rienner.

Call, C. T. 2008. The fallacy of the 'failed state'. *Third World Quarterly*, 29, 1491–1507.

Casas-Cortés, M., Osterweil, M., Powell, D. E. 2013. *Transformations in Engaged Ethnography: Knowledge, Networks, and Social Movements*. Purdue, IN: Duke University Press.

de Certeau, M. 1984. *The Practice of Everyday Life*. Rendail, S. F. Trans. [2006]. Berkeley, CA: University of California Press.

Chambers, R. 1994. The origins and practice of participatory rural appraisal. *World Development*, 22, 953–969.

Chandler, D. 2007. The security-development nexus and the rise of 'anti-foreign policy'. *Journal of International Relations and Development*, 10, 362–386.

Cooper, F. 2005. *Colonialism in Question Theory, Knowledge, History*. Berkeley, CA: University of California Press.

Corbin Dwyer, S. and Buckle, J. L. 2009. The space between: On being an insider-outsider in qualitative research. *International Journal of Qualitative Methods*, 8 (1), 54–63.

Costa Vargas, J. H. 2004. Hyperconsciousness of race and its negation: The dialectic of white supremacy in Brazil. *Identities*, 11 (4), 443–470.

DANIDA. 2004. *Security, Growth-Development*. Copenhagen: Danish International Development Agency.

Das, V. and Cavell, S. 2007. *Life and Words: Violence and the Descent into the Ordinary*. Berkeley, CA: University of California Press.

Deegan, M. J. 2001. The Chicago School of ethnography. In: Atkinson, P., Coffey, A., Delamont, S., Lofland, J., and Lofland, L. (eds.) *Handbook of Ethnography*. London: Sage, 11–25.

Deleuze, G. and Guattari, F. 2008. *Anti-Oedipus*. London: Continuum.

DFID. 2005. *Fighting Poverty To Build a Safer World: A Strategy for Security and Development*. London: DFID.

Donini, A. 2011. *Between a Rock and a Hard Place: Integration or Independence of Humanitarian Action?* Geneva: International Review of the Red Cross.

Duffield, M. 2001. *Global Governance and the New Wars: The Merging of Development and Security*. London: Zed Books.

Duffield, M. 2002. War as a network enterprise: The new security terrain and its implications. *Cultural Values*, 6 (1–2), 153–165.

Duffield, M. 2007. *Development, Security and Unending War: Governing the World of Peoples*. Cambridge, Polity Press.

Duffield, M. 2010. The liberal way of development and the development-security impasse: Exploring the global life-chance divide. *Security Dialogue*, 41, 53–76.

Escobar, A. 1995. *Encountering Development. The Making and Unmaking of the Third World*. Princeton, NJ: Princeton University Press.

Escobar, A. 2000. Beyond the Search for a Paradigm? Post-Development and Beyond. *Development*, 43, 11–14.

European Commission. 2017. *The Agenda for change and in the New European Consensus on Development*. Brussels: European Commission.

Falzon, M. A. 2016. *Multi-Sited Ethnography: Theory, Praxis and Locality in Contemporary Research*. Oxon: Routledge.

Fechter, A-M. 2012. The personal and the professional: aid workers' relationships and values in the development process. *Third World Quarterly*, 33 (8), 1387–1404.

Fechter, A-M. 2017. An excess of goodness? Volunteering among Aid professionals in Cambodia. *South East Asia Research*, 25 (3), 268–283.

Feurgeson, J. 1990. *The Anti-politics Machine*. Minneapolis, MN: University of Minnesota Press.

Fitz-Gerald, A. 2004. Addressing the security-development nexus: Implications for joined-up government. *Policy Matters*, 5, 1–24.

Fluehr-Lobban, C. 2008. New ethical challenges for anthropologists: The terms 'secret research' and 'do not harm' need to be clarified. *Chronicle of Higher Education Review*, 55(12), B11.

Frank, A. G. 1977. Dependence is dead, long live dependence and the class struggle: an answer to critics. *World Development*, 5, 355–370.

Frank, A. G. 1996. The Political Economy of Development and Underdevelopment. In: Jameson, K. P. and Wilber, C. K. (eds.) *The Political Economy Of Development and Underdevelopment*. New York, NY: McGraw-Hill.

Foucault, M. 1977. *Discipline and Punish*. London: Penguin Books.

Foucault, M. 1980. *Power/Knowledge: Selected Interviews and Other Writings, 1972–1977*. C. Gordon Trans. New York, NY: Pantheon.

Frerks, G. 2013. Discourses on war, peace and peace-building in Sri Lanka. In: Hilhorst, D. (ed.) *Disaster, Conflict and Society in Crises: Everyday Politics of Crisis Response*. London: Routledge, 18–36.

Fukuyama, F. 2004. The imperative of state-building. *Journal of Democracy* 15: 17–31.

Gates, R. M. 2010. Helping others defend themselves: The future of U.S. Security Assistance. *Foreign Affairs*, 89 (3), May/June, 2–6.

Ghani, A. and Lockhart, C. 2008. *Fixing Failed States: A Framework for Rebuilding a Fractured World*. Oxford : Oxford University Press.

Gonzalez, M. 2003. An Ethics for Postcolonial Ethnography. In Clair, R. P. (ed.) *Expressions of Ethnography: Novel Approaches to Qualitative Methods*. New York, NY: SUNY Press.

Gonzalez, R. 2012. The world in a bottle. In Stroeken, K. (ed.) *War, Technology, Anthropology*. New York, NY: Berghahn Books.

Goodhand, J. 2006. *Aiding Peace? The Role of NGOs in Armed Conflict*. Boulder, CO: Lynne Rienner.

Goodhand, J. and Sedra, M. 2013. Rethinking liberal peacebuilding, statebuilding and transition in Afghanistan: an introduction. *Central Asian Survey*, 32 (3), 239–254.

Gorman, E. 2011. *Conflict and Development*. London: Zed Books.

Green, E. H. H. 1999. The political economy of empire. In William, A. P. (eds.) *The Oxford History of the British Empire: The Nineteenth Century*, Volume 3. Oxford and New York, NY: Oxford University Press, pp. 346–370.

Gutmann, M. 2005. *The Romance of Democracy. Compliant Defiance in Contemporary Mexico*. Berkeley, CA: University of California Press.

Hall, S. and Jefferson, T. [1975] 2006. *Resistance Through Rituals: Youth Cultures in Post-War Britain*. London: Routledge.

Hall, S., Hobson, D., Lowe, A., and Willis, P. [1980] 2005. *Culture, Media Language: Working Papers in Cultural Studies 1972–1979*. London: Taylor and Francis e-Library.

Hables Gray, C. 1997. *Post-Modern War: The New Politics of Conflict*. London: Routledge.

Hearath, D. 2009. The discourse of development: Has it reached maturity? *Third World Quarterly*, 30, 1449–1464.

Heathershaw, J. 2009. *Post-Conflict Tajikistan. The Politics of Peacebuilding and the Emergence of Legitimate Order*. London: Routledge.

Heller, A. 1985. *Everyday Life*. London: Routledge and Kegan Paul.

Holsti, J. K. 1996. *The State, War and the State of War*. New York, NY: Cambridge University Press.

Hoodge, J. and Hodl, G. 2014. Introduction. In Hoodge, J., Hodl, G., and Kopf, M. (eds.) *Developing Africa: Concepts and Practices in Twentieth-Century Colonialism*. Manchester and New York, NY: Manchester University Press.

Hughes, C., Öjendal, J., and Schierenbeck, I. 2015. The struggle versus the song – The local turn in peacebuilding: an introduction. *Third World Quarterly*, 36 (5), 817–824.

IPA. 2006. *The Security-Development Nexus: Research Findings and Policy Implications*. New York, NY: International Peace Academy.

Jabri, V. 2013. Peacebuilding, the local and the international: a colonial or a postcolonial rationality? *Peacebuilding*, 1, 3–16.

Jarstad, J. K. and Belloni, R. 2012. Introducing hybrid peace governance: impact and prospects of liberal peacebuilding. *Global Governance*, 18 (1), 1–6.

Jolly, R. and Ray, D. B. 2007. Human Security – National perspectives and global agendas: Insights from National Human Development Reports. *Journal of International Development*, 19, 457–472.

Kaldor, M. 1999. *New Wars and Old Wars: Organised Violence in a Global Era*. Cambridge: Polity Press.

Kaldor, M. 2013. In defence of new wars. *Stability: International Journal of Security and Development*, 2 (1), 1–16.

Kalyvas, S. N. 2001. 'New' and 'old' civil wars: A valid distinction? *World Politics*, 54, (October), 99–118.

Kilcullen, D. 2006. Twenty-eight articles: Fundamentals of company-level counterinsurgency. *Military Review*, May–June 2006, 103–108.

Kothari, U. 2005. From colonial administration to development studies: A post-colonial critique of the history of development studies. In Kothari, U. (ed.) *A Radical History of Development Studies*. London: Zed Books.

Laurie, N., Dwyer, C., Holloway, S., and Smith, F. 1999. *The Geographies of New Femininities*. New York, NY: Longman.

Lefebvre, H. 2002. *Critique of Everyday Life*, Volume 2. London: Verso.

Lefebvre, H. 2004. *Rhythmanalysis: Space, Time and Everyday Life*. S. Elden and G. Moore Trans. London and New York, NY: Continuum.

Lemay-Hébert, N. 2013. Everyday legitimacy and international administration: Global governance and local legitimacy in Kosovo. *Journal of Intervention and Statebuilding*, 7 (1), 87–104.

Leopold, M. 2005. Inside West Nile: violence, history and representation on an African frontier. *World Anthropology Series*. London: James Currey.

Lewis, D. 1973. Anthropology and colonialism. *Current Anthropology*, 14, 581–602.

Lewis, W. A. 1954. Economic development with unlimited supplies of labour. *The Manchester School*, 22, 139–191.

Leys, C. 1996. The crisis in 'development theory'. *New Political Economy*, 1 (1), 41–58.

Lilja, J. and Höglund, K. 2018. The role of the external in local peacebuilding: Enabling action – Managing risk. *Global Governance: A Review of Multilateralism and International Organizations*, 24(3), 411–430.
Lottholz, P. 2018. Critiquing anthropological imagination in peace and conflict studies: From empiricist positivism to a dialogical approach in ethnographic peace research. *International Peacekeeping*, 25(5), 695–720.
Lucas, G. 2009. *Anthropologists in Arms: The Ethics of Military Anthropology*. Lanham: Altamira Press.
MacFarlene, S. N. and Khong, Y. F. 2006. *Human Security and the UN: A Critical History*. Bloomington, IN: Indiana University Press.
MacGinty, R. 2008. Indigenous peacemaking versus the liberal peace. *Cooperation and Conflict: Journal of the Nordic International Studies Association*, 43(2), 139–163.
MacGinty, R. 2010. Hybrid peace: the interaction between top-down and bottom-up peace. *Security Dialogue*, 41(4), 391–412.
MacGinty, R. 2014. Everyday Peace: Bottom-up and local agency in conflict-affected societies. *Security Dialogue*, 45(6) (2014), 548–564.
MacGinty, R. and Richmond, O. 2013. The local turn in peace building: A critical agenda for peace. *Third World Quarterly*, 34, 763–783.
MacGinty, R. and Sanghera, G. 2012. Hybridity in peacebuilding and development: an introduction. *Journal of Peacebuilding & Development*, 7(2), 2–8.
Manning, J. 2018. Becoming a decolonial feminist ethnographer: Addressing the complexities of positionality and representation. *Management Learning*, 49(3), 311–326.
Marriage, Z. 2006. *Not Breaking the Rules Not Playing the Game*. London: Hurst and Company.
Maynes, M. J., Pierce, J., and Laslett, B. 2008. *Telling Stories: The Use of Personal Narratives in the Social Sciences and History*. Ithaca, NY: Cornell University Press.
Mazurana, D., Jacobsen, K., and Lacey, G. A. 2013. *Research Methods in Conflict Settings: A View from Below*. New York, NY: Cambridge University Press.
Mbembe, A. and Nuttall, S. (eds.) 2004. Writing the world from an African metropolis. Special issue of *Public Culture*, 16(3), 347–372.
McKinnon, K. 2011. *Development Professional in Northern Thailand: Hope, Politics and Practice*. Honolulu, HI: University of Hawai'i Press.
Millar, G. 2014. *An Ethnographic Approach to Peacebuilding: Understanding Local Experiences in Transitional States*. London: Routledge.
Millar, G. 2018. *Ethnographic Peace Research: Approaches and Tensions*. Basingstoke: Palgrave MacMillan.
Mills, C. W. 1959. *The Sociological Imagination*. London: Oxford University Press.
Mitchell, A. 2011. Quality/control: international peace interventions and 'the everyday'. *Review of International Studies*, 37 (2011), 1623–1645.
Mitchell, J. 2007. A fourth critic of the Enlightenment: Michel de Certeau and the ethnography of subjectivity. *Social Anthropology/Anthropologie Sociale*, 15(1), 89–106.
Mitchell, A. and Kelly, L. 2011. Peaceful spaces? 'Walking' through the new liminal spaces of peacebuilding and development in North Belfast. *Alternatives: Global, Local, Political*, 36(4), 307–325.
Mohanty, C. 1984. Under Western eyes: Feminist scholarship and colonial discourses. *Boundary*, 2, 12(3), Spring–Autumn, 333–358.
Moss, D. and Lewis, D. 2005. *The Aid Effect: Ethnographies of Development Practice and Neo-liberal Reform*. London: Pluto Press.

Moser, C. and McIlwaine, C. 2004. *Encounters With Violence in Latin America: Urban Poor Perceptions From Colombia and Guatemala*. New York, NY: Routledge.

Mosse, D. (ed.) 2013. *Adventures in Aidland: The Anthropology of Professionals in International Development*. New York, NY: Berghahn.

Munkler, H. 2004. *The New Wars*. Cambridge: Polity Press.

Nadarajah, S. and Rampton, D. 2015. The limits of hybridity and the crisis of liberal peace. *Review of International Studies*, 41(1), 49–72.

Nandy, A. 1989. Shamans, Savages and the Wilderness: On the Audibility of Dissent and the Future of Civilizations. *Alternatives*, 14, 263–277.

Newman, E. 2004. 'The "New Wars" debate: A historical perspective is needed'. *Security Dialogue*, 35(2), 173–189.

Nordstrom, C. 1997. *A Different Kind of War Story*. Philadelphia, PA: University of Pennsylvania Press.

Nordstrom, C. and Robbens (eds.) 1996. Introduction. In *Fieldwork Under Fire: Contemporary Studies of Violence and Culture*. Berkeley, CA: University of California Press, pp. 1–25.

OECD. 2007a. *The OECD Principles for Good International Engagement in Fragile States and Situations*. Development Assistance Committee's High Level Forum. Paris: OECD.

OECD. 2007b. *OECD DAC Handbook on Security System Reform: Supporting Security and Justice*. Paris: OECD.

OECD. 2008. *Concepts and Dilemmas of Statebuilding in Fragile Situation: From Fragility to Resilience*. Paris: OECD.

OECD. 2010. *Ensuring Fragile States Are Not Left Behind. International Network on Conflict and Fragility*. Paris: OECD.

OECD. 2018. *Operationalising The 'Nexus': Principles and Approaches For Strengthening And Accelerating Humanitarian, Development and Peace Coherence*. Development Assistance Committee's (DAC). 19 November 2018. Paris: OECD

Ortner, S. B. 2005. Subjectivity and cultural critique. *Anthropological Theory*, 5, 31–52.

Paffenholz, T. 2015. Unpacking the local turn in peacebuilding: A critical assessment towards an agenda for future research. *Third World Quarterly*, 36(5), (2015), 857–874.

Paris, R. 2010. Saving liberal peacebuilding. *Review of International Studies*, 36, 337–365.

Picciotto, R. 2004. Aid and conflict: The policy coherence challenge. *Conflict, Security and Development*, 4, 543–562.

Polman, L. 2010. *The Crisis Caravan: What's Wrong with Humanitarian Aid?* New York, NY: Picador.

Prebisch. 1950. *The Economic Development of Latin America and Its Principal Problems*. UN document no. E/CN.12/89/Rev.1. Lake Success, NY: United Nations.

Price, D. 2011. *Weaponizing Anthropology: Social Science in Service of the Militarized State. Counter-Punch*. Oakland, CA: AK Press.

Price, D. 2014. Counterinsurgency by other names: Complicating humanitarian applied anthropology in current, former, and future war zones. *Human Organization*, 73(2), 95–105.

Pugh, M. 2011. Curing strangeness in the political economy of peacebuilding: Traces of liberalism and resistance. In: Tadjbakhsh, S. (ed.) *Rethinking the Liberal Peace*. London: Routledge.

Rahmena, M. and Bawtree, V. (eds.) 1997. *A Post-Development Studies Reader*. London: Zed Books.

Randazzo, E. 2016. The paradoxes of the 'everyday': Scrutinising the local turn in peace Building. *Third World Quarterly*, 37(8), 1351–1370.

Rantacore, J. 2010. It is strange: a reply to Vrasti. *Millennium*, 39(1), 65–77.
Richards P., 1996 *Fighting for the Rain Forest: War, Youth and Resources in Sierra Leone*. Oxford: James Currey.
Richmond, O. 2009. Liberal peace transitions: A rethink is urgent. Available at: *Open DemocracyNet.org*.
Richmond, O. 2011. *A Post-Liberal Peace*, London: Routledge.
Richmond, O. 2017. The green and the cool: Hybridity, relationality and ethnographic biographical responses to intervention. *Mediterranean Politics*, 22(2), 1–22.
Richmond, O. and Mitchell, A. 2011. *Hybrid Forms of Peace: From Everyday Agency to Post Liberalism*. London: Palgrave Macmillan.
Rivas, A. M. 2018. Vignette 3: Thinking about race and gender in conflict research. In: Rivas, A. M. and Browne, B. Bristol (eds.) *Experiences in Researching Conflict and Violence: Fieldwork Interrupted*. Bristol: Policy Press, University of Bristol.
Rivas, A. M. and Browne, B. (eds.) 2018. *Experiences in researching conflict and violence: fieldwork interrupted*. Bristol: Policy Press, University of Bristol.
Rodney, W. 1972. *How Europe Underdeveloped Africa*. London: Bogle-L'Ouverture Publications.
Rostow, W. 1960. The stages of economic growth. New series. *The Economic History Review*, 12 (1), 1–16.
Sabaratnam, M. 2013. Avatars of Eurocentrism in the critique of the liberal peace. *Security Dialogue*, 44, 259–278.
Sabaratnam, M. 2017. *Decolonising Intervention*. London: Rowman & Littlefield International.
Sachs, W. 1992. *The Development Dictionary: A Guide to Knowledge as Power*. New York, NY: Palgrave.
Scheper-Hughes, N. 1995. The primacy of the ethical: Propositions for a militant anthropology. *Current Anthropology*, 36(3), 409–440.
Scott, J. 1985. *Weapons of the Weak: Everyday Forms of Peasant Resistance*. New Haven, CT: Yale University Press.
Scott, J. 1990. *Domination and the Arts of Resistance: Hidden Transcripts*. New Haven, CT: Yale University Press.
Scott, J. 1998. Geographies of trust: Geographies of hierarchy. In: Warren, M. E. (ed.) *Democracy and Trust*. Cambridge: Cambridge University Press.
Selby, J. 2013. The myth of liberal peace-building. *Conflict, Security & Development*, 13, 57–86.
Sen, A. 1999. *Development as Freedom*. Oxford: Oxford University Press.
Singer, H. [1950] 1975. The distribution of gains between investing and borrowing countries. In *The Strategy of International Development: Essays in the Economics of Backwardness*. London: Macmillan, pp. 473–485.
Smirl, L. 2015. *Spaces of Aid*. London: Zed Books.
Smith, D. 1987. *The Everyday World as Problematic: A Feminist Sociology*. Boston, MA: Northeastern University Press.
Spivak, G. 1985. Can the sub-altern speak? Speculations on widow sacrifice. *Wedge*, 7.
Stewart, F. (2004) Development and security. *Conflict, Security and Development*, 4, 261–288.
Stren, M. and Öjendal, J. 2010. Convergence? Mapping the security-development nexus: Conflict, complexity, cacophony. *Security Dialogue*, 4, 5–29.
Taylor, C. 1991. *The Ethics of Authenticity*. Toronto: Canadian Broadcasting Corporation.
Tschigiri, N. 2009. *The Security-Politics-Development Nexus: The Lessons of State Building in sub-Saharan Africa*. European Report for Development Workshop. Florence, Italy: EC.

UN. 1997. *UN Statement of Common Understanding on Human Rights-Based Approaches to Development Cooperation and Programming*. New York, NY: United Nations.

UNSG. 2004. *A More Secure World: Our Shared Responsibility, Report of the Secretary-General's High-Level Panel on Threats, Challenges and Change*. New York, NY: United Nations.

UNSG. 2005. *Larger Freedom: Towards Development, Security and Human Rights for All*. Report of the Secretary General. New York, NY: United Nations.

UNDP. 1990. *Human Development Report*. New York, NY: Oxford University Press.

UNDP. 1994. *Human Development Report*. New York, NY: Oxford University Press.

UNDP. 2004. *Security with a Human Face: Challenges and Responsibilities. National Human Development Report: Afghanistan*. Kabul: UNDP and the Government of the Islamic Republic of Afghanistan.

Urmitapa, D., Kashimana, A., and Walkling, K. 2016. The everyday peace project: An innovative approach to peace pedagogy. *Journal of Peace Education*, 13(1), 79–104.

Uvin, P. 2002. The development/peacebuilding nexus: A typology and history of changing paradigms. *Journal of Peacebuilding and Development*, 1 (1), 5–24.

Van Bremen, J. and Shimizu. A. (eds.). 1999. *Anthropology and Colonialism in Asia and Oceania*. Surrey: Routledge.

Vaneigem, R. 1967. *The Revolution of Everyday Life*. D. Nicolson-Smith Trans. [1984]. London: Left Bank Books; Rebel Press, 1983

Vrasti, W. 2008. The strange case of ethnography and international relations. *Millennium*, 37(2), 279–301.

De Waal, 2015. *Advocacy in Conflict: Critical Perspectives On Transnational Activism*. London: Zed Books.

Wallerstein, I. 1974. *The Modern World System: Capitalist Agriculture and the Origins of the European World Economy in the Sixteenth Century*. New York, NY: Academic Press.

Waltz, K. 1979. *The Theory of International Politics*. New York, NY: McGraw-Hill.

World Bank. 2011. *Conflict, Security and Development*. World Development Report.

World Bank. 2018. The Security-Development Nexus Conference. Working Group. 18 April 2018, Washington, DC.

Willis, P. 2000. *The Ethnographic Imagination*. Cambridge: Polity.

Zaum, D. 2012. Beyond the 'liberal peace'. *Global Governance*, 18(1), 121–132.

Zoellick, R. B. 2008. Fragile states: Securing development. *Survival*, 50, 67–84.

1 The policy stories

Afghanistan, intervention, and exit

Afghanistan is a country with a long history of foreign invasion. Long before the US-led in intervention in Afghanistan following the events of 9/11, different foreign powers sought to occupy and control the people and the territory. These attempts, which have varied in length and strategy, have been detailed elsewhere by scholars writing on the history of Afghanistan. Suffice to say, this history goes back at least as far as the mid-19th century 'Great Game' between the British and the Russian empires for control of South and Central Asia, in which Afghanistan had something of the status of a 'buffer state'. This chapter focuses on more recent history and provides a brief overview of the international approach to Afghanistan in the 1990s, before moving on to an examination of the post-9/11 international policies, between 2001 and 2012. The long history of empire-building attempts by external powers, however, emerges regularly in reflections and memories of Afghan people and intervening officials interviewed in this research and throughout the book.

This chapter examines the imaginaries of the Afghan state, the Afghan population, and foreign interventions that underlie international policy, and the subsequent frameworks and structures established to support these depictions. The historical and thematic analysis draws upon policy documents, reports, and speeches from intervening countries, the UN and the Afghan government. The policy stories presented here reveal a shifting narrative regarding the purpose of foreign governments and international organisations presence in Afghanistan that runs alongside a continuous depiction of Afghanistan and its people as objects in need of governance and transformation, dependent upon international actors to rescue them from a permanent state of crisis. The global and domestic events and policy debates from the 1990s, outlined at the outset of the chapter, began to link security and development and laid the groundwork for many of the trends shaping international peacebuilding interventions in the 2000s. The exploration of the post-9/11 international policy and statements on Afghanistan, reveals the trajectory and shifts in crucial international agreements and organisational mandates which quickly moved from a narrowly focused intervention to an extensive occupation and reconstruction project. The rest of the chapter then considers the institutional arrangements that attempted to link security and development in practice, the legitimising function of localisation in policy discourse and finally, the transition and transformation policies, which were meant to facilitate the exit of security forces, and the reduction of aid investment in Afghanistan when this study ended in 2014.

Setting the stage – pre-2001

In the early 1990s, the fluid political situation in Afghanistan and growing criticism for UN strategies in conflict situations contributed to the development of an experimental framework for Afghanistan. The UN had operated in various modalities in Afghanistan since 1946 (UN, 1946) providing humanitarian and development aid, and assuming a political function such as the mediation of the 1980s Geneva Accords (Larsen, 2010). In 1998, however, Afghanistan became a testing ground for a new UN approach to development, conflict, and intervention guided by the UN Strategic Framework for Afghanistan (SFA) (UN, 1998). Although other countries were identified as potential experiment sites, Afghanistan was the first country where this approach was tested (Kreczko, 2003). The SFA was represented as 'the first effort by the United Nations system and its partners to put a common strategic framework into place for a particular country experiencing a crisis' (Minear, 1998, p. 1). Afghanistan was chosen as the focal point for this new UN-driven vision of how to conceptualise and practically approach conflict, security and development.

During the Cold War, geopolitics clearly dictated where and to whom assistance would be delivered in Afghanistan by outside countries. Aid was partisan and Western organisations often supplied goods directly to anti-Soviet factions and commanders (Duffield, Grossman, and Leader, 2001; Goodhand and Sedra, 2013). While INGOs and UN agencies attempted to maintain the perception of neutrality, their solidarity with the anti-Soviet *jihad*[1] (Raqib and Barreto, 2014, p. 18) was widespread (Donini, 2011). When the geopolitical divide created by the Cold War ended, UN agencies, INGOs and donor governments involved in Afghanistan found themselves having to make new choices. As a humanitarian worker explained:

> During that time, it was unthinkable to operate in certain areas of the country. Once those political borders fell away, what to do, why and the principles of engagement became foggy.
>
> (187, Geneva)

During the 1990s, two things happened that influenced the international approach to Afghanistan. At the global level, the post-Cold War events outlined in the previous chapter along with the failures of UN missions in the early 1990s in Rwanda, Somalia, and Kosovo had led to calls for changes to the UN's approach to conflict and peacebuilding. UN officials faced growing pressure and requests from member states and the Security Council to analyse what had gone wrong with the 1990s missions and produce recommendations to improve the UN approach to peacebuilding. In response, UN Secretary General Boutrous

Boutrous Ghali's now-famous report *An Agenda for Peace* (1992) proposed a reorganisation in the way the UN managed crisis and intervention through the development of an integrated approach that advocated increased coherence between the political, human rights, and development arms of the UN (Macrae and Leader, 2000). A new era of UN intervention began.

On the domestic front, the UN actors and aid agencies were struggling in the context of a civil war in Afghanistan where the population was increasingly victimised by all sides of the conflict and where the delivery and impact of international aid assistance was questionable (Donini, 2011). After the Soviet withdrawal from Afghanistan 1988–1989, and the collapse of the Najibullah-led communist regime in Afghanistan, the *Mujahidin*[2] who had fought the anti-Soviet war had begun to struggle against each other for power in an internal conflict that took place between 1992 and 1996 (Ponzio, 2007). On the cusp of the Soviet withdrawal there had been an increase in aid agencies and coordination bodies such as Agency Coordinating Body for Afghan Relief and Development (ACBAR) (Elijah, 2001) and new funding incentives and programmes set-up by organisations such as the United States Agency for International Development (USAID), and the UN High Commissioner for Refugees (UNHCR) (Oliker *et al.*, 2004, p. 34).

By the early 1990s, however, the tenuous cohesion between *Mujahidin* groups during an ideological conflict against the Soviet forces had given way to inter-group fighting along ethno-confessional, tribal, and regional lines (Ghulam, 2015; Saikal, 1998). During this time, with the majority of UN and aid agencies based across the border in Pakistan, the cross-border delivery of aid was facilitated by and depended upon relations and negotiations with different warring parties (Goodhand, 2006). These practices took place amidst growing criticism that, at least in part, humanitarian endeavours were helping to fuel the conflict in Afghanistan, rather than to assist the general population. Aid agencies had little oversight over or knowledge about what happened to the aid they provided, and whether it was actually reaching the communities for which it was intended. In 1996, the Taliban, a Deobandi Islamist militia that emerged during the civil war, took power over most of Afghanistan. They established the Islamic Emirate of Afghanistan (IEA), moved the capital from Kabul to Kandahar, and implemented a very specific and strict interpretation of the Islamic *sharia* (see Ghulam, 2015). The change in political circumstances led Western agencies to ponder their approach for the future.

In 1998, in the context of these debates, a new approach to Afghanistan was developed in the form of the SFA, which detailed the establishment of two mutually reinforcing processes, 'a political strategy for peacebuilding and a common programming mechanism for international assistance' (UN, 1998, Article 29). The framework document was produced in the aftermath of a multi-agency visit to Afghanistan in October 1997. Several UN agencies including the Department of Political Affairs (DPA), the Department of Humanitarian Affairs (DHA now OCHA), the UNDP, the World Bank, and Oxfam, held consultations with over 80 Afghan and international participants, from humanitarian, development, and political organisations.[3] The efforts for greater coherence between three pillars, development assistance, politics, and human rights, were to be led by the UN, but also adopted by other external actors working on Afghanistan. While not advocating the merging of the three pillars, the SFA argued that any hope for peace in the Afghan context was dependent on eliminating any 'disconnects' between the political, human rights, humanitarian, and developmental aspects of the international response (UN, 1998, Article 13), and 'enhance[ing] the synergy between the United Nations political strategy in Afghanistan and the international assistance activities' (UN, 1998, para. 3). Thus, the framework represented an early example of the reconceptualisation of development, peace, and security in international policy which stressed the benefits of using aid for strategic purposes. A list of principles, strategies, and broad institutional arrangements were laid out in the document, which outlined a more integrated approach to peacebuilding (Brabant and Killick, 1999). The framework strategy was reliant on framing Afghanistan as a 'failed state', the perceived malleability of the local population, and promoting coherence amongst a group of institutional arrangements set up to guide the engagement of the UN and other external organisations with each other, Afghan officials, and local communities.

A so-called failed state is commonly regarded by other states, multilateral organisations, and INGOs as not providing acceptable political interlocutors. Ultimately, however, the designation of a nation is a subjective exercise often undertaken by hegemonic actors who have the power to frame such viewpoints and is often more reflective of their political aims and values than an objective portrayal of the circumstances of a particular state itself. Therefore, as Goodhand (2004) notes, in Afghanistan, during the 1990s, aid agencies often bypassed the Taliban government whenever possible. Instead they acted as a surrogate government, whereby agencies did not merely provide relief aid, but also delivered basic services to the population and engaged directly with communities at the village level. As the subsequent chapters below will show, many aid agencies have continued to operate in this manner in post-9/11 Afghanistan. Subsequently, the 'failed' label not only legitimises bypassing the government, but it also calls for the identification of other more palatable focal points. One of the only legitimate activities in this context, therefore, is to engage with non-state actors, such as community gatekeepers, civil society organisations, or religious leaders. This approach is commonly associated with what UN and INGO documents refer to as 'building politics from below' (Andrieu, 2010).

Accordingly, one of the strategic aims of the SFA was to build peace from below. The document states that though national ownership of the process is paramount, it is complicated by the 'near total breakdown of national and subnational institutions of governance in Afghanistan' (UN, 1998, para. 14). As a result, one of the main goals of the strategy was to 'increase the capacity of the Afghan people to determine their own priorities and build the conditions for peace' (UN, 1998, para. 14). This strategy, which targeted peacebuilding activities at local communities, had two implications. First, it meant that aid was being directly linked to peacebuilding activities. Therefore, local communities and organisations, not belligerents or the leaders of armed groups, were considered potential interlocutors for peacebuilding. The nature of these peacebuilding activities, however, were rooted in political and human rights frameworks that were not in line with the imperatives of the Taliban regime, or for that matter, local community values. Second, for this approach to succeed it required that aid be channelled through activities that supported local communities to become self-sufficient political actors and their adoption of Western-driven frameworks on issues such as human rights and governance. While the achievement of these goals may have been deemed a peacebuilding success in UN terms, the human rights values central to the SFA may have been contrary to local customs, which are given very little space in the document, and also had regional variations in Afghanistan. The capacity for Afghans to build peace therefore required their malleability in accepting the values and frameworks promoted by international actors through which peace and stability were conceptualised.

The SFA experiment implied that the malleability of local communities and civil society organisations to a liberal agenda and the potential to force behavioural change amongst the Taliban officials were dependent on the effective manipulation of aid by external actors and the weight given to assistance by Afghans. This hypothesis did not acknowledge the limited interaction of Western actors with Taliban authorities (Rashid, 2008), and was based on an exaggerated confidence in Western influence to leverage aid, and aid conditionality (Duffield, Gossman, and Leader, 2002). It also presented a portrayal of Afghan culture and political dynamics as violent yet simple and hence malleable. Furthermore, these violent tendencies required attention and management, while the supposedly simplistic nature of the local culture was assumed to facilitate its malleability. Thus, the underlying assumption was that Afghans suffered from a condition that could be 'cured' through Western intervention.

Finally, the SFA introduced multiple coordination mechanisms which included donors, UN agencies, and the development of an aid community providing a 'range of entry-points for donors to contribute to the overall direction of the humanitarian aid programme in Afghanistan' (Johnson and Jolyon, 2002). Some of the mechanisms put forth in the document were never realised in practice, but several were, including the Afghanistan Support Group (ASG), a donor coordination body, and the Afghanistan Programming Body (APB), an overall coordinating body and a series of thematic, regional, and national structures. As both Johnson (2002) and Harrison (2001) point out, despite the new organisational arrangements, the SFA was unable to overcome the fact that donor countries, UN agencies and NGOs were suspicious of each other, protective of their territories, and unclear as to what the practical realisation of the objectives set out in the SFA really meant. These multiple coordinating bodies and the relationships of the actors within them mirror the structures that later dominated post-9/11 Afghanistan.

The events that took place in Afghanistan after the 9/11 World Trade Center attacks in New York are unique in many respects; however, they must be situated in a broader historical landscape which recognises the political situation of the country, and the roles of foreign governments, the UN, and the aid community in the country. The SFA embodied the changes underway globally and regionally during the 1990s, which shaped how aid, conflict, and security were coordinated and managed through international policies. The framing of Afghanistan as a failed state with a highly traditional yet violent and malleable society made it a prime location for experimentation by international actors. The events in the 1980s and 1990s and the SFA foreshadowed the discursive framings and material arrangements that characterised the post 9/11 era in Afghanistan. After the initial ousting of the Taliban in 2001, the revisionist history of external actors largely discounted the lessons, mistakes, and challenges of the recent past; thus, Afghanistan became a *tabula rasa* for the UN once again.

Post 9/11

Multiple rationales emerged in the post-9/11 era to justify international intervention in Afghanistan, and linked security and development in contrasting and converging ways. The UN-led state-building and reconstruction plan, which promoted democratisation and used the language of human security, emerged alongside the US-initiated Global War on Terror (GWOT) policy agenda, sometimes referred to as the 'Long War'. Both drew on the idea of Afghanistan as a failed state with a violent history that needed to be managed by international actors. Over time the language of the two projects became strikingly similar.

After the initial US-led Operation Enduring Freedom (OEF) military campaign, several US agencies began to airdrop humanitarian aid in the border regions and around Kabul, but no long-term assistance was anticipated; rather, US-led intervention policy revolved around two main elements. First, the invasion was primarily concerned with the perceived national security interests of the US, yet had been framed as part of a global security effort. In speeches directly after 9/11, the national security interests of the US were linked to the framing of al-Qaeda and their alleged protectors the Taliban, as a problem of global proportions. This was done in several ways: the threat of terrorism was constructed not as endangering the US alone, but also the international system. Soon after the attacks, US President George W. Bush opined that al-Qaeda, and by inference the Taliban, wanted to overthrow existing governments in many Muslim countries, including those of US allies such as Egypt and Saudi Arabia, to drive Israel out of the Middle East, and drive Christians and Jews from vast regions of Asia and Africa (Bush, 2001a). Moreover, the base of the threat was not just confined to Afghanistan but also took on global dimensions. As Bush went on to say:

> Our war on terror begins with al Qaeda, but it does not end there. It will not end until every terrorist group of global reach has been found, stopped and defeated.
>
> (Bush, 2001a)

The pursuit of this threat was framed as an international response by all the nations supporting freedom and universal human rights. In fact, then US President Bush described the Afghanistan invasion as being 'the collective will of the world' (Bush, 2001b).

Second, US policies were devoid of any substantive long-term political strategy and focused on the short-term objective of regime change and counterterrorism. OEF was 'designed to disrupt the use of Afghanistan as a terrorist base of operations and to attack the military capability of the Taliban regime' (Bush, 2001a). It was based on the strategy known as the 'Rumsfeld Doctrine', named after Donald Rumsfeld, the then US Secretary of Defence, which advocated the use of technology, information, and airstrikes to root out the enemy while minimising the number of troops on the ground and hence Western fatalities (Graves, 2010). The swift toppling of the Taliban regime in 2001 was perceived as a success for the Rumsfeld approach, and was reinforced by assertions that the US would not 'create the future government of Afghanistan' because 'it is up to the Afghans themselves to determine their future' (Bush, 2001b). Any aid was to be delivered by military actors, be humanitarian in nature, and short-term, as part of the broader counterterrorism strategy. The US approach aimed to form a new Afghan regime that would cooperate with the United States in stamping out any residual terrorist threat (Dobbins, 2008). When asked about any US commitments to Afghanistan, Rumsfeld said:

> We go in and root out terrorists; I don't think that leaves us with a responsibility to try to figure out what kind of government that country ought to have. It certainly does suggest that we would have a humanitarian interest in the people of that country. – I don't know people who are smart enough from other countries to tell other countries the kind of arrangements they ought to have to govern themselves....
>
> (Rumsfeld, 2001)

In retrospect, the irony of his statement cannot be overlooked given the extensive social, political, and economic re-engineering project that was then set in motion. By 2002, the US official discourse on Afghanistan began to shift. Rather than a short-term military action to force regime change, the war in Afghanistan began to be depicted in the official policy as a 'war of liberation' and a first step in the Freedom Agenda of the Bush administration, which would later form the basis for military intervention in Iraq. Thus, in an effort to alter public perception of the US role in Afghanistan, Bush (2002) contended that OEF 'was not sent in to conquer [Afghanistan]; they were sent in to liberate [...] true peace will only be achieved when we give the Afghan people the means to achieve their own aspirations' (Bush, 2002). This was a shift from the previous US position, which had expressed no interest in anything beyond regime change to a construction of the US role in Afghanistan as a partly altruistic endeavour. This shift in US policy attempted to put forth a revisionist version of history that legitimised the invasion of Afghanistan as not only a counterterrorism campaign, but also as necessary for the security of the civilised world, the liberation of the Afghan people, and their escape from poverty and abuse. From 2002, US activities expanded to include state-building goals and longer-term aid assistance, with the important caveat that counterterrorism still remained their principal aim. As US policy continued to revolve around its counterterrorism strategy, the UN began to lead a democratisation and state-building agenda for post-Taliban Afghanistan.

Bonn

The Agreement on Provisional Arrangements in Afghanistan Pending the Re-Establishment of Permanent Government Institutions, signed on the 5 December 2001 (hereafter the Bonn Agreement), was the outcome of the UN-led process which sought to set out the institutional framework which would negotiate a post-Taliban Afghan state. After the military defeat of the Taliban, carried out by a joint US-led coalition and co-opted Afghan *Mujahidin* forces, most notably the Northern Alliance, a series of negotiations began to take place in preparation for meeting in Bonn, Germany, which would set out the roadmap for the next few years in Afghanistan. The ten-day process, led by UN official Lakhdar Brahimi, saw the UN, US, UK, Germany, and several other international bodies, including the EU, met with four groups representing various segments of Afghan society and the diaspora, the Northern Alliance, the Cyprus Group of former *Mujahedin*, the Peshawar group, formed of mainly Pashtun exiles based in Pakistan, and the Rome Group who were composed of the exiles who supported the former Afghan King Mohammad Zahir Shah and the royal family (Chesterman, 2002; UN, 2001a, 2001b). The discussions focused on creating an interim power-sharing arrangement that would facilitate the process to re-establish permanent government institutions in Afghanistan. Though Bonn was often referred to as a part of a peace process, the exclusion of the Taliban precluded a peace agreement from being part of the outcome of the process. Instead, the result of the meetings was the Bonn Agreement, an approximately 30-month state-building and security roadmap for post-9/11 Afghanistan, culminating in a series of national elections.

Characterising a large-scale external intervention as a locally led process is difficult. However, local ownership and legitimacy were important elements of the international rationale for the international presence in Afghanistan, which had been promoted as necessary and desirable at both the global level and domestic level. The transformative process that took place in the aftermath of 9/11 needed to be seen as something the Afghan people wanted. Relatedly, the Bonn Agreement (2001) highlighted the agency of the Afghan population in shaping and owning the reconstruction process. It begins by explicitly 'acknowledging the right of the Afghan people to freely determine their own political future in accordance with the principles of Islam, democracy, pluralism and social justice' (p. 1).

At Bonn, however, Brahimi maintained that even though the Afghan people were not properly represented, history would 'ignore that the meeting was unrepresentative if the participants managed to fashion a process that would lead to a legitimate and representative government' (qtd. in Barnett, 2004). He claimed that it was more important to establish a process that would lead to a legitimate and representative government than to focus on the inclusiveness of the process (Hassan and Hammond, 2011). Therefore, from the outset of the international intervention in post-9/11 Afghanistan, a precedent was set whereby certain parts of Afghan society, not just the Taliban, were relegated to the periphery of the international forums and decision-making processes. This remained the *status quo* for future conferences in London, Tokyo, Paris, and Germany, which also largely excluded significant civil society voices. The representatives at the Bonn meeting were acceptable intermediaries to the Western actors leading the process. Many of these leaders were to become powerful figures in the Afghan government formed after 2004.

The officials forming the new Afghan government after the elections in 2004 and 2005 were a diverse group. The elected Afghan government that was to lead this liberal nation-building exercise consisted of a mix of warlords (Khir, 2012), modernists, and diaspora technocrats, a few civil society members, and others selected for their ethnic and tribal ties (Suhrke, 2007). After the elections, Afghan President Hamid Karzai began to make political appointments in a bid to bring on-side local personalities that opposed the government, including religious leaders. Suhkre (2007, p. 1295) contends that Karzai tried to use 'traditional methods of Afghan statecraft to co-opt and balance political contenders' after the election (p. 1295). This was not a new practice: as Rubin (2002) points out, from the outset of the intervention 'the UN, troop providers and donors, however, also tried to constrain these processes' (pp. 179–180). Ironically, the political appointments that followed the election in an attempt to include the government critics and power holders that had not been involved in the elections or not elected into government were a continuation rather than a challenge to the process initiated by Western actors (Suhrke, 2007).

The Bonn Agreement laid out the interim political structures, the administrative support system, and the roles and responsibilities of key international actors. The plan was to put in place an Afghan Interim Authority, then an Emergency *Loya Jirga*[4] which would decide on the composition of a Transitional Authority (June 2002), to be disbanded after presidential elections (October 2004) and the national assembly and provincial council elections (September 2005), which would signal the completion of the Bonn process. Additionally, a Central Bank, a Civil Service Commission, an Independent Human Rights Commission, a new legal framework and judicial system, and a new constitution (January 2004) would be established. International actors, a new UN mission, and an international security force, would work to support the new Afghan governance bodies. If met, Bonn's short-term institution-building goals were poised to provide much of the architecture through which reconstruction and state-building, perceived as significantly longer processes, would take place.

The roles given to the UN and its partners in the Bonn Agreement differed slightly from previous peace operations, such as Kosovo, where UN-led transitional administrations were put in place. Rather in Afghanistan, a 'light footprint' approach (UNSG, 2002, para. 98) would be adopted. UN involvement would be coordinated through the United Nations Assistance Mission in Afghanistan (UNAMA), taking over from the long-standing UNSMA based in Pakistan, mandated via UNSCR 1401. Bonn also recommended the establishment of an international security force, that later on became the International Security Afghanistan Force (ISAF), which would be UN-mandated but not UN-led (UN, 2001). The ISAF was meant to be a non-combat force mainly confined to Kabul; therefore, it would not interfere with the larger scale and separate US-led OEF operations (UN, 2001a, Annex I). To facilitate this process, the Bonn participants agreed 'to withdraw all military units from Kabul and other urban centres or other areas in which the UN-mandated force is deployed' (UN, 2001, Annex 1). The follow-up to this commitment, however, was inconsistent and largely unmonitored. A key purpose of putting in place a 'relatively lean' UN mission was to signal to the Afghan leadership the process which would ensure a sustainable and a non-dependent government. As discussed below, however, Afghan ownership over the process was highly contested and over time, UNAMA and ISAF's mandates and responsibilities expanded considerably as 'mission creep' took hold.

Bonn posited the UN to be the principal actor in the Afghan intervention project, taking the lead role in supporting Afghan officials, facilitating important aspects of the transition, and coordinating between international civilian and military organisations on the ground. Accordingly, the UN was perceived as being particularly well-suited to playing the leading role in the establishment of the new Afghan governance architecture, due to its identification as an 'internationally recognized impartial institution' (UN, 2001, Annex II). From the outset of the Bonn process, however, the UN was decidedly not an impartial actor. Any perception of neutrality was eliminated as it supported the 'internationally recognized transition government [actors] and against the "spoilers" trying to undermine the transitional process' (Eide *et al.*, 2005, p. 6). Consequently, the UN mission mandate and activities were strongly contested by one or more of the conflict parties (Metcalfe, Giffen, and Elhawary, 2011, p. 47). The 'peace now justice later' approach of Brahimi, who was head of UNAMA from 2001–2004, could be better understood as proposing an emphasis on state-building and security with reconciliation and justice as elements that could be addressed somewhat later (Tondini, 2008). Ultimately, the UN was positioned to support the Afghan government but not to promote reconciliation, building peace, or advance justice, a theme that will be explored in greater detail in the chapters to come. Indeed, a decade later, when the transition period approaches and where this chapter ends, reconciliation began to be considered only as *part* of a possible exit strategy for ISAF contributing nations and donor governments.

The UN-led Bonn Agreement and the US-led coalition policy maintained an uneasy co-existence within Afghanistan, but also converged in some important ways. Both approaches advocated for an intervention project based on a

Western vision of the appropriate nature of the state and society, and both attempted to produce an international consensus on the existence of and need to address the Afghan problem. As the UN, US, NATO, their partners, and other external actors settled into Afghanistan, the merging of security and development in international policy meant that there was an increasing number of situations where development and security met in practice (Gänzle, 2009). This phenomenon is evident in the integrated UNAMA mission structure, the Provincial Reconstruction Teams, and the funding structures that were set up in Afghanistan.

Setting up the structures: integration and coherence

The integrated mission

From the outset, UNAMA was set up as a special integrated mission led by the DPA and the Department of Peacekeeping Operations (DPKO), coordinating over 30 UN agencies and 20 field offices (Earle, 2002). The integrated mission concept was initially discussed during the 1990s in the context of UN reform but the proposal and elaboration on the concept was introduced by the Brahimi Report (UNSG, 2002) which called for the establishment of 'one-stop support for United Nations peace-and-security field activities [that would] extend across the whole range of peace operations' (p. 35). At a basic level, according to former UN Secretary General Kofi Annan's *Note of Guidance on Integrated Missions* integrated is a 'system-wide response … and guiding principle for the design and implementation of complex UN operations in post-conflict situations and for linking the different dimensions of peacebuilding into a coherent support strategy' (UNSG, 2006, pp. 2–3). The rationale behind integration is that greater coherence between different aspects of UN missions (political, development, humanitarian, human rights, rule of law, social, and security) will increase the likelihood of peacebuilding objectives being achieved. There has been little documented evidence of increased efficiency due to the integrated structure, however, nor did the perspectives shared by actors throughout this study reflect that opinion. Instead, the integrated set-up in Afghanistan was marked by several contradictions.

The first conundrum was the choice of the 'two-feet in integration' model that the UN adopted in 2002. There are several possible integration mission models, two-feet-out, two-feet-in and one-foot-out one-foot-in (UNOCHA, 2009).[5] Each model contains a different set of management, coordination, and reporting arrangements between various arms and agencies within UN missions in response to the local context. The two-feet-in model is usually implemented in stable post-conflict settings, where a UN peacekeeping or political mission with widespread in-country support is deployed alongside a United Nations Country Team (UNCT) (OCHA, 2009) facilitating the establishment of a combined Deputy Special Representative of the Secretary General (DSRSG)/Resident Coordinator (RC)/Humanitarian Coordinator (HC) (UNOCHA, 2011).[6]

Practically, in the UNAMA, this meant that the DSRSG, a senior official from the DPKO held a 'triple hat'. They were responsible for providing direct supervision and overall strategic direction for the UN mission, and reported to the Special Representative of the Secretary General (SRSG), the top UN official in the mission. Simultaneously, they were also the RC, responsible for recovery and development operations, and the HC, responsible for the coordination of humanitarian affairs. They also coordinated the UNCT, essentially a political body whose objectives were to support the host government's long-term plans and objectives. The UN classification of Afghanistan as a 'post-conflict' situation in 2002 allowed the 'two-feet-in approach' to be adopted; however, in situations like the Afghanistan where conflict and military operations were still ongoing throughout the country, and the UN was not accepted by at least a portion of the population this model was rarely implemented.

Second, the decision to become a two-feet-in integrated mission and the conflation of responsibilities created as a result of the DSRSG's triple hat raised both operational and political challenges. One the one hand debates arose regarding the appropriate structural arrangements needed to preserve the independence of humanitarian coordination functions of the UN mission and whether a standalone OCHA office should be established or whether these functions should be integrated into the UN mission structure (Metcalfe, Giffen, and Elhawary, 2011, p. 1). On the other hand, actors within and outside of the UN disputed the tendency of integration arrangements to facilitate the prioritisation of political prerogatives over other mission objectives (p. 57). Perspectives shared throughout the book highlight this last issue, in particular, as many UN officials and aid workers expressed frustration at the unwillingness of UN senior management to report honestly on the deteriorating security and humanitarian situation in the country due to their desire to construct a discourse of political success. The stark reality of these decisions for UN staff, aid workers, and district residents is detailed in the forthcoming chapters.

The PRTs

In 2003, the ISAF, now under NATO's command, began to establish PRTs as the main vehicle for their expansion outside of Kabul as mandated by UNSCR 1510 (UNSC, 2003). The new mandate did not only call for an increase in military personnel, but added political and development components to ISAF's previous mission. The PRTs, once described as being to the development–security nexus what light bulbs were to electricity (Petrik, 2016, p. 163), were provincial-level integrated military-civilian structures, staffed and supported by ISAF member countries (NATO, 2008, p. iii). Their origins can be traced back to US-led coalition Humanitarian Liaison Cells, established in Afghanistan in 2002, which comprised of 10–12 troops, and were tasked with both intelligence gathering and the implementation of Quick Impact Projects (QIPs) (Gilmore, 2011). The PRTs, however, described as 'civil–military institutions that are able to penetrate more stable and insecure areas because of their military component and able to stabilise these areas because of their combined capabilities' (NATO, 2010, p. 8) were much larger structures and carried out a range of activities. The increase of international military force was called for to facilitate the expansion of 'the United Nations and other international civilian personnel engaged, in particular, in reconstruction and humanitarian efforts' across the country, and to support the slow roll-out of the Afghan government's authority to the provinces beyond Kabul (NATO, 2010). Ultimately, the PRTs were mandated with three areas of responsibility: security, governance, and reconstruction and development. By 2006, over 400 smaller military bases run by US and ISAF forces were located throughout the Afghan countryside (Stewart, 2012), and a four-phased roll-out of the PRTs was completed. In total, 26 PRTs had been established, with plans for two more in Daikundi and Nimroz provinces[7] (NATO, 2010, 2012), each serving as a laboratory for testing different types of military-political-assistance hybrids.

Although they were conceived of as institutions with significant civilian leadership and/or composition at the outset, the majority of PRTs were comprised of predominantly military personnel, and a smaller group of civilians ranging between 5–25 per cent of the total staff (Haysom and Jackson, 2013). They also varied significantly in size: at any given time the German PRT could have upwards of 375 staff (Mitchell, 2015), the Lithuanian PRT had approximately 130 staff and the US PRTs were smaller with an average of 80 staff (Eronen, 2008). Different NATO nations took the lead for the joint military-civilian teams in selected provincial capitals of Afghanistan. By 2009 the US lead 12 of the PRTs, 14 were led by other nations, and one was jointly led by the US and Poland.[8] The overall supervision of the PRTs, however, was done jointly by both the ISAF HQ and the government of whichever lead nation was involved.

Though the ISAF HQ was supposed to be the primary source of guidance, the domestic governments provided funding for PRTs, and heavily influenced how each PRT team operated. As a result, it was difficult to monitor the extent to which guidelines or directives from ISAF HQ were implemented or if they were ever communicated to the various PRTs. The primacy of national government authority meant that there were different types of operations being conducted from PRT to PRT. For example, the USA PRTs were co-located with a wide range of military officials and special teams actively engaged in counterinsurgency and combat operations, with civilian staff to support the military effort. Conversely, the national policies of certain non-US PRTs placed restrictions on undertaking security-related functions without explicit approval from capitals, operating at night and venturing more than a set distance from camp (Perito, 2005). An added layer of complication was due to the cohabitation of several different nations within one PRT. Of the 26 PRTs, 12 were comprised solely of staff from the lead NATO nation, and 14 PRTs were multinational, often having one lead NATO nation and smaller military contingents from between one to four other countries, which sometimes included the US, and several civilian staff.[9] Therefore, different groups within the same location would undertake divergent activities according to their national policy directives. The PRT system was supposed to increase coherence and coordination between civilian and military actors. Instead, however, they were better characterised by inconsistency amongst the PRTs themselves and fractious relationships between the civilians and military staff both inside and outside of the PRTs, a theme that begins to be explored in Chapter 3.

Funding

In 2000, Afghanistan was the 69th largest recipient of ODA worldwide, receiving 0.3 per cent of total ODA flowing to developing countries. An assessment prepared by the UNDP and several other international organisations projected that recovery and reconstruction in Afghanistan would cost anywhere from 11 to US$18 billion from 2002–2012 (UNDP, 2002). UN Secretary General Kofi Annan asked the more than 60 nations in attendance to pledge US$10 billion for five years; US$6.3 billion were pledged (Reliefweb, 2002). By 2008, Afghanistan's share of total ODA increased again by a massive US$1.3 billion and then to a historic high of US$6.2 billion in 2009, the second-largest amount ever received in a single year by any recipient country after Iraq's US$8.8 billion in 2005 (World Bank, 2019).

Donors who had become established in Kabul after 2002 privileged their own bilateral channels and implementing agencies, and used funding channels in the provinces where their PRTs were present. NATO-member nations were putting significant funds into their PRTs and used them as a way to bypass multilateral channels and promote their domestic agendas. PRTs were engaging in governance and development activities far beyond the reach of what most actors, including the UN, had projected for them. In addition, Western countries funnelled aid bilaterally and through INGOs based in their home countries. INGOs distanced themselves from the UN, because they distrusted the politicisation of UNAMA, but also because they were now flush with funds. A myriad of new Afghan and international organisations appeared on the scene and began vying for the significant amounts of funding now available, but with little accountability as the following chapters will show.

Up until 2005, little to none of the technical assistance from the Asian Development Bank, the European Commission, Germany, Japan, or the United Kingdom was provided through coordinated programmes consistent with government strategy, and only one-third of the analytical work was done jointly (OECD, 2006). The chronic lack of transparency and communication of international donors with Afghan officials was exemplified in a report in which Afghan government officials stated they were unaware how one-third of all international aid assistance given to Afghanistan was spent between 2001 and 2008 (Waldman, 2008). In fact, only a small percentage of the aid funding has been run through government channels. Of the US$17 billion Afghan national budget in 2011, approximately 90 per cent or US$15.7 billion was delivered outside of government channels (Bjelica and Ruttig, 2018). The preference by international donors to *not* funnel aid money through the government contributed to a situation whereby aid agencies, funded directly by the donors rather than the Afghan government, continued to be the main providers of public services and donors, and could thus easily side-step working on national priorities as defined by the government. As a result, information on the programmes and services that were being implemented were often not available to government officials, or communities. This undermined the government and challenged the rhetoric of local ownership, but also, added to community perceptions of governmental and foreign corruption.

Expanding mandates and missions

The policies produced because of more than 20 international meetings that took place in the decade after Bonn – in an approach resembling Cramer's (2006) post-war 'great make-over fantasy' – set out a formula for the complete overhaul of the Afghan political, economic, and social systems, which constantly refer to the linking security to development. The UN-led reconstruction program of action was based on the New York Consensus model, an ambitious state-building guide with a timeline and plan of action to transform failed states into model liberal democracies based on the Western state system (Kahler, 2008). The intervention proposed a universalist vision of the appropriate ways for social and political organisation. The fall of the Taliban gave UN officials the opportunity to resurrect this normative agenda. Brahimi (2004) expressed this wish saying:

> We want to bring about some form of sustainable economic development, we want to change the way people do things, we want to improve the way they run their courts, the way they police themselves, the way they uphold human rights, the way their women are treated.
>
> (p. 3)

By 2005, the international actors, and specifically the UN, were mandated to work on Demobilisation, Disarmament and Reintegration (DDR), Security Sector Reform (SSR), counter-narcotics, and the reform of the justice sector, in addition to the human rights and the election roles laid out in Bonn (UNSC, 2005a). Resolution 1623 (UNSC, 2005b) on Afghanistan begins by recognising 'that the responsibility for providing security and law and order throughout the country resides with the Afghans themselves', but later goes on to say that 'the situation in Afghanistan still constitutes a threat to international peace and security', and therefore the strengthening and expansion of ISAF is welcomed throughout the country (pp. 1–2). The Afghan Compact (Afghanistan, 2006), the EU External Co-operation Programme (EU, 2008), the United Nations Development Framework for Afghanistan 2010–2013 (UNAMA, 2009a) all continue to highlight the interdependence of security, governance, and development, create new monitoring and oversight structures, and call for expansion.

Initially, in line with Brahimi's light footprint approach, UNAMA was meant to deploy approximately 180 civilian expatriate staff and a handful of uniformed military and police advisers, mainly based in Kabul, with 12–15 staff being deployed to each regional office (UNSG, 2002). By 2008, the UN mandate was extended to include leading international civilian efforts to support the Afghan government and to facilitate greater political outreach to Afghan leaders a result of the expanded and sharpened (Metcalfe, Giffen, and Elhawary, 2011). This resulted in a 91.5 per cent budget increase and approval for a staff upturn of 437 (UNSG, 2009a, para. 78).[10] As a result, by 2009, the UN had established offices in 13 provinces: Baghlan, Kandahar, Ghor, Kunar, Khost, Nimroz, Badghis, Faryab, Uruzgan, Badakhshan, Daikundi, Sar-i-Pul, and Zabul (UNAMA News, 2009). In addition, a series of UN resolutions from 2008–2010 created new structures aimed at strengthening the integration of UN bodies, including a 'super envoy' post designated as head of the UNAMA mission created by UNSC 1806 (2008). The expansion of the UN presence and mandates, however, ran alongside a troubling time for the Afghan population and external actors.

In 2006, months after the end of the Bonn process marked by the national assembly and provincial elections, the US policy also changed focus from counterterrorism to counterinsurgency (COIN). The move was guided by the US Army and Marine Corps *Field Manual 3–24 Counterinsurgency* (United States, 2006), in which human-centred security language figured prominently. In fact, the altered approach was represented as a 'people-centred or cultural turn' within US military doctrine (Gilmore, 2011). The US approach went beyond capturing 'hearts and minds', and called for military-centred activities, incorporating heavy development assistance competent which resembled, at least in certain terms, a human security approach. It proposed restrained military operations, coupled with greater investment in reconstruction and development projects, community leader dialogue, gender initiatives, and increased awareness of local cultures. Thus, COIN invoked human security language, but it maintained its goal which was to produce a state and society complaint with the US, described as global, security interests through military operations in service of the War of Terror narrative (Gilmore, 2011). This policy shift, however, lay the groundwork for a more expansive intervention requiring the enhancement of military and civilian staff, sub-contractors, and the establishment of new units to achieve the development and reconstruction goals slatted as fundamental to the COIN approach. This reached its peak in 2009, with the plan for an international military and civilian 'surge'.

The aftermath of the 2005 Afghan elections and incrementally escalating violence, and an emerging culture of impunity, however, began to tear at the 'postwar make-up fantasy' rhetoric (Cramer, 2006). The toppling of the Taliban regime was followed by two rapid elections. These established an Afghan government which had been put in place and by the US, UN, and European officials; this was touted as an initial success of the international intervention. The perceived lack of independence of the Karzai government from Western powers, however, had diminished faith in elected officials and stability of the government.

The 2009 elections, which saw Karzai elected for a second term and the following parliamentary elections in 2010 were marked by violent attacks on polling stations and the intimidation of voters; the voter turnout was approximately 40 per cent, lower than the 2004 and 2005 turnouts (Wilder, 2005). In addition, divisions amongst international bodies became more public. For example, disagreements between the US and European officials and the incumbent Afghan leadership and factions within the higher echelons of the UN concerning the elections process, and widespread fraud cover-ups. The heated disputes between US Ambassador Richard Holbroke, UN Special Envoy Peter Galbraith, and UN Special Representative Kai Eide were widely broadcast in the national and international media and ended with the termination of Galbraith from his post.[11]

In mid-2009, the then US President Obama unveiled a new Strategy for Afghanistan and posed a similar question to that which many Afghans had also been asking of international actors at the time: 'What is our purpose in Afghanistan?' (Obama, 2009). While the George W. Bush administration had focused on 'ideological warfare, and later the virtues of nation-building and the spread of liberal democracy', Obama, elected in November 2008 and taking up office in January 2009, adopted a very different approach looking towards the US exit from Afghanistan (Ul Haq and Zahra, 2009). The new plan, referred to as the *AfPak* (United States, 2009), focused on regional dynamics, and represented a turnaround from the statements of the previous administration. The new US policy sought to address 'the perilous situation' NATO forces found themselves in almost a decade into the Afghan intervention (ibid). The 2009 strategy abandoned the idea of nation-building and refocused and scaled-down US objectives in Afghanistan, moving from focusing on a military campaign to a political solution framed as depending on the will of the Afghan people. The former ISAF Commander, General McChrystal, reiterated this by saying:

> This is a different kind of fight. Our strategy cannot be focused on seizing terrain or destroying insurgent forces; our objective must be the population.
>
> (Gen. McChrystal, 2009a)

The *AfPak* proposed that a significant increase in NATO military forces, aimed at fighting the armed opposition groups and training the Afghan army and police, should be accompanied by a surge in civilian experts who would work on improving development assistance and governance. It stated:

> This new strategy will have no chance of success without better civil–military coordination.… [It] must integrate population security with building effective local governance and economic development.
>
> (United States, 2009, pp. 2–5)

Accordingly, from 2009–2011, to support the surge, troop levels increased from approximately 64,500 to 132,500. The highest numbers of soldiers came from the US (30,000 to 90,000) and the UK (9,000 to 9,500) (NATO, 2012). The troop surge was complemented by a 70 per cent increase in civilian advisers (Erikson *et al.*, 2016). Agricultural specialists and educators, engineers, and lawyers would be recruited to work with the military 'to advance security, opportunity, and justice – not just in Kabul, but also from the bottom up in the provinces' in the hope that, 'assistance benefits would contribute directly to security' (Obama, 2009). Most of the new cadre of experts would be placed directly in Afghan government units on a day-to-day basis, taking on a much more intrusive role than PRT staff had previously had. The *AfPak* surge, however, was limited and was meant to signal the final push before an imminent Western exit.

The 'light footprint approach' that Brahimi (UNSG, 2002, p. 16) had spoken of, which was supposed to acknowledge Afghan leadership and sovereignty, began to give way to an expansion of the roles of both external military and civilian actors within Afghanistan, and along with that a significant surge in the influx of foreign aid money. While the improvements in infrastructure, health, and education were undeniable, the allegations of corruption of both international and local actors were rampant and a focus on quantity not quality had led to uneven access to services (Rivas, 2011). At the same time the insecurity of Afghan people was on the rise, as civilian causalities caused by all belligerents to the conflict were mounting (UNAMA, 2009b). Pre-2007 estimates are difficult to verify, but suggest no less than 6,500 civilian casualties resulting directly from the invasion and armed conflict between 2003 and 2007, with thousands of people dying because of the humanitarian crisis followed (Crawford, 2015; UNAMA, 2007). Between 2007–2011 there were 11,980 civilian casualties, including fatalities and injuries in Afghanistan, attributed to belligerents from all sides of the conflict, including anti-government armed groups, Afghan security forces, and international military forces (UNAMA, 2008, 2010, 2018). Afghanistan was marked by a rise in the violent anti-government activity, mounting civilian casualties, and growing discontent over corruption and both real and perceived government and international failures to improve the lives of Afghan citizens (Nixon and Ponzio, 2007, p. 2). The expanding presence of the interveners, military and civilian, had not brought peace, security, or justice. On the cusp of these events, two new policy agendas emerged: transition and transformation.

Transition and transformation

In 2010, there was a noticeable shift in the international narrative on Afghanistan. The supposedly altruistic 'saviour' trope (Easterly, 2006), which characterised international policy statements of the early 2000s, gave way to more a sombre rhetoric. Donor governments began to express concern that wide-scale intervention in Afghanistan had reached its height and the international community could not continue to invest significant human and financial resources in a failing project. Afghans were encouraged to take responsibility for their problems and control over their destiny, as donors and NATO nations put them on notice that the clock was ticking (UNSC, 2010). Transition and transformation agendas emerged to guide NATO forces and international donors towards an exit from the perceived *impasse* of Afghanistan.

The transition process was a time-bound plan for the handover of all areas of the country from the ISAF forces to the Afghan government and security forces. Planning began in late 2009 for a phased transition to take place from phase was to take place between 2011–2014. The plan involved an immediate short-term increase in human and financial resources aimed at facilitating a swift drawdown and eventual exit of international security forces from Afghanistan (Hassan and Hammond, 2011). In May 2012, the leaders of the 50 countries contributing to the NATO mission in Afghanistan met in Chicago to discuss the future of NATO engagement in Afghanistan. The Chicago Summit Declaration (2012) reaffirmed that the handover to Afghan security forces by the summer of 2013 and the withdrawal of the NATO combat mission forces by the end of 2014 to be replaced by a new mission focused on training, advising, and assisting. The reality of the approaching transition, however, began to set-in, including the lack of clarity about the remaining levels of international military forces, aid funding, and donor interest in Afghanistan. This uncertainty contributed to anxiety within the aid community, UN agencies, the Afghan government, and the wider population. Some suggested the reduction of international military forces could reduce the Taliban incentive for attacks and therefore decrease the levels of violence, allow development agencies to assert their concerns over the politicisation and militarisation of aid, and that less money might drive more effective and efficient programming. A more pessimistic view was that the military drawdown would lead to a significant reduction in aid and interest in Afghanistan globally. Aid agencies were mainly funded by nations that are or were militarily involved in the conflict after 9/11. In total, approximately 92 per cent of the aid committed to Afghanistan between 2002–2011 was given by troop-contributing nations (Afghanistan, 2011). By the end of 2012, overall aid assistance had begun to drop in line with the gradual decrease in troops by several NATO countries including the Netherlands, Canada, and Poland (Dobbins *et al.*, 2019; World Bank, 2019).

The Transformation decade was set for 2015–2024, and focused on development. International policy began to stress more intensely than before the full ownership and sovereignty of the Afghan government over Afghanistan on the path to transition and transformation. Clues regarding the shifting aid agenda emerged in 2010 at two important conferences. The London Conference Communiqué (United Kingdom, 2010), developed at the London conference in 2010 emphasised 'that the Afghan government and the international community are entering into a new phase on the way to full Afghan ownership' (p. 1). The Kabul Conference, held six months later in July 2010, was the first international conference on Afghanistan to be held in the country. The location was meant to symbolise the leadership of the Afghan government over the process and essentially its own future. The Kabul Communiqué (Afghanistan, 2010) begins by 'affirming support for the Afghan leadership in exercising its sovereign authority' (p. 1). It then lays out a plan of action for the Afghan government to implement certain programmes within the areas of security, countering government corruption, the rule of law, fiscal management, social and economic development, gender equality, and several other issues. These steps were meant to 'support the transition to Afghan ownership and leadership' (Afghanistan, 2010, p. 9). The emphasis on ensuring the process was Afghan-led; however, this brings into question the heavy emphasis on local ownership which underlined international policy documents from late 2001 onwards, including the Bonn Agreement.

The transition and transformation agendas placed a significant focus on the accountability of the Afghan government. This is most evident in the Bonn II (2011) and the Tokyo Declaration, which laid out the specific terms for the Transition to Transformation Decade (2015–2024). Bonn II ends by saying, 'recognising that the security and wellbeing of Afghanistan continue to affect the entire region and beyond, the international community strongly commit to a renewed partnership for the Transformation Decade' (p. 6). The documents contain a long list of areas where the Afghan government is seen to have fallen short, and reaffirms the commitment of international donors and organisations to continue to provide support in these areas. This support is, however, conditional upon the increased accountability of the Afghan government and is limited in scope. A few months after I left Kabul, in July 2012, representatives from over 70 countries, international organisations, and non-profit groups met in Tokyo to decide upon the framework for international support for Afghanistan from the end of the transition in 2014 through the Transformation Decade. At the conference, a conditional offer was made of approximately US$16 billion in aid assistance until 2015 along with a commitment to not drastically reduce funding flows to Afghanistan (SIGAR, 2012). The Tokyo Declaration (2012a), entitled *Self-Reliance in Afghanistan*, for the first time specifically prioritises limiting aid flows to Afghanistan and lays down mechanisms for the increased accountability and reporting of the Afghan government's conduct to international donors, on a bi-annual, annual and monthly basis which were set out in the Tokyo Mutual Accountability Framework (2012b). The change in the mood reflected a planned reduction in the scope of the state-building project and a shifting of responsibility for what was increasingly seen as another international intervention failure and its aftermath to the Afghan people and government. In return for the assistance, the Afghan government promised to implement political and economic reforms to improve governance, make public institutions more accountable, and tackle pervasive corruption.

Consequently, the strategies of external actors became largely shaped by the 2014 deadline (Goodhand, 2012). There was a growing recognition that the deals consolidated for the immediate future as part of the transition process could compromise the quality of life for the Afghan population, but that this was just the way it had to be. In 2010, the NATO Senior Civilian Representative acknowledged that several prominent Western leaders began to discuss reconciliation, something Afghan people had been calling for since the initial toppling of the Taliban in the Autumn of 2001, as an alternative to intervention and as a means for withdrawal rather than part of transitional justice (Tellus, 2009; Sedwill, 2011) Paradoxically, it was clear at least in practice that the international intervention no longer aimed to secure or develop Afghanistan. The explicit focus now was now on leaving, while retaining a sufficient presence of security forces to prevent the violence from spilling over into the West.

Changes in the intervention landscape began quickly once the transition and transformation agendas had set in. NATO nations began to prepare to leave. UN agencies and the aid community started evaluating operational reorganisation models. UN who had increased their staff and placed emphasis on opening and resourcing provincial offices began to scale back as the transition process took hold and in the light of budget constraints and security issues. The UN funding began to decrease in 2011 and 'after the 18.7 per cent reduction in funding for UNAMA in 2013' they began to close offices or co-habitat with other agencies (UNSG, 2013, Section VIII); ultimately planning to reduce operations to only 13 field offices in 2014, down from a total of 23 in 2012 (UNSG, 2013, Section VIII). Afghan and international agencies began to prepare for an impending drop in funding. In fact, despite commitments made by international donor governments at the Tokyo Conference aid disbursed to Afghanistan declined from an annual average of US$6.1 billion between 2008 and 2011 to around US$4.2 billion in 2015 (World Bank, 2019). International and local aid organisations who had assumed provision of many of the basic services usually provided by the government began closing down their programming and scrabbling for funds. Civil society networks busied themselves planning advocacy campaigns aimed at preventing donors from making drastic reductions in aid funding; aid workers, private security experts, UN staff, EU diplomats, and many others began looking for work elsewhere. Conversations in offices, coffee houses, and kebab shops in Kabul debated what the future held. As Afghanistan moved from transition to 'transformation', the poverty rate actually increased by 4 per cent 2008 between 2012 (Afghanistan, 2019).[12] Many Afghans remained hopeful, despite being increasingly disillusioned with the widespread impunity, inequality, and violence across the country.

It was amidst this dynamic yet very reflective period, ten years after the US-led intervention and the UN-led Bonn Agreement, in the midst of transition and in preparation for Tokyo, that my research commenced. The next four chapters, drawing upon interviews, focus groups, personal communications, and my own participation in activities and observations collected in Afghanistan and the West, explore security and development as understood by the people who live and work in Afghanistan, and how their understanding of these has influenced their relationships, identities, and everyday lives. These stories provide insight into the practices, contradictions, and experiences of intervention, specifically knowledge production, the circulation of power, hierarchies and relationships, and everyday violence.

Notes

1 Arabic word which literally means to strive or struggle, especially with a praiseworthy aim, with another person or group or with oneself.
2 Plural of 'mujahid' meaning one who engages in jihad. Often used to refer to guerrilla fighting to protect Islamic lands against foreign domination and/or unjust state violence.
3 The SFA was complimented by the Principled Common Programming (PCP) developed in 1998. The PCP was seen as being more field-led and elaborated on the principles for assistance, and mechanisms for the priority setting, and coordination, based on the SFA. (For further details see: Making a reality of Principled Common Programming. Item 3: Afghanistan: Assistance Strategy Paper 3. Prepared by UNOCHA, the Inter-Agency Standing Committee Working Group XXXIIth Meeting 3 June 1998, Geneva).
4 A *jirga* is a gathering or circle but also used to refer to a traditional conflict resolution mechanism in Afghanistan, used mainly be Pashtuns. A *loya jiga* is a grand council or mass national gathering that brings together representatives from the various ethnic, religious, and tribal communities in Afghanistan (See Wardak, 2009. Defining the Gaps: the Case of Afghanistan: From Education Reforms to Sustainable Development. Kabul: Ministry of Education. See Ahmed and Yousaf, 2018. Pashtun Jirgas, Their Potential in Pak-Afghan Reconciliation and National Reconstruction. South Asia Research, 38, 57–74).
5 The 'two-feet-out' is used in situations characterised by widespread conflict, the absence of a peace process, a lack of acceptance of the peacekeeping force, or the existence of spoilers, groups or persons trying to undermine a peace process. Thus, the Humanitarian Co-ordinator and UN Office for the Co-ordination of Humanitarian Affairs (OCHA) would thus remain entirely separate from the rest of the UN, to preserve their independence and neutrality, and their ability to engage with NGOs. The second approach is 'one-foot-in, one-foot-out', implemented in countries coming out of conflict with a political process in place and decreasing humanitarian needs. In the case the Deputy Special Representative to the Secretary General, Resident Coordinator (RC), and HC, are combined, but OCHA sits outside of the UN mission.
6 However, the HC role may be removed and OCHA may not be present or only present in a limited capacity.
7 Despite initial discussions no PRTs were ever established in Daikundi or Nimroz.
8 The PRT lead nations included: US, Canada, UK, The Netherlands, Germany, Sweden, Hungary, Poland, Norway, Italy, Spain, Lithuania, New Zealand, Turkey, and the Czech Republic.
9 The US was present in some capacity in 25 of the 26 PRTs.
10 This included an increase of 115 international staff, 57 national professional staff, 249 national support staff and 16 United Nations Volunteers.
11 For more information see: *The Guardian*, 10 December 2010, New direction for US in Afghanistan following Richard Holbrooke death; Radio Free Europe, 28 August 2009, Holbrooke, Karzai Reportedly Argue Over Alleged Afghan Vote Fraud; *New York Times*, 30 September 2009, After Clash Over Afghan Election, UN Fires a Diplomat; *New York Times*, 11 October 2009, UN Acknowledges 'Widespread Fraud' in Afghan Vote.
12 As of 2016/2017 the poverty rate in Afghanistan is 55 per cent.

References

Afghanistan. 2006. *Afghanistan Compact*. London Conference on Afghanistan, London, 31 January–1 February 2006.

Afghanistan. 2010. *Kabul Conference Communique*. The Kabul International Conference on Afghanistan. Kabul: Ministry of Foreign Affairs.

Afghanistan. 2011. *Development Cooperation Report*. Kabul: Ministry of Finance.

Afghanistan. 2019. *The Afghanistan Living Conditions Survey*. Kabul: Central Statistics Office.

Ahmed, Z. S. and Yousaf, F. 2018. Pashtun Jirgas, their potential in Pak-Afghan reconciliation and national reconstruction. *South Asia Research*, 38, 57–74.

Andrieu, K. 2010. Paradigm civilizing peacebuilding: Transitional justice, civil society and the liberal. *Security Dialogue*, 41, 538–558.

Barnett, R. R. 2004. Crafting a constitution for Afghanistan. *Journal of Democracy*, 15, 5–19.

Bjelica, J. and T. Ruttig. 2018. *The State of Aid and Poverty in 2018: A new Look At Aid Effectiveness in Afghanistan*. Kabul: Afghanistan Analysts Network.

Bonn. 2011. *Bonn II: From Transition to Transformation in Afghanistan*. International Conference on Afghanistan. Bonn. 5 December.

Brabant, K. V. and Killick, T. 1999. *The Limits and Scope for the Use of Development Incentives and Disincentives for Influencing Conflict Situations*. Case Study: Afghanistan. Paris: OECD.

Brahimi, L. 2004. *Strategies for Economic Reconstruction and Post-Conflict Management*. Berlin: German Ministry of Foreign Affairs.

Bush, G. 2001a. *Address to a Joint Session of Congress and the American People Office of the Press Secretary*. 20 September 2001. Washington, DC.

Bush, G. 2001b. *Presidential Address to the Nation*. The White House Archives. 7 October 2001. Available at: http://georgewbush-whitehouse.archives.gov/news/releases/2001/10/20011007-8.html

Bush, G. 2002. *Remarks by the President to the George C. Marshall ROTC Award Seminar on National Security:* President Outlines War Effort: Cameron Hall, Virginia Military Institute Lexington. Richmond, VA: Office of the President.

Chesterman, S. 2002. Walking softly in Afghanistan: The future of UN state-building, *Survival*, 44(3), 37–45.

Chicago Summit Declaration. 2012. *Issued by the Heads of State and Government participating in the meeting of the North Atlantic Council in Chicago*. 20 May 2012.

Cramer, C. 2006. *Civil War Is Not A Stupid Thing: Accounting For Violence In Developing Countries*. London: Hurst & Co.

Crawford. C. 2015. *War Related Death, Injury and Displacement in Afghanistan and Pakistan 2001–2014*. Cost of War Project. Watson Institute. Boston: Boston University.

Dobbins, J. 2008. *After the Taliban: Nation-Building in Afghanistan*. Washington, DC: Potomac Books.

Dobbins, J., Campbell, J. H., Mann, S., and Miller, L. E. 2019. *Consequences of a Precipitous U.S. Withdrawal from Afghanistan*. Washington, DC: Rand Corporation. January 2019.

Donini, A. 2011. *Between a Rock and a Hard Place: Integration or Independence of Humanitarian Action?* International Review of the Red Cross. International Committee of the Red Cross.

Duffield, M., Grossman, P., and Leader, L. 2002. *Review of the Strategic Framework for Afghanistan*. Kabul: AREU.

Earle, C. 2002. *Rebuilding Afghanistan: The United Nations Assistance Mission in Afghanistan (UNAMA)*. Stimpson Background Papers. Washington: Stimpson Centre.

Easterly, W. (2006) *The White Man's Burden*. Oxford: Oxford University Press.

Eide, E. B., Kaspersen, A. T., Kent, R., and Hippel, K. V. 2005. *Independent Study for the Expanded UN ECHA Core Group*. Report on integrated missions: practical perspectives and recommendations. New York, NY: United Nations.
Elijah J. 2001. NGOs and the economic recovery of Afghanistan. *Development in Practice*, 11(5), 633–636.
Eriksen, P., Hassan, M., Killian, L., LaForge, G., Levit-Shore, S., Rhode, S., and Sholes, K. 2016. *Lessons Learned from the U.S. Civilian Surge in Afghanistan*. Graduate Policy Workshop January 2016. New York, NY: Woodrow Wilson School of Public Policy.
Eronen, O. 2008. PRT Models in Afghanistan: Approaches to civil–military integration. *Finald Civilian Crisis Management Studies*, 1, 1–58.
EU. 2008. *External Co-operation Programme: Afghanistan*. Kabul: European Union.
Gänzle, S. 2009. *Coping with the 'Security-Development Nexus': The European Community's Instrument for Stability – Rationale and Potential. DIE Research Project 'European Policy for Global Development'*. Bonn: German Development Institute.
Ghulam, M. 2015. Afghanistan: A study in internal conflict and national cohesion. *International Journal of Multicultural and Multireligious*, Understanding, 2.
Gilmore, J. 2011. A kinder, gentler counter-terrorism: Counterinsurgency, human security and the War on Terror. *Security Dialogue*, 42, 21–37.
Goodhand, J. 2004. From war economy to peace economy? Reconstruction and state building in Afghanistan. *Journal of International Affairs*, 58(1), 155–174.
Goodhand, J. 2006. *Aiding Peace? The Role of NGOs in Armed Conflict*. Boulder, CO: Lynne Rienner.
Goodhand, J. 2012. *Contested Transitions: International Drawdown and the Future State in Afghanistan*. Oslo: Norwegian Peacebuilding Resource Centre.
Goodhand, J. and Sedra, M. 2013. Rethinking liberal peacebuilding, statebuilding and transition in Afghanistan: an introduction. *Central Asian Survey*, 32, 239–254.
Graves, T. C. 2010. Al-Qaeda, The revolution in military affairs, and the future of warfare. In: Yarger, H. R. (ed.) *Short of General War: Perspectives On The Use Of Military Power In The 21st Century*. Carlise, PA: Strategic Studies Institute, pp. 23–39.
Harrison, P. 2001. The strategic framework and principled common programming: A challenge to humanitarian assistance. *Humanitarian Exchange*, 19.
Hassan, O. and Hammond, A. 2011. The rise and fall of American's freedom agenda in Afghanistan: counter-terrorism, nation-building and democracy. *The International Journal of Human Rights*, 15, 532–551.
Jackson, A. 2011. *High Stakes: Girls Education in Afghanistan*. Kabul: Oxfam GB.
Johnson, C. 2002 *Lessons for a Post-Taliban Afghanistan. Humanitarian Exchange: Humanitarian Practice Network (HPN)*. London: Overseas Development Institute (ODI), pp. 19–21.
Johnson, C. and Jolyon, L. 2002. *Coordination Structures in Afghanistan*. Background Research for Humanitarian Policy Group Report 12. London: Overseas Development Institute (ODI).
Kahler, M. 2008. Statebuilding in Afghanistan and Iraq. In: Paris, R. and Sisk, T. D. (eds.) *Statebuilding After Civil War: The Long Road to Peace*. New York, NY: Routledge, pp. 287–303.
Khir, I. 2012. *A Look Into the Reconstruction of Afghanistan, Searching For a Security-Peacebuilding Nexus*. Law Review.
Kreczko, A. 2003. The Afghan experiment: The Afghan support group, principled common programming and the strategic framework. *Disasters*, 27, 239–258.

Larsen, I. H. 2010. UNAMA in Afghanistan: Challenges and opportunities in peacemaking, state-building and coordination. *Security in Practice*. Oslo: The Norwegian Institute of International Affairs.

Macrae, J and Leader, L. 2000. *The Politics of Coherence: Humanitarianism and Foreign Policy in the Post-Cold War Era*. London: Humanitarian Policy Group (HPG).

Metcalfe, V., Giffen, A., and Elhawary, S. 2011. *UN Integration and Humanitarian Space*. An Independent Study Commissioned by the UN Integration Steering Group. December 2011. Washington, DC: Humanitarian Policy Group.

Minear, L. 1998. *Report to the Headquarters Colloquium on the Interagency Strategic Framework Mission to Afghanistan*. UN Interagency Mission to Afghanistan Special Report. New York, NY: United Nations.

Mitchell, D. 2015. Blurred lines? Provincial reconstruction teams and NGO insecurity in Afghanistan, 2010–2011. *Stability: International Journal of Security and Development*, 4.

NATO. 2008. *CIMIC and PRT Operations in ISAF*. Brunssum: NATO.

NATO. 2010. *PRT Handbook*. Brussels: NATO.

NATO. 2012. *International Security Assistance Force (ISAF): Key Facts and Figures*. Brussels: North Atlantic Treaty Organisation (NATO).

Nixon, H. and Ponzio, R. (2007) Building democracy in Afghanistan: The statebuilding agenda and international engagement. *International Peacekeeping* 14: 26–40.

Obama, B. 2009. *A New Strategy for Afghanistan and Pakistan*. Washington, DC: White House Briefing.

OECD. 2006. *2006 Survey on Monitoring the Paris Declaration*: Afghanistan. Paris: OECD.

Oliker, O., Kauzlarich, R., Dobbins, J., Basseuner, K. W., Sampler, D. L., McGinn, J. G., Dziedzic, M. J., Grissom, A., Pirnie, B., Bensahel, N., and Guven, A. I. 2004. *Aid during Conflict: Interaction Between Military and Civilian Assistance Providers in Afghanistan, September 2001–June 2002*. Santa Monica, CA: RAND Corporation.

Perito, R. 2005. *The U.S. Experience with Provincial Reconstruction Teams in Afghanistan: Lessons Identified*. New York, NY: USIP.

Petrik, J. 2016. Provincial reconstruction teams in Afghanistan: Securitising aid through developmentalizing the military. In Brown, S. and Grävingholt, J. (eds.) *The Securitization of Foreign Aid*. New York: Palgrave Macmillan, pp. 163—187.

Ponzio, R. J. 2007. Transforming political authority: UN democratic peacebuilding in Afghanistan. *Global Governance*, 13, 255–275.

Raqib, M. and Barreto, A. A. 2014. The Taliban, religious revival and innovation in Afghan nationalism. *National Identities*, 16, 15–30.

Rashid, A. 2008. *Descent Into Chaos: How the War Against Islamic Extremism is Being Lost in Pakistan, Afghanistan and Central Asia*. London: Allen Lane.

Reliefweb. 2002. *Afghanistan: Donors Pledge $4.5 Billion in Tokyo*. See: reliefweb.int/report/afghanistan/afghanistan-donors-pledge-45-billion-tokyo.

Rivas, A. 2011. Health and education in Afghanistan: ten years later – quantity not quality. *Working Paper*. Afghan Coordinating Body for Afghan Relief (ACBAR).

Rubin, B. R. .2002. *The Fragmentation of Afghanistan: State Formation and Collapse in the International System*. New Haven: Yale University Press.

Rumsfeld, D. 2001. *News Briefing*. Department of Defence. Washington, DC: Government of the United States.

Saikal, A. 1998. Afghanistan's ethnic conflict. *Survival*, 40 (2), 114–126.

Sedwill, M. 2011. *Afghanistan: Transition & Partnership*. Speech for Asia Society in New York on 28 March 2011. Accessed at: www.nato.int/cps/en/natolive/opinions_71995.htm.

SIGAR. 2012. *Quarterly Report to the US Congress on Afghanistan.* Washington, DC: Office of the Special Inspector General for Afghanistan Reconstruction. 30 July 2012.

Stewart, A. 2012. Military base growth in Afghanistan: A threat to scorpion populations? *The Journal of Arachnology*, 40(2), 245–248.

Suhrke, A. 2007. Reconstruction as modernisation: The post-conflict project in Afghanistan. *Third World Quarterly*, 28: 1291–1308.

Tellus, A. 2009. *Reconciling with the Taliban? Toward an Alternative Grand Strategy in Afghanistan.* Washington, DC: Carnegie Endowment for International Peace.

Tokyo. 2012a. *The Tokyo Declaration: Partnership for Self-Reliance in Afghanistan From Transition to Transformation.* 20 July 2012.

Tokyo. 2012b. *Tokyo Mutual Accountability Framework.* Agreed by the Afghan Government and the International Community at the Tokyo Conference on Afghanistan, 20 July 2012.

Tondini, M. 2008. From neo-colonialism to a 'Light-Footprint Approach': Restoring justice systems. *International Peacekeeping*, 15 (2), 237–251.

Ul Haq, N. and Zahra, N. 2009. *Contours of U.S. 'AFPAK' Strategy.* Islamabad: Islamabad Policy Research Institute.

UN. 1946. *Resolution 8 (1946).* 29 August. New York, NY: United Nations.

UN. 1998. *Strategic Framework for Afghanistan: Toward a Principled Approach to Peace and Reconstruction.* New York, NY: United Nations.

UN. 2001a. *Agreement on Provisional Arrangements in Afghanistan Pending the Re-Establishment of Permanent Government Institutions. The First International Bonn Conference on Afghanistan*, December 2001, Bonn: United Nations.

UN. 2001b. *Security Council Endorses Afghanistan Agreement on Interim Arrangements Signed Yesterday In Bonn, Unanimously Adopting Resolution* 1383 (2001). Press Release. 6 December 2001.

UNAMA. 2007. *Report of the SG on Protection of Civilians in Armed Conflict.* Kabul: United Nations.

UNAMA. 2008. *Report of the SG on Protection of Civilians in Armed Conflict 2007.* Kabul: UNAMA Human Rights Unit.

UNAMA. 2009a. *United Nations Development Framework for Afghanistan 2010–2013.* Kabul: United Nations.

UNAMA. 2009b. Afghanistan: *Annual Report on Protection of Civilians in Armed Conflict, 2008.* Kabul: UNAMA Human Rights Unit.

UNAMA. 2010. *Report of the SG on Protection of Civilians in Armed Conflict 2009.* Kabul: UNAMA Human Rights Unit.

UNAMA. 2018. *Report of the SG on Protection of Civilians in Armed Conflict 2017.* Kabul: UNAMA Human Rights Unit.

UNAMA News. 2009. *UN Expands Presence in Afghanistan With New Office in the North.* 9 May. Kabul: UNAMA News.

United Kingdom. 2010. *The London Conference Communique.* The London Conference: Afghan Leadership, Regional Co-operation. London: International Partnership. 28 January 2010.

UNOCHA. 2009. *OCHA's Structural Relationships Within an Integrated UN Presence.* New York, NY: United Nations Office for the Coordination of Humanitarian Affairs.

UNOCHA. 2011. *Aid Worker Security Report: Spotlight on Security for National Aid Workers: Issues and Perspectives.* Geneva: United Nations for Coordination of Humanitarian Affairs.

UNSC. 2003. *Resolution 1510 (2003) on Afghanistan.* New York, NY: United Nations.

UNSC. 2006. *Resolution 1662 (2006) on Afghanistan*. New York, NY: United Nations
UNSC. 2008. *Resolution 1806 (2008) on Afghanistan*. New York, NY: United Nations.
UNSC, 2010. Afghanistan's Transition to Greater Responsibility for Its Own Destiny Requires Realignment of Aid with Priorities, Security Council Told. 6464th Meeting (AM). SC/10142. 22 December 2010. New York: Security Council.
UNSG, 2000, *Report of the High Panel on United Nations Peace Operations*. Chaired by Lakhdar Brahimi. 17 August 2000: U.N. Doc. A/55/305. New York, NY: United Nations Security Council.
UNSG. 2002. *The Situation In Afghanistan and its Implications for International Peace And Security*. Report. S2002/278. New York, NY: United Nations Office of the Secretary General. 18 March 2002.
UNSG. 2005a. Resolution 1589 (2005) on Afghanistan. New York, NY: United Nations Security Council.
UNSG. 2005b. Resolution 1623 (2005) on Afghanistan. New York, NY: United Nations Security Council.
UNSG. 2006. *Secretary General's Note of Guidance on Integrated Missions*. New York, NY: United Nations Office of the Secretary General.
UNSG. 2009. *The situation in Afghanistan and its implications for international peace and security*. Report. A/63/751-S/2009/135. New York, NY: United Nations Office of the Secretary General. 5 March 2012.
UNSG. 2013. *The Situation in Afghanistan and its Implications for International Peace and Security*. Report. A/66/728-S/2012/133. New York, NY: United Nations Office of the Secretary General. 5 March 2013.
UNDP. 2002. *Afghanistan: Preliminary Needs Assessment for Recovery and Reconstruction*. New York, NY: United Nations.
United States. 2006. *Field Manual 3–24 Counterinsurgency*. Washington, DC: Department of the Army.
United States. 2009. *White Paper of the Interagency Policy Group's Report on U.S. Policy toward Afghanistan and Pakistan*. Washington, DC: United States Office of the President.
Waldman, M. 2008. *Falling Short: Aid Effectiveness in Afghanistan*. ACBAR Advocacy Series. Kabul: ACBAR.
Wardak, H. A. 2009. *Defining The Gaps: The Case Of Afghanistan: From Education Reforms To Sustainable Development*. Kabul: Ministry of Education.
Wilder, A. 2005. *A House Divided*. Kabul: Afghanistan Research and Evaluation Unit. December 2005.
World Bank. 2005. *Assessment, Afghanistan Reconstruction Trust Fund (ARTF) Final Report*. Kabul: World Bank.
World Bank. 2019. *Net Official Development Assistance and Official Aid Received (Current US$) – Afghanistan*. Available at: https://data.worldbank.org/indicator/DT.ODA.ALLD.CD?end=2015&locations=AF&start=2010.

2 The intervener stories

One dusty day in Kabul I sat at the Flower Street Café a popular meeting place for ex-pats and Afghans working with INGOs. There, I mapped out the locations in the city where my interviews had taken place over the first six months of fieldwork. Most of my discussions in Kabul had been with interveners, a diverse array of external actors who were working in Afghanistan during the period of my field research. The majority had arrived there as part of the intervention architecture, working for aid agencies, military forces, political missions, international organisations, or private companies. The interveners were also independent consultants, restaurant owners, and journalists, who, while not necessarily working for an external organisation, had livelihoods that were attached economically to the international intervention. The interveners were not only those that came after 9/11: a few of them had been in Afghanistan for decades. When our paths crossed, however, they were funded by or were working for organisations or governments that fuelled the intervention project. Mapping the geography of my interviews was also a way to reflect on the diversity of the interveners. Visits to large UN or military compounds or smaller INGO buildings helped to reveal the different sub-cultures that existed within this broad category, each location distinct in terms of its built environment, the daily routine, the makeup of the staff. Beyond this, however, were layers of complexity which went far beyond organisational affiliations.

This chapter explores everyday realities of intervention through an exploration of the narratives and experiences of the interveners. The analysis here draws upon interviews and conversations with interveners and locates these experiences in context. Kabul City forms the backdrop for the chapter, as it is the location with the largest numbers of interveners and where most of my interviews and interactions with them took place, though insights from those based in other provinces are also explored. The chapter focuses on three themes. First, it pulls apart the dense mosaic of actors that I categorise as 'the interveners'. It does this by providing a brief overview of the demographics of the assemblage, and exploring the multiple ways that this diverse group develop knowledge of their surroundings, move through and negotiate the Afghan environment and relationships with the local population. Second, the chapter explores interveners' discourses and practices. The narratives here demonstrate the struggle with, contestation against, the social reproduction of institutional frameworks and policy guidance on the intervention, security and development, and access. Lastly, questions are raised throughout the chapter regarding the paucity of information and the relationship between knowledge and power in the context of intervention; mainly, how do we know the interveners and how do the interveners come to know Afghanistan and the intervention project they participate in?

Coming to Afghanistan: experience, hardships, and turnover

A persistent critique of the intervention is that the chaotic and contradictory policies and outcomes in Afghanistan can partially be attributed to an international workforce that was largely young, inexperienced in conflict dynamics and/or had little knowledge of Afghanistan, and high a staff turnover (Donini, 2009). Autesserre (2010) suggests that the UN recruitment practices generally favoured technical expertise over context-specific experience, and that this was an important driver of ineffectiveness in peacebuilding missions. Therefore 'expert' status is dependent on the ability to employ the policies and frameworks developed by international agencies rather than on the knowledge of the local context and people (Autesserre, 2014). The growth of donor interest and funding in post 9/11 Afghanistan opened the way for new aid agencies and private companies to establish themselves in the country, and for those already there to expand their operations and staffing levels.

An industry was created that required the rapid recruitment of thousands of Afghans, diaspora, and foreign professionals. Hundreds of short-term international staff were needed to work on the various elections that took place from 2004–2010, the growing UN mission, and the expansion of the international security forces which also needed civilian support. Given that Afghanistan was not a location that had received major aid assistance and that international agencies, for the most part, operated out of Pakistan during the 1980s and 1990s, the numbers of aid and security professionals, in the early stages of the intervention expansion in 2002 and 2003, with contextual or on-the-ground knowledge was limited. Of the non-military personnel, I interviewed only 10 per cent had experience in Afghanistan before 2001; however, 85 per cent had worked in post-conflict situations before coming to Afghanistan, and 75 per cent had worked in at least two other countries. In addition, several UN staff been locally recruited staff in Sierra Leone, Congo, Sudan and the Balkans or other conflict-affected countries, who had then come to Afghanistan as international staff. Though I spoke to a relatively small number of people compared to the thousands that work in Afghanistan, the trend within this group did reflect that few people had previous experience in Afghanistan, although many interveners had previous conflict experience.

Surprisingly, a small group of those I interviewed suggested that the knowledge of what they considered to be modern or Western ideas and ways of doing was more imperative than contextual knowledge and experience working in conflict-affected areas experience. These perspectives came mainly from international advisers to the Afghan government and diplomatic officials. I had an extensive interview with a senior ISAF official, in charge of a programme which placed international advisers across 20 non-security focused government ministries, such as Women's Affairs and Labour, Social Affairs, Martyred and Disabled, said. The advisers gave advice, and showed the Ministry staff how to plan, develop training programmes, solve problems, and communicate with each other and across ministries. Indeed, those tasks sound similar to that of most government advisers/consultants in any country, however, as the official went on to explain the rationale and recruitment practices a more problematic picture emerged. He said, 'We are there to show the Afghans what to do' (I51, ISAF, Kabul), and then explain that contextual or even topical expertise of the different areas where the ministries worked, was not important for advisers because they worked at the strategic level. He summed up the project by saying, 'We try to help them govern Afghanistan in a way that is acceptable to us. This way they can develop strong institutions that are legitimate and functioning' (I51, Kabul). Furthermore, in another interview with an American working for the ISAF Joint Command (IJC) he said succinctly:

> In the villages people think they know what development is but they don't. They cannot because they have never developed. We need to start modelling behaviour for the Afghans to follow.
>
> (I60, Kabul)

The interview with the official was quite long and he spent time reflecting on what he felt the contribution of the international intervention was to security and development in Afghanistan. Recruitment practices were informed by the belief that Western knowledge was universally applicable and superior to local culture. Accordingly, being bearers of this knowledge alone seemed to give the official and his staff the authority and legitimacy to guide Afghans in the acceptable ways of being. Not everyone shared this viewpoint, however, and Kamini discussed the problems that could arise when advisers were placed in the ministries for their Western expertise.

Kamini

Kamini had been in Afghanistan for four years (2010–2014). She had held different positions but was now working as an adviser to one of the central Afghan ministries after two years working with Afghan civil society organisations. Before coming to Afghanistan, she worked for seven years with the EC, based in New Delhi, covering rural development bilateral programming in India and Bhutan. Ten years before that in the UK working cross-sector for UK government, the CBI, Environment agency as well as other organisations, which involved high-level representation on both EU and international working groups covering issues from climate change to biotechnology. She reflected on her experience in Kabul and the problems she observed at her latest job in the Ministry during a conversation one afternoon saying,

> Vast amounts of aid funding are coming into the country, to the extent that spending it effectively was always going to be near impossible due to the absorptive capacity in country. As a result, a quasi-governance structure (civil service) was put in place whereby Afghan civil servants were being paid more than handsomely to manage Donor programmes. Some International Advisers were attracted to the financial packages being offered, despite the environment being somewhat 'dangerous' not only to live in, but effectively implement successful programmes. Working at the Ministry as an advisor, I am constantly shocked by the attitudes of the international staff and the way they treat even senior Afghan officials. There is a colonial approach that is reflected in some local staff really disliking the advisors … and I don't blame them.
>
> (C23, Kabul)

Scholars and policymakers have suggested that the insecurity of Afghanistan, which characterised it as a 'hardship posting' appealed less to more experienced older senior officials who had the ability to choose their postings and those with families (Brinkley, 2013; Reis and Bernath, 2016, pp. 30–32). It was difficult to assess the average age amongst such a large and diverse group of interveners. While many of those I met were in their late 20s and early 30s there were also many aid workers, UN staff, and private consultants in their 40s and beyond. Aid agencies tended to have younger staff on average than any other organisations, but whether this is specific to Afghanistan or a reflection of the staffing composition of NGOs globally was not clear. The career opportunities provided by working in Afghanistan and the incentives offered by international agencies and INGOs, however, often outweighed any hesitation to work in a dangerous environment.

A common comment by those interviewed was that Afghanistan's high profile internationally was a draw for them. Afghanistan was grouped with the Balkans, Iraq, the Democratic Republic of Congo, and Sudan amongst others as a high-profile mission. Working in one of these countries was a rite of passage for interveners who were serious about career-making in the field of conflict, security, or development. The wide range of organisations that were present in Afghanistan and the scope of their operations created an opportunity for interveners to make strategic decisions which could advance their careers quickly. For example, interveners based in the field mission could apply for jobs at higher pay grades or with more responsibility, which may not have been the case if they were located in headquarters. Therefore, Afghanistan experience held professional benefits for both junior and senior-level staff.

Incentives are given to staff who work in locations classified as 'hardship postings', including frequent paid rest and relaxation leave and substantial financial benefits. For example, the UN classifies Afghanistan as a non-family

'Class E' posting, reflecting the highest level of difficulty in working conditions. Both international and national staff receive additional salary benefits. Table 2.1 below lists the additional financial benefits for internationally recruited UN staff in Afghanistan. Depending on personal circumstances several other incentives were also available (See Table 2.1: UN Staff Class E Posting Benefits). The UN incentive package was extensive, but other international organisations such as the European Commission also provided additional benefits for staff in what they referred to as Category C postings (EC, 2014) and even small aid agencies topped up employee salaries with additional benefits. Undoubtedly. the difficulty of working in an area affected by conflict, and the inability of staff to bring family members along with them served as a disincentive for some officials. However, as Nigel's story below shows, the hardship benefits offered by various organisation overrode those concerns for some and played a role in why people came to and stayed in Afghanistan.

High staff turnover is also regularly cited in the literature and was mentioned by several participants as contributing to poor coordination, due to the resulting lack of contextual, and institutional memory amongst workers. Outside of the European Commission and UN, both large organisations with many career-track permanent employees, it was unusual for staff working in smaller organisations to remain in a post in Afghanistan for more than a couple of years. International

Table 2.1 UN Staff Class E Posting Benefits (International Civil Service Commission, 2019)

Allowance	*Explanation*	*Amount (US$)*
Danger Pay	A special allowance established for internationally and locally recruited staff who are required to work in locations where very dangerous conditions prevail	19,200 annually (1,600.00 per month)
Hardship Allowance	To compensate for the degree of hardship experienced by staff in hardship duty stations	17,440 to 23,250 annually depending on job classification
Non-Family Duty Station Allowance	This is an incentive for staff to undertake assignments at non-family locations and recognises the increased level of financial and psychological hardship incurred by involuntary separation from their families, including additional service-related costs.	19,800 annually ($1,650 per month) for staff with eligible dependants, 7,500 annually ($625 per month) for staff with no dependants
Mobility Incentive	Intended to encourage geographic mobility	Between 6,500 and 14,625 annually depending on job grade and number of assignments
Total Annually		50,640 (low-end no dependants) 76,875 (high-end with dependants)

organisations, aid agencies, private companies, and even the international military forces were constantly recruiting for staff to fill new and vacant positions. Therefore, it was easy for an intervener to move around between different organisations and 'agency hopping' was a common practice. Leaving an agency, however, did not mean leaving the country. For example, the Head of ECHO at the time had previously worked with Afghan civil society; the head of a large Afghan NGO had previously worked with the OCHA; and people moved between UN agencies and INGOs sometimes. In these cases, whatever situational knowledge interveners had gained from their time in Afghanistan moved along with them as they hopped from agency to agency.

The common critiques mentioned at the beginning of the section characterised some of the problematic recruitment practices of international organisations in Afghanistan, but did not reflect the complexity of the international workforce mosaic. Indeed, professional experience in conflict elsewhere tended to outweigh familiarity with the Afghan context. Sometimes being from the Global North alone was a sufficient qualification for expert status. However, the disincentive of working in a conflict zone was often countered by the professional opportunities and financial incentives offered by agencies, and while staff turnover was common, in-country experience could travel with interveners between organisations. These factors are important in understanding the demographics of the external actors, how and why they found themselves in Afghanistan, and the knowledge they brought with them.

Knowing Afghanistan

In intervener circles, it was rare for people to describe themselves as experts on Afghanistan, instead there were temporal and spatial markers which were used to signal the extent to which one 'knew Afghanistan'. Few expatriates that I met, aside from two anthropologists, considered themselves experts in history, culture, or politics of Afghanistan. Rather, the tendency was to define one's expertise by one's educational background, or professional training. More importantly, the greater the time spent in the country, the more places they had travelled to or worked in, their housing arrangements, gender, and language abilities were criteria used to by some to signal 'knowing Afghanistan', or the ability to speak with some authority about the political and cultural dynamics of the country. One evening at a restaurant owned by a French Afghan businessman, Jenny who was an independent journalist and communications consultant explained:

> There are so many people that come in and out of here it's ridiculous. Most of them stay in Kabul, and maybe do a few trips to the provinces, probably Bamiyan and Mazar, if at all, and then after a few months they talk as if they are experts in the place. They don't know Afghanistan. I know this place, I have been here for 5 years and I have never lived in a compound like the UN or embassy people.
>
> (C20, Kabul)

In 2011, of the non-military interviews I conducted in Afghanistan, 30 per cent of people had been in the country for two years or more. Military timelines varied, but were rarely longer than one year and officials had less choice in the lengths of their deployments, whereas civilians had more agency over whether they stayed in Afghanistan or moved on to somewhere else. Two years is not a lengthy period in which to grapple with the diversity of Afghan culture and history, and the complexity of the international intervention. Indeed, after living there for over five years and more than a decade of research I personally am still left with many more questions than answers. Two years, however, is a substantial period of someone's life and seemed to be the dividing line amongst international civilians, with the majority of people staying less than two years. Since Afghanistan was classified as a 'hardship posting' for UN staff, permanent staff could request rotation to another mission after two years (ICSC, 2019). This was not mandatory, however, and people could stay much longer if they wanted. In total eight of the people interviewed had been working on or in Afghanistan for over ten years.

The group that had been in Afghanistan for longer than two years could be divided into different categories. First, were those who worked in Afghanistan with the UN or NGO community in the 1980s and 1990s but were based in Pakistan, often in Peshawar, a city near the eastern border of Afghanistan with a large Afghan refugee population. They often had a good understanding of migration issues and Afghan civil society, which had also largely functioned from outside of the country during those years. Second, a minority of mainly Americans and Europeans had worked with NGOs, often in faith-based organisations such as the International Assistance Mission in Afghanistan, during the Taliban years and previously. As missionaries, they often raised their families in the country as well. Third, were those I met who arrived in Afghanistan for the first time soon after 9/11 and never left. This group included UN staff, private security contractors, and aid workers. Fourth, and representing most of the interveners who had been in Afghanistan for more than two years, were those who had worked in-country for a few years and then returned sometime later, usually for a longer period of time. Therefore, ten years after the US-led intervention began, enough time had passed to mean that some UN staff, aid workers, journalists, private security contractors and private company employees had been in Afghanistan for the better part of a decade.

Another commonly noted variable revolved around housing arrangements. Where someone called home largely depended on whom they were working for. International security forces lived on their base; PRT civilians usually lived on the base as well. Civilians that worked with the military in Kabul could stay on the base, but in some cases also had the option of finding their own accommodation elsewhere in the city. All UN staff was required to live in places which met the UN Residential Security Measures (RSMs) which are a set of guidelines detailing residential security advice and training, procedures and restrictions, and the installation of security enhancements in or around staff residences (United Nations Department of Safety and Security [UNDSS], 2012, p. 142), which changed depending on the directives given by the UN Senior Management Team. Until 2008, many UN staff lived in rented houses in Kabul City or the provincial centres where they were based. In 2009, after an attack on a UN guesthouse in Kabul, the UN reviewed its security protocols which dictate the security infrastructure for office compounds and the RSMs. By, 2011 UN staff in Kabul were could only live in a few locations around the city, including two UN compounds and a handful of large international hotels. The majority, such as Nigel, lived at the UN Operations Centre in Afghanistan (UNOCA).

Nigel

I first met Nigel in 2005 when I was working with an international organisation in Kabul. At that time, he had already been in Afghanistan for three years. Nigel came to Kabul in 2003 to work with UNAMA as they were setting up the new Afghanistan mission. He was originally from Latin America and the Caribbean where he had worked with the state security forces when he was recruited by the UN. Afghanistan was his first UN posting. When Nigel first arrived in Afghanistan, he lived in a small shared house with four other UN colleagues in the city. The house was guarded by Afghan Quick Response Forces around the clock. In 2007, when the security situation began to deteriorate, Nigel moved to the UNOCA. When I returned in 2010, he was living at the UNOCA compound which was located on Jalalabad road out the outskirts of Kabul City, and approximately 45 minutes from the city centre.

UNOCA is an extremely large compound. It takes at least 20 minutes to walk from the entrance on Jalalabad road to the main centre of activity inside the compound, which can only be reached after going through at least two security checkpoints. The compound housed several UN offices as well as living quarters. The accommodation was varied but included hostels with shared rooms, studio-like containers with no cooking facilities, and small one- and two-bedroom self-contained apartments. There were two cafeterias, a few restaurants, a 'Superette', and three small shops with a limited assortment of canned and frozen food, basic toiletries, cigarettes, and household items. UNOCA also had a social centre, a small sports field, a gym, and a small library with books and DVDs.

Nigel said he found living there easier because it was close to his office, which was in the compound, and he did not have to fight through the rush hour traffic. Since so many staff were in the same compound, meetings required less coordination. He also liked not having to go out into the city to buy goods or access services.

His family was still living back home, but he said the eight-week leave rotation policy allowed him to visit them regularly. The salary and benefits he received were substantially better than he could get at home, or in many other UN missions. After eight years he felt comfortable in his job and had close relationships with his staff, several of whom had worked with him since his arrival in 2003. Nigel never took language classes in the local languages of Dari and Pashto; however, he could hold a conversation about the geopolitics of the intervention, but he felt that was not part of his purpose in Afghanistan. He said:

> Life here is okay. It's simple and I know the staff well. I travel to the regions sometimes. I don't go into the city much anymore but over the years I have seen a lot of this country so I just rely on that knowledge and what my staff tells me. For me it is more about the interactions with the people.
>
> Nigel left Afghanistan for a new job in Africa in 2013 after ten years in Kabul.
>
> (C21, Kabul)

Aid workers, development company staff, and private contractors lived in the city either in an office/guesthouse compound, in a separate house with other colleagues, or on their own. The shared office and living spaces could consist of one house where the living and working quarters were arranged on separate floors, or a small compound with two of three small structures each with its own purpose. Residences that were separate from the office would usually take the form of one shared house or small complex with three or four apartments. It was rare for aid agencies to have national or international armed guards at their gates, and equally as rare for private development companies to be without them. Several people, journalists, independent consultants, researchers, private security, and some aid workers, lived on their own or with their spouses in small houses.

Living in the city, and not working for the UN, usually also meant more flexibility with how one travelled and where you could go. UN staff travel in Kabul armoured vehicles, were not permitted to walk in the streets, and had a 23:00 curfew. Visits to shops or other locations in the city were point-to-point only, and staff were not allowed to stay in shops or groceries for long periods of time. UN staff could dine at local restaurants in the city if the restaurants were approved by the UN Department of Safety and Security. For most of 2010 and 2011 all eateries were off-limits to UN staff. No other civilian organisation restricted their staff to this extent, but each agency had its own security rules, which usually involved a list of places to avoid, protocol for travel within and outside of the city, and a curfew.

Outside of Kabul the rules in regional offices UN staff were also required to adhere to RSMs, which placed greater limits on their housing and movement than aid agencies and private companies. Staff were confined to their office or housing compounds except for essential movement to meetings and other UN approved guesthouses in most regions of the country. UN interveners based away from the panopticon of the HQ in Kabul, however, often tried to bend the rules occasionally without fear of immediate reprisals. The Western and the Northern regions' aid workers and private company employees lived in similar conditions as they did in Kabul, and had very few limitations on their movement. They could drive around the urban centres, go shopping, visit markets, go to historical sites, and go to restaurants. In the central, eastern, and southern regions, where military operations and/or armed conflict was ongoing, the numbers of international staff were limited, but movement within and around the city was usually without restriction. It was not unusual to see NGO vehicles parked in the markets, or outside of shopping centres, parks, and local restaurants waiting for international staff. The ability of non-UN civilian interveners to live in the city in closer proximity to the local population and their comparative freedom of movement was translated as a greater ability to partake in the everyday life in Afghanistan.

Knowing Afghanistan was also associated with the extent of one's embodied experiences outside the boundaries of Kabul. Outside of the aid workers I came across in the eastern region when doing research on Behsud, many of the people I met were based in and had spent the bulk of their time in Kabul. A smaller number of people had worked in several different regional or provincial offices, and one or two had only worked outside of Kabul. When someone had first arrived in Afghanistan seemed to be an important factor in whether they had travelled outside of the province; likewise, the *type* of transport they used to travel was significant. It was not uncommon for interveners who had come to Afghanistan before 2007 to have visited several regions of the country and often travelling by road. For example, the former head of a UN regional office reminisced about the 16-hour journeys from Northern Afghanistan through the Khyber Pass during winter to Kabul; he would make such journeys every few months in 2004. After 2007, when attacks against aid workers sharply increased, aid agencies and the UN began to drastically restrict road travel. UN staff only travelled outside of the province by air. Trips to the provinces by aid workers usually took place by aircraft too. Private security and contractors would drive or fly if they took a local airline, or were able to get on the flight manifests of one of the international organisations[1] that maintained its own aircraft fleet. Ironically, the road infrastructure that had been laid connecting provinces throughout Afghanistan since 9/11 could no longer be used to travel by the UN and many aid agencies due to lack of security.

Expatriates based in Kabul tried to get out to the provinces on short trips ranging from a day to a week, to 'experience' the regions. These short trips added to their knowledge of the country, but also provided them with 'street credibility'. Even short trips spent mainly in office compounds were deemed as providing sufficient information to comment on the situation in those areas. An EC official based in Kabul City whom I met during fieldwork, maintained an extensive travel blog, where he chronicled his time in Afghanistan, including his visits to the regions. These trips, lasting a day or two, usually entailed meetings with government officials, lunch with the staff of an aid agency that were being funded by the EC, a community visit, and a trip to the local market. He explained the importance of these visits:

> Quite a few of my colleagues [in Kabul] have been getting out to the regions. So, I was feeling left behind as if they were getting a better sense of the country than I was … but it is difficult to arrange travel. You have to

> justify the reason you need to go somewhere, but I have figured out how to do that now so I have a few more trips lined up in the next few months. And I have already seen Mazar and will go to Bamiyan for skiing.
>
> (C3, Kabul)

A few weeks later we spoke again. He had just returned from a field trip to a rural community outside Kabul where he held discussions with the community leaders. He reflected:

> I thought it was interesting. They told me many of their problems. It is awful to see the way some of them have to live. They have ideas but they need us to help them organise themselves and figure out what to do. They can learn from us and then apply it to their own situation … but they need guidance. That is obvious.
>
> (C3, Kabul)

Amongst the EC official and his colleagues, a causal link was made between how many locations one had seen and the level of knowledge one held about Afghan society. Attached to this was a special status given to those who were well travelled. The substance and depth of one's understanding, however, seemed less important. Essentially, more time in-country and visits to more locations outside of Kabul added to the 'knowledge credit' of the intervener.

Finally, language was also regarded as an important part of being able to know Afghanistan. The influx of international workers, many of whom were coming to Afghanistan for the first time, and did not speak either Dari or Pashto, creating an overnight industry for language tutors. Individual tutoring classes ranged from US$15 to 50 per hour. Small group classes were slightly more expensive. Some tutors, usually young Afghan men, would be hired directly by organisations to provide Dari lessons for the expatriate staff, and simultaneously give English lessons to the Afghan staff. Though taking Dari classes was a common practice amongst civilians, fluency developed in-country was rare and there was often only a fleeting commitment to learning the language for effective communication. Ultimately, most expatriates communicated through translators or with basic language skills. Speaking one or both of the official languages, however, was a premium skill and people with this capability were perceived as having insight into a world few foreigners could access.

The temporal and spatial positioning of interveners and their communication skills were used as yardsticks to denote those who 'knew Afghanistan': the number of years of experience in Afghanistan, exposure to its diverse regional cultures and landscape, the ability to live and travel within the community, and local language capacity are all very important factors in learning about the social, political, and cultural dynamics of the country. There were many interveners that I met and spoke to who had years of experience in Afghanistan, had lived in or travelled around the country, lived within Afghan neighbourhoods, and spoke more than basic Dari or Pashto. As many of the stories in this and the following chapters will demonstrate, however, even these factors did not always smoothly translate into a heightened knowledge of Afghanistan, or a deeper understanding of the impact of policy decisions and most importantly, into a genuine respect for Afghan culture or people.

Distancing

I was constantly struck by the ways in which the everyday practices of international intervention brought many people together but simultaneously created distances between them. The literature on the built environment of humanitarian agencies (Smirl, 2015) and bunkerisation and risk aversion practices (Duffield, 2010, 2012; Weigand and Andersen, 2019) has touched on this by focusing on the international retreat from local populations. Beyond the structures that physically divided interveners from Afghans, however, other modes of separation existed. Indeed, I was constantly struck by the distances that were created and maintained between people within shared everyday spaces of which much less has been written. Between interveners and Afghans one such place was the office environment and amongst interveners divisions often existed in large housing compounds.

Regular interaction between interveners and Afghans took place most frequently from Sunday to Thursday at the workplace, whereas socialising during the evening or weekends was less common. Interveners depended on their Afghan colleagues to be their 'ear to the ground' providing insights into the political dynamics of the government and local communities. The office was also the same that close professional relationships and friendships could be forged. Nigel, for example, developed a good rapport with his Afghan staff over a period of years in-country. Naila, a key member of my research team, and I first began our relationship as colleagues when I worked for an NGO in Afghanistan years before this research project. Interveners could take advantage of their time with Afghan colleagues to further their understanding of the environment and develop bonds of trust. Even within the shared space of the office compound, however, divisions existed that created distance between interveners and Afghans.

Suzanne

Suzanne was a young woman in her early 30s who had worked in Afghanistan for two years for an international organisation located outside of the large UN compounds. We meet just a few weeks before she left Kabul to return home to North America. At university she had studied Persian history and culture and she spoke Persian and Dari. She reminisced about the office culture of the organisation she had worked for saying,

> We had weekly management meetings with all of the program managers, who were all international staff. The only time Afghan staff came to a meeting was if their line manager was away. I just found it so strange how

> once a week all of the senior international staff would gather in this container and have a meeting while the Afghan staff were excluded from. It was like this protected space where internationals discussed things that the local staff were not supposed to know about. The local staff found it strange as well ... but of course they would never say anything ... that we could understand anyway.
>
> The local staff also had their own stuff going on that most international were oblivious to. For example, there was this on-going dispute between two local staff members and it had been escalating for a few weeks. One afternoon the two guys had a fight just outside of the office gates. For the 20 minutes or so when the whole thing went down the majority of the Afghan staff had gone outside to witness what was going to happen. The office compound was almost empty and it seemed like none of the international staff noticed. Then the local staff just came back and went back to work ... even the guys that had been fighting. I spoke to my staff about it afterwards and they said everything was ok now ... it wasn't but the fight was over. A few of the international staff came to know about the disagreement a few days later but not many. The local staff, however, were talking about it all the time in their offices and in front of the ex-pat staff.
>
> Looking back, it is kind of funny. Like there were different worlds existing in the same office compound....
>
> (C24, Kabul)

Suzanne's experience was not uncommon. The exclusion of local staff from the weekly management meetings reflected the staffing structure of the organisation which did not include any Afghan senior managers, which was unusual for international organisations or aid agencies or even private sector companies. It was commonplace, however, for different worlds to exist within the workplace that were dominated by either local staff or interveners within a larger shared space. Sometimes, the separation between locals and interveners in the workplace took on a physical dimension. For example, office compounds could have a local cafeteria that was separate from the international eating area and served local food. At other times, however, as in Suzanne's story, the cultural and discursive distances between interveners and Afghan staff engendered multiple realities which unfolded in the same room and at the time. Afghan staff engaged in many practices in an attempt to control the situation. For example, shifting through resumes that were dropped off at the office compound by potential applicants for open job positions before they reached the human resources office was another common practice (W2, Jalalabad). This theme is picked up again in Chapter 5 on Behsud. These distances were both deliberately and unintentionally created by both interveners and Afghans.

Many of the restaurants in Kabul were either not approved for UN staff or served alcohol and therefore, could not allow Afghan clients. After work socialising was rarely an option for Afghan women, however, due to their responsibilities at home and cultural norms. There were several eating establishments and meeting places where meals could be shared or socialising after work could take place, however, between interveners, even UN staff, and Afghans, usually male colleagues. In addition, weddings and sometimes funerals were large events where interveners were often invited to attend by their Afghan colleagues. Meeting someone's family, having a meal at their home and other casual activities, however, were less uncommon but not unheard of. For example, Kamini, saw getting to know her colleagues socially an important part of being in Afghanistan and her work, regularly went out with her Afghan colleagues including attending a weekly games night.

Views varied, however, on what it meant to socialise outside of work. One interviewee, suggested that social distancing was also in part due to the fact that Afghans and interveners just led different lives, saying

> It's nice to hang out with my Afghan friends but they have real lives, and commitments. We are just here to work, most [interveners] are single out here on their own. It's a lot to ask Afghans to accommodate us in their private time....
>
> (I59, Kabul)

Catherine, who had been in Afghanistan on and off for seven years felt differently and expressed a sentiment that was shared by several others that I spoke to, saying, 'it is just better to keep things separate. There are a lot of cultural things that are different between us and them and I just feel more comfortable with ex-pats' (C25, Kabul). Ultimately, more personal interactions and friendships depended upon security regulations which the intervener had to follow but more so on the individuals, both the interveners and Afghans involved. Within an environment racked by conflict, violence, and intervention the bonds of trust needed to build such relationships were difficult to establish and for some undesirable. Distances also existed amongst interveners, of which much less has been said. In ex-pat dominated spaces these separations became very clear.

Green Village and Maria

One evening I had dinner with two friends at the Green Village (GV), which was a large securitised housing and office complex near the Kabul airport and Mikrorayon apartments.[2] The advertising brochure described GV as 'a safe, secure and protected … oasis of cool and green in Kabul, containing gardens, relaxing areas, and restaurants'. My friends lived in a one-bedroom apartment located near the back of the extensive 1,800-room compound. The complex housed the EU Police advisers, UN staff, international advisers, private sector employees, and contractors. Some organisations had whole accommodations blocks allocated to their staff only. The EU Police advisers, for example, lived in a separate area of the complex.

To get to GV you travel down a long busy paved street called Jalalabad road, which leads to UNOCA and then out of the city to the eastern region of the country. The turn-off to GV takes you down a wide dirt and rock road that is peppered with a few local shops and high stone barriers that alternate positions down the middle of the road that the Toyota Corolla that I was travelling in was forced to weave through. As we got closer to the compound, armed guards began to appear along the road. Upon arrival at the entrance my car went through a vehicle checkpoint outside the complex and then was allowed to drive to the GV entrance. From the road nothing inside the compound was visible. The only thing one could see was the large perimeter wall. Since, I did not live in the compound, I had to leave the car behind and continue on foot. On the other side of the entrance gate, Hescos, and barriers I went through a checkpoint. After exiting the checkpoint booth, I entered an enclosed parking lot of a similar in size to a small shopping centre parking area. After walking across the lot, manned by a guard tower, I arrived at another checkpoint. Upon clearing the third checkpoint booth I stepped out into the distant edge of the green oasis, where my friends met me. It would be another seven minutes to their accommodations. That night while getting dessert I struck up a conversation with one of the cafeteria staff, named Maria.

Maria had been working at the GV for two months. Before that she was working at one of the logistics camps which provide supplies for the military bases and a few other locations. She had been recruited by a private company from her home in the Philippines to come to Afghanistan. She said she knew it would be dangerous but the money was good and the company provided insurance and safe accommodation. Also, she had made friends during her time in Afghanistan.

Maria only went from home to work and back again and only left the compound to go shopping once a week. She had also gone carpet shopping once but didn't feel safe so came back quickly. There was a lot of work to do every day and organising transportation was difficult, but more so she was scared to leave the compound. She said, 'Inside it's okay, but every time I go outside its scary. These people … you never know what will happen. It's crazy'. For months Maria's only interaction with Afghans was with the local staff that worked in the compound and at the supermarket where she shopped. Jalalabad road is heavily travelled and the site of frequent explosions, which could often be heard inside of the GV. Spending her day nestled deep inside GV she felt safe, but also increasingly fearful of the world and people outside the securitised complex (C22, Kabul).

The interveners that lived in GV rarely mixed with the contracted compound staff. Neither of my friends had ever really noticed Maria, though they did occasionally speak to some of the compound staff. Like Maria, most staff were from the Global South, earned lower wages, and had less secure contracts and benefits than UN or international advisers. Essentially, Maria and her friends were an imported labour force. Employing international compound staff was meant to signal to residents that GV had a higher level of service and was a safer environment compared to a similar establishment with mainly local Afghan staff. The contracted GV staff were viewed by residents as slightly different than other international workers.

The physical distance of GV from the main road, the obstacles along the way and the dozens armed security staff were all meant to act as a deterrent to attacks from AOG. My friends and Maria felt being inside the compound gave them refuge just as the brochure promised and respite from the world outside the GV walls. Within the compound, however, people also distanced themselves from each other. GV was a microcosm of social ordering and global hierarchies. The compound exemplified the way in which global hierarchies were manifested in intervention, not only between locals and interveners but also amongst the interveners.

Coming undone: the security–development nexus

Despite the diversity of interveners and the multiple ways in which they moved through Afghanistan, one unifying factor for many interveners was the logic of the nexus which purports that security and development are inextricably linked, which in turn underlined the policies of the organisations that they worked for and programmes that they implemented. Interveners are often perceived in the literature and policy as embodying their organisational mandates. However, little empirical work has been done to tease out how interveners translate the policies they are meant to uphold. In the context of my research, this meant interrogating intervener understandings of the relationship between security and development in Afghanistan, and the policy frameworks which guided their work. Therefore, this became the departure point for many of my interviews with interveners: during those discussions three nexus narratives emerged: the nexus as an unequivocal truth; the nexus as a possibility; and no nexus.

The first narrative, the nexus as truth, was the most commonly held belief amongst the external actors with whom I spoke. The officials that maintained that the security–development nexus was a certainty came from a range of institutional backgrounds. They were often senior civil servants in their various governments, or with agencies such as DFID and USAID, or political advisers within international organisations, such as the NATO Senior Civilian Representative Office and aid workers. The credence given to the nexus, however, was tied to an unreflective acceptance of Western approaches to global problems.

My interviews usually began by discussing security and development, and then the relationship between the two. It became clear early on in my field research that many of the interveners had never questioned the existence of the nexus or how it was constituted, but rather blindly accepted it based on policy documents and discussions with other foreign officials. In one of my first interviews, an ISAF civilian official in charge of advising NATO officials, explained:

> I have never thought about that before. All of the information and books I read about Afghanistan before coming here talk about the security–development

> nexus and that is how I informed myself about the situation. Nobody really questions that. It is just assumed.
>
> (I26, Kabul)

The push for the greater integration of development and security in policy has overtaken the understanding of how the two relate (Tschigiri, 2005). This is not surprising, when as Duffield (2005) points out,

> th[is] claim … [has been] repeated to the point of monotony in countless government reports, political statements, UN documents, NGO briefs, academic works, and so on.… [To the point that] it now qualifies as an accepted truth of the post-Cold War era' (p. 142). Youngs (2008) echoes this point when he states that 'few in the EU would doubt that security and development go together.
>
> (p. 420)

Interestingly, a senior European diplomat, who had also argued that security was a process of modernisation, acknowledged this saying:

> Of, course, we circulate knowledge among ourselves and that becomes the truth and translated into policy. We only invite the Afghans sometimes, but it is difficult to engage with them.
>
> (I44, Kabul)

It was unclear what the official meant by 'difficult'; however, his main point was that even if the nexus was a constructed truth amongst interveners it was sufficient to inform international approaches to intervention in Afghanistan, and that local perspectives were useful but not necessary. Several others said they were rarely asked to account for whether the nexus existed or upon what evidence their assumptions were based. Instead, a problem-solving rather than a critical approach (Cox, 1981) was adopted, where the nexus was perceived as an ontological reality and epistemological questions were left unasked.

The nexus was the premise upon which these officials worked towards, rather than a relationship that they sought to understand. As a result, the, constructed truth of the nexus was reproduced through everyday practices. This phenomenon was demonstrated by two officials that worked for USAID and DFID. The USAID official explained their feedback process:

> Of course, there is a direct link between security and development. We do not need to question that. We all know it, and we expect our operations in the field to do their jobs based on the link. That is what the PRTs were constructed to do.
>
> (I43, Kabul)

In conversation, the DFID official, who had previously explained that she saw development as necessary regardless of its contradictions, stated that the security–development nexus was a definite reality. When asked why she held this belief, she responded:

> That is a good question. I had not thought of it before. We get information from our implementing partners … but I suppose all of our programmes are based on that reality so the information that we get back reflects that.

She expanded:

> We look for sources of strategic knowledge, however, like looking back at what led to the rise of the Taliban … but there is a gap between what we know and what we do, but we have to continue to work on what we have access to.

Finally, she said:

> The linkage between security and development is accepted by most of us. DFID, definitely, and the US as well. You see it evidenced in ISAF papers, policy documents and positions papers. It shapes the direction of [our] programming.
>
> (I33, Kabul)

Both women designed programmes, decided who received funding, and the benchmarks against which those projects were assessed. They were heavily guided by the policy frameworks discussed above in Chapter 2, and reproduced this knowledge in their own work, such as in the framing of requests for projects and funding calls and the language in which project reports were required to be written. They also played a role in shaping policy, selecting projects and were key informants to institutions in North America and Europe.

More senior officials tended to be confined to Kabul, so they often had little exposure to outlying areas of the country. The trips they did take usually focused on meeting within government or institutional structures and perhaps short staged meetings with local leaders or trips to the villages to speak to groups of women. The DFID official who stated the security–development nexus was a definite reality, clarified that she rarely left Kabul, saying 'I cannot go to the field because of our security regulations. It is very rare that I would go to the field and it can be quite difficult to organise' (I33, Kabul). Technical or operational staff often had more experience in the provincial capitals outside of Kabul. A senior official based in one of the PRTs commented, 'The head of our agency, no, he rarely comes down here. He does not want to get his boots dirty. It is too *in the field* for him' (I6, Telephone). The same senior USAID official mentioned above verified this in a separate interview:

> I rarely get out to the field. I work more at the strategic level. Setting policy and advising the administration back home. We get information from the field and the PRTs, but it is slow and watered down.
>
> (I43, Kabul)

For these participants, the process of acquiring knowledge of the context worked from inside outwards. Rather than having their lens shaped by the environment which they were in, international policy provided the filter through which they constructed the environment. The nexus discourse provided a framework to organise thinking about intervention in Afghanistan, and a lens to interpret and translate information received, ultimately reproducing the same discourse it sought to describe.

In the second narrative, the security-development nexus was a possibility but that external actors did not have enough knowledge about what was happening in Afghanistan to understand it. This position was explained in detail by the Ambassador of a European Embassy, who was formerly the Head of an NGO that had worked in Afghanistan for over 35 years. He suggested that there could be different ways of thinking about the relationship between security and development that were not necessarily part of the dominant international approach. The Ambassador acknowledged that in his new position, movement was difficult and though he tried to engage with Afghan communities and organisations this was a challenge. Therefore, he drew upon mainly military and diplomatic sources of information, and local contacts, journalists, other media sources and his own previous experience as an NGO director. He began by saying:

> Strong development with advocacy for issues such as gender equality can cause social violence and conflict. If the military becomes associated with NGOs doing this type of work, it can compromise their operations. Then the military becomes associated with an agenda, which is not security-related, but a western rights agenda. Whereas, NGOs that become associated with military operations can also be targeted.
>
> (I50, Kabul)

The Ambassador did not discount the nexus logic completely, but rather proposed that more needed to be done to unravel the complicated relationship between security and development in the context of the intervention. He went on to explain that better understanding of the realities of intervention and the experiences of local communities was obscured at times by a lack of honesty within amongst civilian actors. In particular, he said the aid community and UN often constructed the work that they did in a positive light while failing to grapple with the sometimes violent impact of some of their interventions. In fact, the constant references to the Do No Harm Framework,[3] participatory development approaches and human security in everyday conversations overshadowed the material realities of their everyday practices and provided a discursive diversion from the dangerous and unaccountable aid programming.

The director of an NGO that had struggled to define itself amidst the vigorous debate between development and humanitarian agendas, gave his perspective saying:

> If you do development well, then, you achieve development goals, but the relationship between security goals and development is not something that

> automatically exists but rather something that may exist and in any case is very specific and contextual.
>
> (I28, Kabul)

The NGO director said that interveners lacked the knowledge, particularly of the rural Afghan communities that represented most of the population, to be able to unequivocally make that claim. He went on to say:

> Honestly, sometimes it is hard to know what we are doing in this context. There are many questions you constantly ask yourself: Are we doing the *right* job? Are we doing the *job* right? Are we doing development or are we trying to solve security issues with development? And a lot of the time … we don't know, and we don't know how these things relate.
>
> (I28, Kabul)

The context of the conflict was most commonly stated as a confusing factor in figuring out what the link between security and development might be. Little time or space was allocated for the development of alternative approaches which could challenge dominant policies. As described above, there was power in being able to claim knowledge about what was really going on and what communities wanted. The head of a regional sub-office of an organisation that did mainly humanitarian work, and who had been in and out of Afghanistan for 5 years, explained this conundrum:

> Everyone has something to say about what is really going on here. But we really don't know. Actually, how little we know is shocking. The pressure to produce and reproduce the conventional ideas that are circulated is high … and everything is urgent. Often there is no time to reflect. You just have to move ahead with what you think and often that is driven by ideas that are circulated amongst internationals.
>
> (I68, Mazar–Kabul)

Another interviewee disagreed, feeling the lack of alternative discourses on security and development was not necessarily because of a lack of time and the constant pressures to take action. He suggested, however, that a deference to policy guidance rather than contextual realities characterised what was an inherent practice of aid workers and other interveners. He explained:

> In the international development field, broadly speaking, there is a great divide between the thinkers and the doers. Aid workers tend to be doers … which means that thinking too far beyond the operation is often seen as an impediment to progress rather than an asset.
>
> (I67, Kabul)

This second group tended to recognise the possibility of other ways of knowing, and the limitations of interveners in Afghanistan to reimagine security and development.

In the last nexus narrative, the main argument was that there was no nexus because no evidence of any nexus existed. In addition, the lack of clarity concerning this putative relationship was intended to serve the strategic purposes of international civilian and security agencies. A senior UN official, who had spent over 20 years in the region and had sat on the UN country team for several years (although he was leaving within days of our interview), explained his frustration saying, 'Some people say that development is key ... but it has not led to security for local communities, international actors or at a global level and in areas with security it has certainly not facilitated development'. He went on to explain:

> Even though many of us on the ground knew things were not going well, security was not leading to development and development initiatives were not contributing to government legitimacy, there was no space for an alternative discourse to that of success. No one was interested. Funding and resources had increased to tremendous amounts and saying that our footprint was having no effect was not an option.
>
> (I27, Kabul)

The official suggested that the on-the-ground realities were subordinated to political rhetoric about the perceived success or failure of the international intervention and strategic goals of interveners. Therefore, the investment of external organisations, including the one he worked for, in justifying their actions and this international experiment in addressing global crisis outweighed the desire to address the growing insecurity, persistent poverty and the growing humanitarian crisis.

A second but divergent perspective in this last group was put forward by an architect of the transition policy discussed in Chapter 2, when he candidly stated:

> Transition is not about linking security and development. At this point it is about prioritising. Security comes first. Development may come later but maybe not. Countries are not willing to support development anymore and we are only looking at minimal security conditions to exit now.
>
> (I41, Kabul)

His statement was unique, but his position, as one of the framers of the policy that would shape the exit of the intervening NATO nations from Afghanistan added to the weight the comment. He went on to explain that the international community run out of patience with Afghanistan. The persistent insecurity and underdevelopment were attributed to the failures of Afghan governance structures and society. Therefore, local problems could no longer be global ones.

There was an interesting dynamic between the comments of the UN official and those of the NATO adviser. The two comments speak to the shifting focus of the intervening nations over the ten years of the intervention, and the constructed nature of the changing discourse which was firmly rooted in the interests of external actors.

All three nexus narratives were propagated by interveners working for organisations that espoused the inextricable linkage of security and development as *the* foundation for international policy and practice. The first story supports the nexus but demonstrates how the logic is reproduced through narratives and practices of interveners. The second questions the nexus and highlights a lack of knowledge and critical reflection amongst interveners, which hinders the ability to construct an alternative narrative. The last rejects the nexus as being an external political construct divorced from the everyday realities of Afghanistan. However, in each story the nexus as a universal ontological grounding has come undone.

Access?

Beginning in 2006, there were growing concerns about diminishing aid agency *access* to local communities as armed attacks in Kabul began to increase (Lee, 2011) and the UN was named as a specific target by the main Taliban groups.[4] Subsequently, in 2007 and 2008 several aid workers were killed in Afghanistan in incidents that received worldwide attention.[5] The Afghanistan NGO Safety Office (ANSO) began their 2007 annual report by saying, 'In a few years from now, 2007 will be considered the year that the Taliban seriously rejoined the fight', and this broader and deeper conflict that would result in difficulties *in access* for the aid community (Lee, 2007). An NGO director, from a small INGO explained the access problem aid agencies were facing:

> If the community does not provide security for us, then there is *no access* or *development*. If something happens, we go to the community and ask them to sort it out. If they cannot, we leave.
>
> (I58, Kabul)

Anti-government groups could be a potential threat to national security and the stability of the Afghan state actors and international military forces, seen as belligerents in the conflict. Armed non-state groups were automatically perceived as a threat to security for communities and aid agencies. If the groups targeted the aid agencies, however, then development work, referring to a wide range of projects taking place at the community level, would be halted. The director went on to explain:

> We depend on the community for security and let them know that development is tied to their willingness to guarantee our safety. A few months ago, in one of the districts where we have been working for some time, six of our

> staff members were kidnapped. The community tried to intervene, but they could not stop it. Eventually five staff were let go and one was killed. We left the community because they could no longer guarantee our safety.
>
> (I58, Kabul)

An aid worker from another large INGOs explained how violence and insecurity had affected access and their programming choices:

> We had an office in Kandahar until 2005. But we could not continue the operation there. Communities are the core of security, but after 2004 they could no longer guarantee security. So, we closed the office and shifted our focus to Heart and Ghor provinces and expanded our programmes there.
>
> (I57, Kabul)

Both stories suggest that access is dependent on community trust, and therefore community agency was a determining factor. If the community wants development, defined here as NGO projects, they will ensure the security of those that bring aid, and if that security is maintained the area will become developed. I shall revisit this debate in the context of Qarabagh District in a later book. Conversations on how to provide aid in insecure conditions focused on the need for increased security measures for aid agencies, the use of remote management tools, and the benefits of greater localisation.

There was no unanimous consensus, however, that access was decreasing. The director from above, who was unsure of the nexus, commented that his organisation had indeed reduced their number of programmes, but this was more due to funding flows and a shift in community perceptions about the organisation (I28, Kabul). Others rejected the reframing of the debate by the aid agencies outright. A UN official, who had been working in the region for 20 years, commented that most NGOs had been working in the same areas for years and while the number security incidents had increased, little had changed in terms of access for aid agencies. What had changed, he felt, was the amount of money required for insurance and agency security needs, and the dangers attached to road travel (I30, Kabul). Additionally, the former Head of Agency concurred with this, expressing frustration at what he thought was the skewing of facts by INGOs saying, 'Access? What is the issue with access? They have no proof. It is just a way to justify poor results and lack of impact'. He continued, 'It just justifies remote management. Do the UN even leave [their main compound] on Jalalabad road anymore?' (C7, Kabul). He suggested that the flurry around diminishing access in part served as a way to relieve aid agencies from responsibility for the impact of their project on the communities, and therefore accountability not access was being diminished.

More research is needed to fully understand the substance of either claim. Indeed, little analysis has been done regarding the linkage between financial flows, security incidents, and changes in INGO programmes in Afghanistan. The aid community in Afghanistan have consistently resisted national mapping exercises which could provide detailed evidence regarding the relationship between the conflict, violence, and the operations of agencies (I30, Kabul). Indeed, even the number of aid agencies in Afghanistan is hard to confirm due to several factors including, a reluctance to register with the government by some organisations, an inconsistent understanding of what defines an NGO within the country. For example, from 1999 figures range (Afghanistan, 2012) to 701 (Mitchell, 2017).

One of the few attempts to research and map NGO activity has been completed by Mitchell (2017) who compiled a database of NGO activity and presence in Afghanistan from 2000–2014. According to his research the number of NGOs, defined as international or local independent, non-profit organisations engaged in humanitarian, development, human rights, or advocacy work, in Afghanistan, steadily increased from 2000 and reached its peak at 701 in 2012. There was then a swift decline between 2012 and 2014 dropping from 701 to 617 agencies. The decrease aid agency numbers coincide with the gradual reduction of aid funding to Afghanistan, from US$6.66 billion in 2012 to US$4.943 billion in 2014 (World Bank, 2019), that aligned with the onset of the transition period and international troop drawdown.

Despite critical voices emerging in certain parts of the intervener community, the perception that access was gradually being decreased because if insecurity was very real amongst many aid workers. A scan of the statistics on aid worker fatalities does not provide a much clearer picture of the situation, with regular fluctuations in either direction occurring between 2010–2014 (See Table 2.2: Aid Workers Fatalities and Causalities in Afghanistan, 2010–2014). In 2011, to address concerns being communicated by aid agencies, OCHA drafted a *Humanitarian Access Strategy*. In its opening section the report highlights the fact that there is little statistical evidence to support the lack of access claims being made by aid agencies. It goes on to say a significant obstacle to understanding the issue is the difficulty in collecting such data in a conflict situation. Ultimately, several NGOs and civil society organisations rejected the report.

Table 2.2 Aid Workers Fatalities and Causalities in Afghanistan, 2011–2014

Year	*Total Victims*	*Total Deaths*	*Total Kidnapped*	*Total Injured*	*Total International*	*Total National*
2010	123	34	59	30	17	106
2011	92	31	32	29	2	90
2012	105	11	49	45	8	97
2013	166	44	79	43	16	150
2014	123	42	59	22	11	112

Source: Table complied from data provided by the Aid Worker Security Database.[1]

Note

1 See Aid Workers Security Database, Humanitarian Outcomes. Available at: www.humanitarianoutcomes.org/projects/aid-worker-security-database-awsd

The access debate highlights another way in which security and development were linked through the practices and discourses of aid agencies. Without a detailed and historical picture of types of activities, working modalities, funding flows, community feedback, and narratives from aid workers on the psychological impact of attacks, however, it is difficult to draw conclusions about the linkage between insecurity and aid agency access in Afghanistan. The dynamics of the debate, however, emphasise the important role of perceptions amongst interveners, which are central to much of the discourse on institutional identity, purpose, and coordination with other actors discussed further in subsequent chapters.

Reflections on the interveners

This chapter has sought to explore who the interveners are, how they move through and develop knowledge about the context in which they operate and what this means for how they understand security and development. The overview of the interveners at the beginning of this chapter complicates popular constructions of who the external actors in Afghanistan are. Researchers often attempt to make sense of complex environments by slotting people into generalised categories. During this study, however, a richer and more granular picture has emerged regarding the distinctions between and within interveners. They are far from being a cohesive community, a group of organisations of individuals who subscribe to shred norms and practices, but rather they represent a diverse group of organisations and individuals in a shared space, the site of intervention. The breakdown here goes beyond simple institutional categorisations to piece together a multi-layered mosaic of organisations and also challenges assumptions about the whiteness and Western-ness of interveners (Rivas, 2018). The staff within the organisations vary in terms of nationality, age, gender, professional background, and contractual obligations. These individuals influence and are influenced by the space in which they live and are connected to each other. Therefore, the everyday of intervention is characterised by global politics and hierarchies of power which are reflected not only in the interaction between the internationals and locals, but amongst the interveners themselves.

Deconstructing the intervener 'community' has also enabled the exploration of common critiques of intervention focused on the youth and inexperience of interveners, their lack of contextual knowledge, and high staff turnover, which only provides a partial picture of the diversity of interveners in Afghanistan, and the relationship between knowing Afghanistan and time in the field. Interveners spanned a wide range of ages, often had some experience in conflict or aid assistance, and though usually coming to Afghanistan for the first time many went on to spend years there. Experience in-country did not necessarily translate to a knowledge of the context or respect for the culture. This nuanced understanding of who the interveners are has raised questions regarding how interveners come to know Afghanistan.

The time spent in the country, exposure to regional diversity, organisational protocols, living arrangements, language skills, and identity all influenced the embodied experience of interveners and the means through which they moved through the sites of intervention. Each factor played a role in their experience in the country, their exposure to different scenes and people, and their ability to understand what was being said around them. They also signalled the process through which interveners constructed themselves in relation to each other. The next chapter develops this theme and explores the construction of organisational hierarchies. Ultimately, one's access to different places and people was influenced by identity and hindered or facilitated by the built environment and the regulations which governed movement. An even more critical factor, however, was the filter through which they chose to understand these experiences.

The intervention in Afghanistan has been used as a prime example of the bunkerisation of aid workers (Duffield, 2007, 2010), the creation of a risk management infrastructure, and governance techniques which are facilitated the retreat of external actors from the populations they are supposed to be assisting (Duffield, 2012). This trend is perhaps best exemplified by the tightening security regulations on UN and diplomatic staff housing and travel, and the debates around access. Some aid agencies also encouraged staff to coalesce in agency-run housing. The extent of these shifts, however, are not clear: many aid agency staff still maintained residences in Afghan neighbourhoods. The spatial distancing of interveners from local communities created obstacles to understanding the impact of international policy directives and of aid assistance on communities. As the district case studies below will show, the lack of accountability of aid agencies may diminish incentives to change their practices. More importantly, closer proximity to local populations could facilitate a better understanding of the environment, or conversely it may not. The problematic comments of officials throughout the chapter reflected the colonial legacy through which several interveners constructed Afghanistan and their roles there. However, attempts were made by others who were confined to compound life like Nigel, and Suzanne, to understand the context and reflect on their positionality. Undoubtedly the conflict environment and the bunkering of some interveners from Afghans exacerbated a culture of fear, and limited opportunities for engagement but the narratives in this chapter suggest the need to look beyond structure and at a combination of factors and to take a nuanced approach to understanding the means through which divisions are created and bonds are built. Indeed, some of the most striking distances between people occurred in shared everyday spaces. Suzanne's story and the story of Green Village demonstrate how intersectionality, power and agency combine in different ways to produce distance amongst interveners and between interveners and Afghans.

The nexus stories are not merely a matter of linking various conceptualisations of how people see the relationship between development and security. Rather, they reveal how actors located themselves within these projects, both institutionally and individually, and how they came to know, or claim to know,

Afghanistan. Paradoxically, working for an organisation even for long periods of time does not necessarily equate to a belief in or acceptance of the institutional discourse. Each nexus story challenges the perceived logic of the security–development nexus in a different way. They also demonstrate, however, the means through which the disconnect between policy and everyday realities are discounted. Therefore, many of the problematic everyday practices of the international experiment in Afghanistan remain unchallenged. Even when failure is acknowledged, the solutions developed by external actors often remain uncontested, as responsibility for the chaos is transferred to the locals, constructed as 'unruly'.

A contradiction emerges in the chapter between the lack of information and the desire to speak with authority. Amongst the interveners being seen to 'know Afghanistan' was a claim to a certain kind of power. The physical, cultural, and symbolic distance that was maintained between interveners and Afghans varied, but always acted as a barrier to gaining knowledge. Therefore, officials, security forces, NGO workers were always searching for avenues to learn about the Afghan environment. Ironically, the practices they used often militated against developing a deeper understanding of the context, or having a more meaningful engagement with the local population. The local perspectives were much sought-after, but paradoxically easily discounted, whereas knowledge circulated within expatriate circles was generally perceived as valid. Also, there was little reflection on the ways in which officials often obliged others to reproduce aspects of international policy discourse in programme reports and related documents. The external knowledge despite being uninformed was, perhaps oddly, perceived as being superior to local insights: this is reminiscent of the colonial approach to encounters with the Other. For some interveners Afghanistan was 'mysterious' and 'unknown'; yet also completely knowable in the same instance.

Further, interveners did not just struggle with their knowledge of local dynamics, but also with themselves. The lacunae in the knowledge that was produced contributed to the persistent convolution of the dynamics of the intervention. In the case of the access debates this facilitated the furthering of INGO claims that they had to reduce their operations due to increasing insecurity. The increase in the violent deaths of aid workers and the fear that is undoubtedly produced when colleagues are killed may have indeed led to a programming retreat by aid agencies. Without detailed information, INGOs could control the narrative. At the same time, it hindered greater understanding of the extent of the violence aid agencies were facing, the extent of the transfer of risk to local staff, and the impact of insecurity on local communities. Ultimately, this had the effect of diminishing the possibility of a deeper understanding of the relationship between (in)security and (under) development. The next chapter explores further the relationships, tensions, and consequences of institutional arrangements that were constructed as part of an international approach to intervention which sought to bring together different groups of interveners.

Notes

1 There were several international organisations that had a regular flight schedule to provincial centres outside of Kabul, including the UN, ICRC, and USAID.
3 The Mikrorayon apartments were constructed of this complex of Soviet-style prefabricated residential buildings built in Kabul between the 1960s and 1980s.
4 For more information on the Do No Harm Framework, see: Collaborative for Development Action (CDA), 2004, The Do No Harm Handbook (The Framework for Analyzing the Impact of Assistance on Conflict), The Collaborative for Development Action Inc, Cambridge, MA.
5 According to UNDSS personnel, during 2007, intelligence was provided where the Taliban clearly singled out the UN as a potential target. This was a break from the past where UN compounds or staff may have been involved in an attack but the organisation itself had not been specifically or publicly named as a target or enemy of the Taliban.

References

Afghanistan. 2012. *List of International and National NGOs*. Kabul: Ministry of Economy.
Autesserre, S. V. 2010. *The Trouble With the Congo: Local Violence and the Failure of International Peacebuilding*. New York, NY: Cambridge University Press.
Autesserre, S. V. 2014. *Peaceland: Conflict Resolution and the Everyday Politics of International Intervention*. Cambridge: Cambridge University Press.
Brinkley, J. 2013. MONEY PIT: The monstrous failure of US aid to Afghanistan. *World Affairs*, 175(5), 13–23.
Cox, R. 1981. Social Forces, states and world orders: Beyond international relations theory. *Millennium*, 10, 126–155.
Donini, A. 2009. *Humanitarian Agenda 2015: Principles, Power, and Perceptions. Afghanistan Case Study*. Feinstein International Center, Tufts University. Available at: http://wikis.uit.tufts.edu/confluence/display/FIC/Humanitarian+Agenda+2015-Afghanistan+Country+Study
Duffield, M. 2005. Getting savages to fight barbarians: development, security and the colonial present. *Conflict, Security & Development*, 5, 141–159.
Duffield, M. 2007. *Development, Security and Unending War: Governing the World of Peoples*. Cambridge: Polity Press.
Duffield, M. 2010. The liberal way of development and the development-security impasse: Exploring the global life-chance divide. *Security Dialogue*, 41, 53–76.
Duffield, M. 2012. Challenging environments: Danger, resilience and the aid industry. *Security Dialogue*, 43, 475–492.
EC. 2014. *General Information On Entitlements and Benefits for Echo Humanitarian Experts*. Brussels: European Commission.
ICSC. 2019. *A Guide to the Mobility and Hardship Scheme and Related Arrangements*. New York, NY: United Nations.
Lee, N. 2007. *ANSO Quarterly Data Report and Annual Summation* (Q.4 and 2007) 1 January 2007 to 31 December 2007. Kabul: ANSO.
Lee, N. 2011. *ANSO Quarterly Data Report and Annual Summation* (Q.4 and 2011) 1 January 2011 to 31 December 2011. Kabul: ANSO.
Mitchell, D. F. 2017. NGO presence and activity in Afghanistan, 2000–2014: A provincial-level dataset. *Stability: International Journal of Security and Development*, 6(1), 5.

Reis, C. and Bernath. T. 2016. *Becoming an International Humanitarian Aid Worker*. Oxford: Butterworth-Heinemann.

Rivas, A. 2018. Everyday development practices. In: Shilliam, R. and Rutazibuwa, Olivia U. (eds.) *Routledge Handbook of Postcolonial politics*. London, Routledge: 166–196.

Smirl, L. 2015. *Spaces of Aid: How Cars, Compounds and Hotels Shape Humanitarianism*. London: Zed Books.

Suhrke, A. 2007. Reconstruction as modernisation: the 'post-conflict' project in Afghanistan. *Third World Quarterly*, 28, 1291–1308.

Tschigiri, N. 2005. *Security and Development Policies Untangling the Relationship*. Presented at the European Association of Development Research and Training Institutes Conference September 2005. Bonn: EADI.

UNDSS. 2012. *Handbook for United Nations Designated Officials for Security*. New York, NY: United Nations.

Weigand, F. and Andersson, R. 2019. Institutionalized intervention: The 'Bunker Politics' of international aid in Afghanistan. *Journal of Intervention and Statebuilding*, 13(4), 503–523.

World Bank. 2019. *Net Official Development Assistance and Official Aid Received (Current US$) – Afghanistan*. Available at: https://data.worldbank.org/indicator/DT.ODA.ALLD.CD?end=2015&locations=AF&start=2010

Youngs, R. 2008. Fusing security and development: Just another Europlatitude? *Journal of European Integration*, 30, 419–437.

3 Civil–military stories

Structures, boundaries, and hierarchies

In post-9/11 Afghanistan, civilian and military officials, even those with experience in conflict or post-conflict situations elsewhere in the world, found themselves in circumstances that were very different from anything they had encountered previously. This cacophony of actors precipitated the creation of specific inter-agency forums, policy guidelines, and working arrangements. The PRTs and the integrated UN mission structures were both attempts to integrate, coordinate, and accommodate different groups of actors in their everyday lives and work. While limited success was achieved in meeting these goals, the institutional arrangements also created frustration, and division between and amongst 'interveners' and others, both within and outside of these structures. Furthermore, efforts at integration came to represent physical and symbolic boundaries against which these actors defined and positioned themselves vis-à-vis others.

This chapter presents interviews, personal narratives, and related data gathered for this research from military and civilian actors, including UN and diplomatic staff, international and national aid workers, military officials, private contractors working in, or who had worked in, Afghanistan, and several of whom we met in the preceding chapters. It explores some of the relationships that emerged between civilian and military actors inside the PRTs, the external and internal contradictions that arose as the UN attempted to position itself as a neutral coordinator between civilian and military actors, and the impact on and responses by aid workers and civil society groups. The chapter explores two themes. The main theme throughout the chapter is the tension that emerged when attempts at integration created the opposite effect. The narratives below emphasise the ways in which the structures which represented the push to be closer created an urgency to fight for space, reinforced boundaries, and crafted distinct identities. A second theme is the pervasiveness of everyday violence and uncertainty. In particular, the stories in this chapter provide insight into the role of fear in the production of boundaries and hierarchies between and amongst military and civilian actors.

The PRTs

In state-building projects, intervening governments have tended to adopt idiosyncratic theories of change, assuming certain causal links between the actions they engaged in and the outcomes they hoped to achieve. The PRTs, each led by a particular intervening country, served as laboratories to test different types of hybrid combinations of military, political, and development assistance deployment and differed widely in set-up, approach, and policy (Abbaszadeh *et al.*, 2008). Despite mounting evidence to the contrary[1] (Khalilzad, 2005; McNerny, 2006; Olson and Gregorian, 2007; Gheciu, 2011) political officials held a seemingly unwavering belief in the PRTs' capacity to integrate security, governance, and development (Ratman, 2015). While coordination on some level could not be avoided because of cohabitation within the same location, the integrated PRT structure did not necessarily facilitate effective coordination. Rather, officials often found themselves struggling to make sense of a seemingly established set of prescriptions. These divisions came to the fore at a large workshop which I observed that took place outside of Afghanistan in 2009 on Civil–Military Relations and the Comprehensive Approach.

The workshop

As I settled into a large workshop held on a NATO base, I looked around the room at the military officials, civilian contractors, NGO staff, and former diplomats also in attendance and wondered if this meeting would be less tension-ridden than those I had attended in Afghanistan in previous years. This was not to be the case. The day started with a presentation by a former UK diplomat outlining the tenants of the comprehensive approach, and its importance to Afghanistan. The first round of comments reiterated the timeliness of the approach as the international community realised a political solution was the way forward in Afghanistan. About 20 minutes into the discussion, however, frustrations boiled over from several people in the room who had recently come from Afghanistan or were still based there. In particular, three military officials, who had just returned from Afghanistan where they had been based in a PRT in the south of the country, vented their disillusionment with their civilian counterparts and what they saw as disinterest by senior officials to respond to the reality on the ground. One of the officers explained:

> They [civilians] never stay at the base [in the field] for long. They just rotate in and then head back to Kabul whenever they can. While they are there, they can't go anywhere because of security protocol, so we have to go to all of these meetings in town. We get there and then aid workers do not want us there. And most of those meetings are a waste of time anyway. The civilian staff just see their time here as something to write home about. And then we have to respond to the people back home who have absolutely no idea what is happening here.

Another official from the same group, who had been in Afghanistan for two rotations, added:

> We are all doing the same thing, or we are supposed to be and you couldn't be here without us so why do civilians or aid people pretend otherwise. You're all just not honest with yourselves.

A woman across the room introduced herself as a consultant and former development worker who had spent time in a PRT in Northern Afghanistan; she retorted, ‘It is always like that dealing with you people. We are not doing the same thing. You have guns, you kill people … and that is the whole problem’. After a fraught and seemingly unending period of silence, a variety of responses emerged from other parts of the room. The first person who spoke was a civilian who had formerly worked at a PRT in the central region of Afghanistan but had now become a consultant. She said: ‘we are not doing the same thing, but we need to work better with each other’. The military official that began the debate observed, ‘Everyone gets these guidelines and pressure to co-ordinate but nothing changes on the ground. Those are just high-level discussions’. The discussion continued with general agreement that coordination between military-civilian and development actors remained *ad-hoc*, that communication tended to be poor, and that improvement was needed in both areas; however, guidance from national headquarters was disconnected from the field offices (W5, USA).

The struggles for autonomy and authority between civilian and military staff within the PRT structures did not arise solely because these actors came from different organisational cultures. These conflicts were shaped considerably by the difficulties of organisational communication and bureaucratic coordination, and competition for influence in their home countries. New jargon, such as, ‘whole of government’, ‘joined-up government’,[2] and ‘comprehensive approach’[3] was deployed to describe the different approaches being implemented to house civilian and military staff under one roof on the ground in Afghanistan, and within the national administrations of the intervening nations back home. However, no amount of jargon could mitigate conflicting perspectives and bureaucratic discontent. Hyrchuck (2009) explains that while actors in the Canadian PRT had some autonomy on the ground, they were nevertheless strongly influenced by bureaucratic management and national politics in Ottawa. While general operational policy on merging military and civilian actors within PRTs was understood, internal domestic tensions emerged over previously neatly carved-out bureaucratic territories, areas of responsibility, and funding. As a result, the dynamics between civilian and military departments in the capital were often reflected in the PRT camps in Afghanistan.

On the ground in Afghanistan, the atmosphere across the PRTs varied in part because of leadership and communication norms specific to the different intervening countries involved. Successive military and civilian leaders used what autonomy they had to conduct day-to-day operations as they saw appropriate, adding a personal element to an already complex organisational dynamic. A former PRT commander explained to me that civil–military coordination was less a function of guidelines and more something that was decided on a case-by-case basis:

> Personal relationships mattered. There were a lot of tough discussions but we were able to have the conversations depending on who the people were most of the time.
>
> (I65, Kabul)

A senior USAID representative, who had management responsibilities including the oversight of all staff in a provincial American PRT, further concurred:

> whether co-ordination was possible depended a great deal on the PRT and the personalities and leadership of the people there at the time. One shift of the latter and an entirely new dynamic was created and not always a good one.
>
> (I43, Kabul)

While individual leadership style and personality contributed to setting the tone of each particular PRT, coordination also required regular communication between civil and military staff members active in the PRT. Different professional jargons, management and communication styles, and norms of personal interaction differed greatly; as a result, nuance was constantly 'lost in translation' at meetings. In some PRTs it was not uncommon for coordination meetings to be spaces where seemingly obvious questions were posed, punctuated by frustrated head-shaking and negative body-language, even the throwing of occasional insults and walkouts. Often, even those meetings deemed productive were frustrating experiences for those involved. A DFID official who had spent some time working with PRTs contended that there were regular gaps in communication between civilian and military actors. She felt this was due in part to the 'military mindset', which devalued civilian work, saying: 'We have not done a very good job of explaining to the military how development works and many civilians have unrealistic expectations of the military' (I31, Kabul). She added that communication was hindered by negative assumptions on both sides, and an unwillingness to listen, cooperate, and learn from each other.

The significance of the struggles between military and civilian actors within the PRTs should not be underestimated. However, they varied at times in intensity depending on how factors such as the contextual background, the varying of military and civilian actors, and organisational culture interacted: depending on the national PRT model involved, there was diversity amongst the military actors; similarly, civilian actors came from different government departments, had various professional and educational backgrounds, and held different political views. Civilians tended to be specialists in foreign affairs, development, defence, immigration, agriculture, health and other fields. Some were trained in trades, and had NGO experience, or came from the private sector; others held relevant PhDs and had undertaken scholarly research. Diversity amongst the military was overshadowed by an overarching military identity whereas, amongst civilian staff, the differences were more pronounced and groups tended to coalesce around similar professional backgrounds. That said, the military identities and the understanding of the role of the military in peacekeeping and state-building could vary according to the intervening country involved in a given PRT.

Civilian bureaucrats, with little previous experience of working with the military, or with people from academic or NGO backgrounds, tended to see themselves not only as distinctly different from their military counterparts, but also as engaged in opposing rather than complementing the military campaign. From their perspective, the military was there for security; this was achieved by the coercive deployment of military force, which contradicted peacebuilding. Accordingly, civilians were in Afghanistan for development purposes, although this was to be achieved through state-building and reconstruction. Being housed in the same compound did not seem to diminish the desire on the part of the various civilian actors to reinforce boundaries between the disparate groups, which manifested itself in their communications and physical distancing during day-to-day interactions. For instance, during dinner and other events, such distance between civilian and military staff tended to be an easier task for those in larger, more resourced PRTs, where there was more freedom of movement inside larger, better-resourced compounds, and harder for those in small outpost-like compounds. Here circumstances could enforce the sharing of space and inter-stakeholder communication.

Those civilians who had military backgrounds tended to find the PRT space easier to navigate. The American PRTs, in particular, had large numbers of civilians who had also served in the military or the Peace Corps. An Australian civilian working for USAID based at an American PRT explained that working with the military in the PRT was just like being back in the military itself. Though he had a different role from the roles he had had in his military career, he understood the military culture and was happy to contribute to the military effort. He was overseeing infrastructure and road projects on the outskirts of Kabul City that were funded with money from USAID, supported by the military and constructed by a largely Afghan and regional labourers from India and Pakistan. He saw his work as providing support to the military and said his background helped him to understand the military approach, which some civilians struggled with. He felt, however, that the communication problems amongst different actors within the PRTs lay elsewhere; he explained, 'I am under no illusions why I am here. Development works in service of security. I think civilians just don't want to accept that. But that is what this is' (C11, Kabul).

Sarah's story was slightly different; she takes us beyond issues relating to how civilian bureaucracy relates to the military. A female civilian contractor without military or government experience based in the PRT, her voice that is rarely represented in literature or policy on civilian-military relations or intervention in Afghanistan.

Sarah

Sarah was a young woman from Norway, a journalist by training. She had been in Afghanistan for 12 months when we met in 2011. She had recently accepted a job based at a PRT in the western region of Afghanistan, which she was enjoying a lot more than her previous stint, where she was based at the PRT in Ghor province. Civilians employed by international organisations or INGOs and working on projects being implemented in a province with a PRT could live at the base or stay there for short periods of time. In such instances the project funding usually came from the PRT lead nation. Aid workers stayed at the PRT's 'secure guesthouse' either because they were unwilling or unable to find other accommodation.

The last time we meet, she was in Kabul for a meeting with her manager. The headquarters of the international organisation she worked for was in a small suburb of the city called Kolala Pushta, where several INGO offices and guest-houses were located. We met at a nearby café: Sarah was helping to set up a local radio station and training women and youths to create radio shows. As a journalist-cum-aid worker she did not subscribe to humanitarian principles as such, and felt her project was characterised as development work. She was given a special contract so that she could be based in a province where the living arrangements, both housing and office, would be outside the normal security regulations for international staff in her organisation. Special contracts, like Sarah's allowed organisations to absolve themselves of responsibility for the safety of those staff members, and to implement projects that they otherwise would not be able to do. It also enabled organisations to work closely with structures like the PRT, while maintaining a contractual, physical and symbolic distance.

Sarah was picked up and dropped off outside of the PRT each day by one of her Afghan colleagues, and spent the day at the radio station site or in meetings. She worked through a translator for most of the day and usually finished work by 15:00 in the afternoon. Other organisations in the region run by Afghan and/or the Afghan diaspora implemented similar projects. Sarah said it was easier for them to find places to stay, but as a Western woman on her own the only place she felt safe was at the PRT; she found the internal dynamics of the PRT fascinating; here she describes the microcosm of PRT life:

> I am not the only civilian. There are lots of different types of people there … the embassy people, aid corporation staff, EU officials sometimes and contractors, US military. The civilian aid staff and the military don't really get each other. Anyway, civilians don't stay for long periods of time. They are always trying to go back to Kabul.... But the military also has issues internally, and that creates tension on the base. I am fairly independent though, so no one bothers me. I have started to do most of my work at the base. The food is really good and comes from abroad mainly. There's no way I would be up there without the PRT.
>
> (C15, Kabul)

Sarah did not have a military, humanitarian, or aid background and hence had no affinity with any of those groups. The PRT structure, however, made her feel secure and she saw them as facilitating her work. Sarah left Afghanistan a few months later just before the end of her project. On her way out, she said life at the PRT had started to wear on her, but she had also begun to question what she was doing. In our last conversation she said:

> I didn't feel pressured for information or uncomfortable with the military, but I just am not sure of the purpose of that project. To be honest I was

> hardly leaving the base anymore. No one really seemed to care what happened just that something was being done. Even though they were funding the project. Development projects should have some plan that might work. You could never do that in Norway … also I started getting scared. The environment … I don't know. Also, I'm just not sure what was really going and what I was contributing to.
>
> (C15, Kabul)

The project that Sarah was working on was eventually completed. A few months later, after she had settled into a new job in East Timor, this time with the UN, she heard from the head of the radio station that she had liaised with regularly, while in Afghanistan. A few of the women had been hired by the station and were putting on programmes, but most had moved on to another project or were staying at home. In her last email to me she said, 'I'm happy to know that everything worked out and it's all up and running. I'm still not sure what it will be used for though … but at least the community is getting some good from it' (C15, Contractor, Kabul).

Sarah, like many others on special contractors, negotiated several different spaces. She was contracted by a company, reported to a large international organisation, lived at the PRT, and had an office at a local radio station. Her free-floating status meant she was unattached to some of the larger debates in the country about civil–military relations and development, humanitarian and political divides. For aid agencies involved in the humanitarian space discussion, Sarah represented a dangerous phenomenon: someone potentially perceived as an aid worker working for specific local communities, was but completely embedded in a military space, therefore totally blurring the lines between the military and civilian actors. For the international organisations, sub-contractors facilitated work they wanted to be funded to do but, remained at arm's length from them; as for the military, she was perceived by military actors to be easy to accommodate. For the local staff such distinctions were of little importance. Ironically, contractors like Sarah often had the most intimate day-to-day interactions with local professionals and communities. For Sarah she was just doing her job. The ambiguous nature of her positionality eventually took its toll. Even though her interactions with Afghan project staff and local women were unproblematic Sarah began to feel fearful of the environment outside the PRT.

PRT civilian and civilian relations: inside and outside

The animosity held by some aid actors towards the PRTs or military actors was attributed to the ongoing militarisation of aid, and duplicating the work of humanitarian and development agencies in Afghanistan. As such, aid actors sometimes thought that the blurring of military–aid put relationships with communities at risk (Donini, 2011; Fishstein and Wilder, 2011). Many aid workers felt uneasy that PRTs funded and engaged in reconstruction projects, and that they did not have long-term objectives, but aimed at 'winning hearts and minds' to combat insurgency. Civilian PRT staff, however, saw themselves as having more in common with and sharing the ethos of public society and civilian staff outside of the PRTs of the UN and the INGOs – but they stressed commonality whenever possible. INGO workers outside of the PRTs rarely shared this view: civilian PRT staff were viewed as political actors, or as civilians pushing counterinsurgency from a different angle. A representative of ACBAR, the largest NGO coordinating body in Afghanistan, summarised this perspective:

> The militarisation of aid is not the problem. We don't expect the military to stop trying to gain support from the people. The problem is the political actors and the politicisation of aid … and this is most apparent in the civilian government officials working in the PRTs.
>
> (I55, Kabul)

Over the course of one night in Kabul, I observed how the militarisation and politicisation of aid influenced the dynamics between civilian actors whose spatial positions placed them differently along the dividing lines of these debates.

Dinner, debates, and Jonathan

In May 2011, during a particularly hot summer evening in Kabul, there was a social gathering at the guesthouse of an INGO working on legal training and human rights law with the Afghan Ministry of Justice, USAID, and the Italian government. Italy was the international lead nation on justice. To promote good relations, the INGO had invited the USAID staff overseeing their project to the event. The heightened military presence and the numerous armoured vehicles in front of the house was an early indication that at least a portion of the guest list would be military. There were three guests from the US embassy compound in Kabul, and a PRT from the eastern region. All guests had been based in a PRT at some point, as it was common to be rotated between locations depending on their position.

The conversation revolved around how pleasant it was to be outside of the embassy compound and the PRT. A senior staff member commented, 'after working with the military, it is nice to be with civilians who understand what you're talking about'. After a brief pause, some of the other guests, mainly NGO and UN staff, responded by nodding their heads empathetically, and sharing stories about their experiences with the various security forces operating in the region. The comments reflected the desire to reaffirm boundaries between civilian and military PRT staff to an external audience by highlighting cultural and practical differences between them and the military, searching for ways to forge links with other civilians.

The confinement of the embassy compound restricted contact with Afghans for local staff members and those who had been met on organised community trips. So, while the conversation focused mainly on work issues and the funding and progress of the NGO's planned activities, one embassy staff member asked several questions about life in Kabul and opinions about the conflict. While the questions themselves were not out of the ordinary, there was a hesitation on the part of the two other guests particularly to engage further in conversation.

Jonathan, a young man from the PRT in the eastern region and an academic by training, talked at length about his interactions with the local community and the development work they were doing. When asked how he travelled to the communities, he paused, knowing what was coming, and then responded, 'Yeah, I go with the military and they are always armed, and I know that is not how you guys do it but it still works'. Later that night, I asked Jonathan what his experience in the eastern region was like. He began by saying that working with the military was challenging. He had been an aid worker and an anthropologist, and had spent several years working with the Peace Corps. He had never worked in a conflict zone or in Asia before, but felt drawn to the situation in Afghanistan. The poverty and lack of human rights that people endured in Afghanistan were significant factors influencing him; he wanted to make a positive contribution to Afghanistan's reconstruction, and felt that this was the moment the Western countries could really make a difference. He said he knew how to work with the locals for their development, based on his time with the Peace Corps and as an anthropologist doing research in Sub-Saharan Africa and South America. However, the attitude of the military officials he worked with bothered him. He said they took racist stereotypes for reality, and it was difficult to watch their interactions with local security forces. Consequently, Jonathan tried to spend as much time as possible on his own when he had to be on base, or he spent time with his Afghan colleagues. In addition, however, he suggested that the resources available to him could go a long way with better coordination with other people working in the development field. He said:

> I understand the NGO's perspective. They don't want to be too close to the military. I am just like them. We have the same background.... Neither do I ... but I'm not the military and if they worked with us better things could be much better for the local communities. Sometimes I think they get in the way of development for their own sake despite what the community wants. I really know what's going on the ground.
>
> (C18, Kabul)

Over the course of the 14 months I conducted research, other PRT staff made similar comments to me. They reflected an insider-outsider dilemma, in which the border demarcating the insider from the outsider seemed to be the perimeter of the PRT.

Jonathan and his colleagues left earlier than most of the other guests to make their curfew: staff curfews were common amongst embassies, UN agencies and INGOs. Depending on the organisation that one worked for, some NGO staff also had a curfew and/or a nightly check-in to confirm their safety and location via cell phone or radio communication with their respective operational bases.

After their departure, several new guests arrived who had driven by the guest-house earlier, but had decided to turn back when they saw the military personnel and a long row of armoured vehicles outside the gate lining the gravel road where the guesthouse was located. It was common for expatriate workers from NGOs, the UN, or private companies to travel in military 4x4s and armoured cars. By comparison, the staff from PRTs and embassies were often accompanied by military personnel, who waited in the vehicles while staff members were in meetings or socialising. This entourage signalled a location to be avoided for some NGO workers, both for reasons of their personal security and for preserving their humanitarian reputations with the Afghan community. First, the visible military presence was seen to increase the likelihood of the location becoming a target for attack by armed or criminal groups; second, for reasons of reputation and credibility, they wanted to distance themselves from being seen to associate with the military.

As the evening progressed, a telling conversation arose regarding the recently departed guests from the embassy compound and the PRT. One guest said: 'You need to be cautious around people like that and do not share any information. You never know if they are civilian development bureaucrats or intelligence'. The host of the event, who was a senior manager of the NGO working with the Afghan Ministry of Justice, retorted, 'Nobody here was working for the CIA. Come on, we speak to them regularly. It was good to have them around sometimes because it lets them feel connected to the aid world, even though they are not development people'. A staff member of the same NGO as the host added, 'I think they're fine as people, but they just don't understand what they are doing vs. what we are doing. They fund us but we are working towards different purposes'.

Another guest suggested,

> I think the problem is that they believe what they are doing is development work and for the good of this country, but they know that development cannot be tied to military occupation and killing people! There's a contradiction here, so they associate themselves with us more.

One of the latecomers stated,

> Development is always political. In their case, they are pushing the politics of the US and NATO in another country and that [is] the difference between them and us. NGO workers have independence; our mandate is not to push the agenda of some foreign power. It [is] completely different and that is clear to everyone else. They just don't want to see it or believe in what they are doing.
>
> (C19, Kabul)

The fact that PRTs contained both civilian and military actors within a single compound contributed to the perception by many aid organisations that anyone working within a PRT was tainted with violence. American staff, due to the role of their country in leading the intervention, were often viewed with distrust and kept at a distance, which was not necessarily the case for PRT staff members from some of the other NATO participating countries, such as Turkey or Germany. Nevertheless, civilians within PRTs were not often viewed as aid workers or development professionals by civilians outside of the PRTs. Some aid workers considered them to be part of the politico-military apparatus of the intervention, and thus they were perceived as dangerous, due to the conflation of the security agenda with that of civilian development actors, such as NGOs. In response, civilian PRT staff sought to align themselves to other expatriate civilians, such as civilian aid actors living within, but ultimately separate from, the perimeters of the PRTs and the military architecture in Afghanistan. The final comment made at the dinner also reveals an interesting dynamic where the identity of aid agencies associated with being independent from the military and political arms of the intervention that was taking place. Yet, few aid agencies actually operated independently of the security forces or the political actors. As discussed further on in the chapter, however, aid organisations were constantly reasserting the boundaries between themselves and other interveners and amongst agencies.

The UN and the international military forces

The UNAMA mandate identified a crucial coordination role as being with the military: the relationship between the UN and International Military Forces (IMF) was enshrined in Security Council Resolution 1974, which highlighted 'the synergies in the objectives of UNAMA and of ISAF' and the importance of 'a comprehensive approach in addressing the challenges in Afghanistan to successful transition to Afghan security leadership' (UN, 2011). From the outset ISAF was mandated in UNSCR 1386 (2001) to 'work in close consultation' with the UN. In addition, the UN was supposed to play a key coordination role between the military and aid agencies. To this end, a series of coordination mechanisms were set up between 2004 and 2011: in 2004, the PRT Executive Steering Committee (ESC); in 2008, the Civil–Military Working Group (CMWG); and in 2010, a high-level coordination group, consisting of the Commander and Deputy Commander of ISAF, the NATO Senior Civilian Representative (UNSCR), the UNAMA Deputy Special Representative of the Secretary General and six ambassadors. There was also a Joint Intelligence Board and *ad-hoc* meetings between UNAMA and ISAF on an issue-by-issue basis.

While formal mechanisms existed, coordination was limited, and both military and civilian actors felt attendance at meetings was often a waste of time. The PRT ESC (2004–2007) was established to provide policy guidance and clarity on the roles of PRTs and external relations. The members only met a few times during its short existence, but managed to 'issue several policy notes to guide PRT operations and interaction with external actors with regards to disarmament, development activities and coordination with humanitarian actors'

(Haysom and Jackson, 2013). The dissemination and use of the guidance notes, however, were not widespread, and there was a lack of clarity as to how many military and civilian actors even knew of their existence. In 2008, the Guidelines for the Interaction and Coordination of Humanitarian Actors and Military Actors in Afghanistan were finalised by the CMWG (2008).[4] The document was a response to the confusion expressed by several NGOs concerning the weakness of the UN and the way civilian agencies were interacting with the military, as well as an attempt to provide a set of guidelines specifically suited to the Afghanistan context for both civilian and military actors to follow. The guidelines were completed in November 2007, but finalisation and endorsement took a further six months. They detailed over a dozen coordination mechanisms for civil–military interaction at different levels within Afghanistan (pp. 7–8) and recognised the role of the PRTs in 'security, stabilization, reconstruction, development, good governance, and security sector reform efforts' (pp. 10–11). However, this belated attempt at instilling coherence and a unified approach amongst different actors ultimately failed. As one interviewee put it:

> The problem with the Civil–Military Guidelines is we wrote them because some NGOs with loud voices requested them and then everyone decided to ignore them.
>
> (I40, Kabul)

Accordingly, even when the various directives and guidance documents did trickle down from Kabul to the field level in the PRTs, UN or aid agency offices: generally, when oversight on implementation was carried out, it was not sufficiently stringent (Abbaszadeh *et al.*, 2008).

The military often expressed frustration at the UN's inability to coordinate amongst aid agencies and their hesitation to work closely with the PRTs in the 'hearts and minds' campaign activities. Commonly cited military frustrations included: the UN's lack of experience with counterinsurgency, its limited capacity, in terms of staffing and the sparse spread of offices around the country; its status as a non-implementing agency with a few exceptions, such as UN-Habitat and the IOM. Conversely, for UN staff, there was no reason to have previous experience with counterinsurgency, and the short-term approach of the 'hearts and minds' campaign ran contrary to the long-term objectives of development projects. However, as discussed previously, many did agree that security was necessary for development, and *vice versa*. Ironically, both the military and the UN experienced regular staff turnover, and struggled with a lack of understanding of the local context which impeded their internal operations and external coordination. Another common counterargument by UN actors was that the military misunderstood the UN's role as a neutral actor in the conflict. However, as established in Chapter 1, the UN was not a neutral actor in Afghanistan. A deep contradiction lay in the fact that the UN was tasked with coordinating its activities with the IMF and the government, and simultaneously maintaining an independent stance to fulfil their monitoring function. This included holding the

IMF, the Afghan government, and armed opposition groups to account for committing civilian causalities amongst the Afghan population (UN, 2011). While the UN, ISAF, and aid agencies were debating with each other on the above, there were increasing levels of violence throughout Afghanistan. At the field level the differing attitudes of UN staff towards the military added to the contradictory nature of the UN's positionality in Afghanistan.

In certain regions of the country, military personnel in uniform regularly attended meetings at UN compounds, despite being advised against the interaction with the military at meetings in the CM guidelines. Further, it was not uncommon, in some areas, for military officials to be invited for dinner at UN guesthouses. UN staff in the provinces lived in shared houses located near to or even in the UN office compounds themselves. During such events, those UN staff who were cautious of creating the perception of or developing close relationships with the military might delay returning home by working late in the office until the military had left the guesthouse. As Jeffery, a UN staff member in the eastern region, explained,

> We have to live together and we are all adults so there is nothing I can do. But it worries me that people in the neighbourhood see us having military over as dinner guests. It's dangerous. I just can't be bothered to fight with my housemates anymore about this. I'm going to move next month.
>
> (C16, Kabul)

Jeffery lived in a large house with five other UN staff colleagues. Military dinners were not common, but occurred sufficiently often to make him feel uncomfortable. While this practice caused discord in the house itself, this internal dissension was not evident to the wider public. However, not everyone in the house felt the same. Neel, who had a security background, and often visited the PRTs on the weekend when they held local markets in the outer perimeters of the compound, had a different perspective. He suggested that these meetings were a form of strategic relationship-building; he explained:

> the military have a lot of resources. Building a relationship with them works as a give and take. We share information sometimes cautiously but it is also about other things. They get really good food shipped in, but they are confined to the base. Having them over for home-cooked food in a more casual setting is a big gesture. And if we ever get attacked and need their help little things like this will make a difference … and none of my housemates that do not want to sit down to dinner with them would refuse help then. I am sure.
>
> (C17, Kabul)

Interestingly, a very similar conversation occurred around having Afghan staff or neighbours over for meals. The concerns regarding Afghan staff were twofold. First, the UN staff were concerned that their Afghan neighbours might think it was inappropriate for Afghans to be coming in and out of a Western guesthouse. Second, there was a general distrust of the local staff and worry that they might share or sell information to local criminal or armed opposition groups, or even be members themselves. Accordingly, both the military and local Afghans were perceived as potential security threats by different UN staff within the same guesthouse.

Military personnel in uniform regularly came to the UN compound in the Western region for meetings organised by UNAMA. This practice continued even though other UN agencies expressed concern about the meetings continuing to take place at the compound, which was subsequently threatened and attacked by rockets several times during the course of the research for this book: on a few previous occasions the staff were assisted and evacuated by the local PRT. In August 2008, over 900 families were affected by an IMF aerial bombardment in the Shindand District of Herat province in the western region. The problematic UN public response to the civilian casualties and destruction that occurred as a result of the raid, and the internal disconnects within the UN were touched upon in a letter sent out to all NGOs and UN agencies in September 2008 by a Kabul-based UN humanitarian officer, before he resigned, to a senior UN official:

> Dear [xxx],
> Just before I leave UNAMA, I should like to bring to your attention an issue which I feel you may want to think about and discuss [...] UNAMA recommended after its mission of 25 August to Shindand, that 'ISAF should be encouraged to build a school, health centre and some wells in Nowabad Village as soon as possible'.
>
> This recommendation takes no account of the fact that schools are being attacked at this time, and such a blatant linkage of development assistance to the campaign to 'win hearts and minds' risks further exposure of school facilities, staff and students to those hostile to the overall efforts of the international community [...]. When the UNAMA Western Region Office initiated the response [...] UNICEF and WHO were reluctant to support it.
>
> The UN is already alarmingly associated with the military in many parts of the country. I believe that most UNAMA Heads of Regional Offices do not appreciate these distinctions, either because they do not understand them or because they do not consider them important within the context of the political mission, they are engaged in. Could I therefore request that you [...] raise these issues and explain to them the positioning of the UN (not just UNAMA, but the whole system)....
>
> (Anonymous)

The letter suggests that the response of the UN officials at the regional office in question could be explained in a variety of ways: a strategic choice; a disregard for the lives of the local population compared to the political goals of the UN mission; and/or ignorance concerning principles of coordination and the boundaries of interaction with military forces. The official's resignation, as well as the subsequent resignations of the rest of his team from the UN shortly afterwards, was based upon the realisation that his own understanding of the mission he was involved in may not have been closely aligned to what was happening on the ground. The struggle in this case was not between civilian and military actors *per se*, but between civilian actors within the same organisation, in this case the UN, with divergent understandings of other actors, each other, and their roles in the intervention project.

It should also be noted that attacks on UN compounds happened sporadically in different regions of Afghanistan throughout my time there. In April 2011, for example, a demonstration at the UN compound in Balkh province, which took place after the burning of the Quran by an American Pastor in Florida, took a tragic turn. The protest became violent and UN staff members were hunted down inside the building and the compound was set afire. The attack resulted in the deaths of four UN security officers from Nepal and three international UN staff members, two of which were beheaded, and over 20 Afghans injured (UNSG, 2011; BBC, 2011). After 2006, when there occurred a marked rise in armed opposition group activity, the attacks on UN compounds often fuelled questions regarding the blurring of the lines between the UN, aid community, and the international military forces. It is imperative not to diminish the tragedy of the injuries and loss of life of UN staff that have occurred since 9/11 in Afghanistan nor to dismiss the fact that the majority of these incidents have been armed groups specifically targeting the UN because of perceptions of it as a Western political actor. The fear instilled by the experience of seeing or knowing your colleagues have been subjected to such stark violence cannot be understated, and weighed heavily in the perceptions and emotions of many if the interveners and Afghans working for international organisations and aid agencies that I spoke to while conducting research. In a few cases however, the targeting and attacks on the UN offices were arguably a result of practices carried out by UN staff members that the community found unacceptable, including inappropriate personal relationships or attempts to influence political actors or processes. Missteps of this sort were rarely acknowledged by the UN, nor did the feature in public debates about the role of the UN in Afghanistan.

The contradictory nature of the UN mandate contributed to the internal chaos amongst UNAMA and the UN agencies; however, another important factor was the everyday practices of the staff, and the relationships they developed. At times, such as in the example above, the translation of everyday practices into discourses about insecurity and development provided a skewed picture of the realities on the ground. These contradictions created internal struggles for some of the UN staff which were only resolved by leaving Afghanistan. Another source of tension, however, was the integrated structure of the UN mission itself.

Fighting for space and the integrated mission

The UN integrated mission structure was intended as a means to facilitate coordination between UN agencies and to strengthen the capacity of the UN to coordinate with other actors involved in peacebuilding and post-conflict reconstruction. As discussed in Chapter 1, although the concept of integrated missions was not new, the post 9/11 intervention in Afghanistan provided an opportunity to test the reforms to the structure suggested in the *Report of the Panel on United Nations Peacekeeping Operations* (UNSC, 2000), written by Lakhdar Brahimi. Also known as the Brahimi Report and written in the aftermath of the first integrated mission in Kosovo in 1999, the document suggested a revised formula for UN mission integration. Afghanistan, virtually a perpetual experimentation site for foreign actors, provided the UN with their first chance to implement his recommendations. Integration is supposed to be flexible, and relevant to local contexts. Rather than producing coherence between actors and facilitating coordination, however, the integration arrangements of the UN in Afghanistan contributed to efforts to forge and maintain distinct identities within the mission and in relation to the UN. The reestablishment of an OCHA office in Afghanistan provides a clear example of how these internal frictions played out.

The OCHA had operated in Afghanistan since 1991, with its activities coordinated remotely via the regional office in Islamabad, Pakistan.[5] In 2002, OCHA staff and operations were subsumed within the integrated UNAMA structure. This created discord within the UN structures, as the limited role allotted to the humanitarian advisers caused them to feel that their roles had been reduced, and that the political focus of the UN mission at the time diminished the attention given to the humanitarian needs of the Afghan people. As these humanitarian needs increased, Afghan communities, INGOs, Afghan civil society, and Afghan government officials repeatedly called for recognition of the worsening military and security conditions, particularly in the more remote rural areas of the country, which was at least in part a consequence of the large-scale international military intervention and increase in AOG attacks. Indeed, UNAMA reported a 40 per cent increase in civilian casualties from 2007 to 2008 (UNAMA, 2009). In addition to the increased violence, extreme poverty, drought, and displacement were persistent problems.

At the time, there were also intense debates on what was perceived as a shrinking humanitarian space in Kabul. The term ‘humanitarian space’ broadly describes ‘the situation of shifting conflict dynamics and geopolitics, particularly since 9/11, have combined to limit or restrict the capacity of humanitarian organisations to safely and effectively provide material relief to populations suffering the ravages of war’ (Brassard-Boudreau and Hubert, 2010).[6] Humanitarian actors are supposed to base their activities on universal principles: humanity, impartiality, neutrally, and independence – that are enshrined in International Humanitarian Law. In Afghanistan this space was argued to be shrinking by humanitarian agencies due to a variety of factors. These included: the integrated PRTs; the UN integrated mission structure; and the large number of aid agencies, some of whom may have branded themselves as ‘humanitarian organisations’ while working directly with or being funded by the military. Humanitarian agencies in Afghanistan argued that of these factors contributed to the blurring of boundaries between humanitarian organisations and other actors with other agendas.

A reluctant UN response to the continued pressure from the aid community and Afghan civil society came in the establishment in 2007 of a Humanitarian Unit within UNAMA, which was staffed by only a handful of people, several of whom resigned within a year of commencing their roles. In 2008, demands from the aid community for a less biased UN coordinator led to a joint letter from over 200 organisations to the UN Emergency Co-ordinator in New York. This letter called for the removal of OCHA from under the auspices of UNAMA, and a re-establishment of an independent OCHA office in Afghanistan to deal with what the Norwegian Refugee Committee (Afghanistan NGO Community, 2008, p. 1) described as the 'growing humanitarian needs that were being subjugated to the UN political agenda and the security aims of the international community'. After numerous field visits to Afghanistan, OCHA headquarters in New York responded negatively. They had decided that a separate HC was not needed in Afghanistan. Now furious, civilian aid agencies and several international organisations argued that the situation in Afghanistan was no longer one where the two-feet-in approach was appropriate, and therefore it was no longer acceptable for OCHA to turn down the request. Consequently, and with great reluctance, in 2009 the OCHA set up an office in Afghanistan. The establishment of OCHA in Kabul was significant because it symbolised the UN's recognition of Afghanistan as a conflict zone, and challenged any narrative of success claimed by NATO regarding the military effectiveness of the intervention in Afghanistan.

In 2009, UNAMA adopted a one-foot-in-one-foot-out approach (UNOCHA, 2009), which allowed OCHA to be located outside the UN compound, but still to report to the DPKO. The physical separation of the OCHA from the UN compound aimed to strengthen the perception of OCHA's independence from UNAMA in the eyes of non-UN actors. The separate office also allowed the agency to have increased autonomy of operation. As defined by their mandate, the central purpose of OCHA was to coordinate humanitarian actors both within and outside UN structures. It was hoped, and initially realised, that those NGOs that did not want to be too closely associated with the UN mission might be encouraged to meet with OCHA in a separate compound. However, a few years later, 2011–2012, none of the agencies I interviewed believed that OCHA had made a positive contribution to this situation. In fact, the majority of the people I spoke to, including representatives from other UN agencies, expressed disappointment with the OCHA. The director of an organisation that had signed the letter requesting the presence of OCHA in Afghanistan remarked that, 'OCHA has not really made a difference. They have tried but they do not have the capacity' (I57, Kabul).

OCHA's return to Afghanistan, however, was plagued by such problems that their first chief of mission resigned in frustration. Paramount amongst these issues was the lack of support OCHA received from the UN structure, rather than the shrinking humanitarian space that so often dominates the discourse

(Glad, 2011; Donini, 2011; UNOCHA, 2011b). After setting up the office in 2009, the OCHA struggled to hire staff, and to obtain vehicles and basic office resources such as computers and telephones. The UNAMA was hesitant to coordinate with OCHA or provide it with the necessary resources to monitor activities and play a coordination role. A turf war emerged where OCHA staff were viewed as encroaching on UNAMA's territory and faced resentment from other UN agencies. A senior UN official explained, 'OCHA is supposed to be coordinating NGOs and facilitating discussions between civilian and military actors, but coordination really takes place at a higher level' (I34, Kabul). The OCHA's difficulties, however, did not just lie within the UN integrated structure.

The humanitarian aid community in Afghanistan had not been effectively coordinated for almost 10 years, and some argue that this had been the modus operandi since the 1980s (Baitenmann, 1990, p. 79). Aid agencies had called for OCHA to play a coordinating role, but were reluctant to surrender their freedom and work together in a truly collaborative manner with each other and with OCHA. Miguel, a senior official who had worked on civil–military relations with the OCHA said:

> UNAMA was unable to undertake that co-ordination role within its mandate and that is why OCHA was called in to set up a presence. The NGOs were unhappy and the DSRSG did not have the capacity. But then, when OCHA came, they were unwilling to give up what they see as the power they had over the situation. Essentially, they did not want to work with the UN but they did not really want OCHA either. They felt it challenged their authority....
>
> (I32, Kabul)

Miguel eventually changed jobs because of his frustration with the situation at the OCHA. He and moved on to a senior position with a large NGO network where his work was mainly focused on advocacy and coordination. A few months after his move we spoke again. His level of frustration had grown even greater and he said quite unequivocally,

> I do not want to ever work with NGOs again. The lack of transparency and accountability among these agencies is shocking. Coming from Iraq I thought Afghanistan would be easier but it is much more convoluted.
>
> (I32, Kabul)

Another UN senior official, who had been part of a previous task group which gathered information on the activities of civilian organisations in Afghanistan, commented:

> For years we have been trying to gather information for a 3W database and have been unable to do so ... not because it is a difficult task, it is actually

> very simple … but because NGOs refuse to provide the information. No one wants anyone else to know exactly what they are doing, where and funded by whom.
>
> (I30, Kabul)

During the fieldwork, it became apparent that the resistance to participating in the 3W exercise was not only resistance to being coordinated but also to being defined by the type of work that an agency was doing. The OCHA example thus demonstrates how friction, not coherence, emerged from UN attempts to institutionally integrate political, development, and humanitarian pillars in Afghanistan. The reluctance of UNAMA to acknowledge the limitations of their politically charged mission created internal and external conflicts. The aversion to coordination in practice amongst aid agencies, however, also raised important questions about the actual challenges were that aid actors were facing, and the relationship between discourse, strategy and practice. The next section examines the relationships and dynamics between different aid actors.

Constructing a hierarchy of aid agencies

The wide range of aid organisations in Afghanistan presented a full spectrum of actors: these ranged from NGOs willing to operate in conflict zones with government funding and military support, to those that adhered strictly to purely humanitarian principles. The NGOs that were adamantly opposed to the integration of security and development tried to distance themselves from other civilian actors that openly communicated their willingness to accept funding from the US government and other NATO troop-contributing nations, to coordinate with the PRTs and, in some cases, the Afghan government. This distinction was far more complex than a simplistic development vs. humanitarian agency divide. Aid agencies often did both humanitarian and development work, and even those that were more development-focused sometimes tried to maintain a distance from the security forces. This mixed bag of responses led agencies that saw themselves as independent to regularly reaffirm their identity as the *real* aid actors in Afghanistan, one step above the for-profit development corporations that regularly engaged with political and security actors. Ultimately, these efforts to distinguish one actor from another created a hierarchy of development actors, but also reflected the impact of violence on aid agencies.

The NGO Code of Conduct (ACBAR, 2005) was developed by the five largest civil society and NGO coordinating networks in Afghanistan, which were composed of local and international agencies: ACBAR; the Afghan NGOs' Coordinating Bureau (ANCB);[7] the South-West Afghanistan Balochistan Association for Coordination (SWABAC);[8] the Afghanistan Civil Society Forum Organization (ACSFO),[9] and; the Afghan Women's Network (AWN).[10] The 21-article Code, reminiscent of the Principled Approach proposed by the UN during the Taliban period, was updated in 2013 to reflect the changed context in Afghanistan.

The preamble defines the Code as 'a set of shared norms, principles and values that aims to guide the conduct of NGOs in Afghanistan' (ACBAR, 2013, p. 2). NGOs were asked to commit to transparency, accountability, good governance, and non-discriminatory practices. Its general principles focused on a commitment to international humanitarian principles and human rights law, and the non-maleficent principle of 'Do No Harm' (Ibid., p. 3). A Code Observance Mechanism, which was a major change in the 2013 version, was designed to ensure better CoC implementation. The Code Observance Mechanism was intended to be monitored by an 'Observance Committee' of representatives from organisations involved in formulating the CoC. The Code reinforced boundaries to resist the conflation of development and security actors, and was an act of resistance to the emergence of a number of large development corporations within Afghanistan, of whom ACBAR members saw as unprincipled agencies, either because they worked as for-profit companies, were co-opted into the counterinsurgency agenda through funding, or were armed.

One of the main aims of the Code was to formally distinguish between NGOs and for-profit development organisations, many of which were registered as NGOs with the Afghan government (Michaels, 2011). The urgency to develop and secure the country opened a space for non-traditional aid actors, such as DAI and Chemonics, to set up operations. The ACBAR felt that this rush of new agencies negatively affected the standards that principled aid agencies operated by, such as 'Do No Harm' (I55, Afghan and International NGO, Kabul). For example, the ACBAR (2010) attempted to distinguish principled from non-principled aid organisations by releasing the results of a poll that showed that only 6 of the 90 agencies surveyed used Private Security Companies (PSCs). The director of ACBAR at the time stated that 'real' aid agencies did not use armed guards (IRIN, 2010).

One NGO staff member explained, 'It is important to clearly differentiate yourself in the field … not just from the military guys but also the other agencies that are only development agencies in name' (I29, Kabul). This director suggested that the problem was with the private contractors and development corporations like DAI, whose bottom line was profit, not development (I29, Kabul). The Code drew a line between organisations that were engaged in work that 'contribute[d] to the empowerment of communities for the improvement in the quality of life of the people of Afghanistan', and those that squandered funds, worked closely with the military and did harm within the communities where they worked (ACBAR, 2013, p. 3). Though the Code was signed by only 90 organisations, it represented an attempt to clearly demarcate between organisations, and reinforce an identity driven by principled action; however, even amongst these 'principled' aid actors, inconsistencies emerged regarding the practical application of those principles.

Although both the SWABAC and the ACBAR were involved in drafting the Code of Conduct, their interpretation and compliance with the Code varied. For instance, the Provincial Development Committee (PDC) was a general meeting that took place monthly in each province. The IMF, national military and

Afghan government officials, as well as members of civil society, gathered at PDCs to coordinate activity plans. SWABAC was the lead agency for the Local Co-operation and Co-ordination Sector of Kandahar's PDC (I56, Kabul). ACBAR, however, advised its members not to participate in PDCs, arguing that they blurred the lines between development and security actors by including representatives from both the development and the security domains (I55, Kabul). Thus, while one organisation perceived it essential for independence and impartiality to distance themselves from the PDCs, another viewed such distancing as unnecessary or even counterproductive.

One of the key factors contributing to the different understandings of the Code revolved around the NGOs' spatial distance from the fighting, and where the organisation was based. For instance, a large Afghan NGO coordination agency based in the southern and eastern regions of Afghanistan met regularly with the PRT in the provinces where it was located; at times, meetings were held at the military bases (I56, Kabul). The director of this coordinating agency explained that local NGOs were finding it difficult to operate in the area, due to increasing violence on the part of military and insurgent actors. In addition, there had been a rise in the number of civilian casualties in the province and the local community's anger towards the military forces had increased. Consequently, in 2011, the coordinating body reduced the frequency of their meetings with the PRT, but still maintained regular contact them. The local coordinating body had also attempted to establish a third-party mechanism,[11] but that also failed. The director remarked that the PRTs were problematic because they often did not understand local dynamics, local culture, or the work of NGOs, and they lacked accountability to the Afghan people. He also mentioned that several local agencies had reported that staff members had been killed, likely due to the agencies' associations with the military. Regardless, the director explained that the PRT was a major player in the province and could be helpful in certain situations with logistical and medical support; therefore, they felt it was essential to maintain good lines of communication.

The act of categorising agencies into a hierarchy was not only a matter of principle; it was also intended as a source of protection for aid workers who were 'real' development actors. Signatories to the Code of Conduct, for example, were supposed to carry a copy of the Code with them in the field to show to armed actors, including national and international military forces and non-state actors such as the Taliban or other armed groups. The document stressed the independence and neutrality of NGOs in the hope of differentiating NGO staff from other actors to avoid attack or harm. However, as the following chapters show, this distinction was not always recognised within local communities, who differed in their perceptions of the different intervening actors. Thus, the director of a large NGO argued that this differentiation was critical:

> It is important to not confuse the local communities. There needs to be clear lines between us and the other agencies that do bad development

> work [for money]. NGO workers have lost their lives because of this confusion … and many of the local staff as well.
>
> (I57, Kabul)

Ironically, this comment came from the director of an NGO that was heavily funded by USAID and had several projects tied to the stabilisation and counter-insurgency effort.

The perception of the Code as an important barrier to violence was not shared by all NGOs or even all of the signatories to the Code. Some felt that the Code was useful, but that the distinctions between agencies depended upon the type of programming that an agency implemented. The director of an agency that re-evaluated their position in Afghanistan after they lost several female staff in an armed attack, which took place while the young women were travelling back to Kabul from another province and who had raised questions about the access debate in the previous chapter, explained why the Code was not useful for them:

> We have withdrawn from the Civil–Military Working Group and several other forums. Many of them are a waste of time, and we don't agree with what is done and said a lot of the time. We have developed our own bilateral meetings privately with those that matter … this allows us to do things our way and not get confused with the other agencies. That way, we maintain our identity and way of doing things … and this has worked for us and helped our reputation with the communities. If we had done this before, those three staff members may not have been killed … but we also can't know that.
>
> (I28, Kabul)

For this agency, it was important to distance themselves not just from the for-profit agencies and security actors, but also from many of the other 'real' development actors. There is little evidence, however, that such distinctions had any impact on the levels of violence inflicted upon aid workers.

Many of the aid workers witnessed acts of violence that occurred on a regular basis: these included spectacular insurgent attacks such as suicide bombings and military operations involving 'collateral damage'; but they also included more everyday acts of violence such as stabbings, physical assaults, and abuses of power (C12, Kabul). Actors often commented that they felt the potential for some kind of violence was always present. For example, one researcher commented,

> I have seen more violence in the last few months than my entire life … but it is strange, you just accept it and forget about it because then you can't function … but you don't really forget about it because it must affect the way we do things.
>
> (C4, Kabul)

The impact of the violence was also clear in a statement made by an international adviser working for the Afghan National Government:

> Every time there is an attack, my family and friends always send emails and everyone wants to know if you are ok … most of the time you are but what they don't know is that it is the everyday small acts of violence that you see on the way to work or in the street that really slowly chip away at you and affect the way you see things.
>
> (I24, Kabul)

A review of the statistics on violence against aid workers presented in Chapter 2 suggests that it is difficult to identify any clear trends. A scan of the number of incidents over time does little to illuminate the situation. The greatest increase in the number of attacks, meaning the actual number of incidents, on aid workers in Afghanistan was between 2009 (26 attacks) and 2010 (57). This spike was followed by a slight decrease in 2011 (51) and then a slight increase in 2012 (56) until 2013 (81) when the numbers began to go down again in 2014 (54). Nonetheless, Afghanistan was the country with the highest number of incidents taking place against aid workers in the world from 2009–2014.[12] On a global scale this is significant, and feeds into the perception real or imagined that aid workers are under fire in Afghanistan. For many of the signatories, the Code represented a claim to knowledge of the local security dynamics and, therefore, to have an increased ability to control their environment, and perhaps an attempt to feel as though they had power over their circumstances and their survival.

The Code created and entrenched the hierarchy of agencies, where some were seen as legitimate and others as distorting the landscape with their drive for profit and work with military and political actors. While being a signatory was meant to symbolise the commitment to certain principles the practical application of those ideals varied. The Code also represented a shield to protect those organisations from becoming potential targets of attack, despite uncertain evidence of the effectiveness of this strategy. It was a mechanism of control for aid workers within a violent context that allowed them to feel justified in their work and presume a degree of control over their lives.

Reflections on structures, boundaries, and hierarchies

This chapter has sought to deconstruct the complex web of relationships that existed between military, UN, and civilian interveners in Afghanistan. It would be unrealistic to expect an environment entrenched in ongoing conflict and violence, fuelled by vast amounts of money, and where so many different types of organisations, agendas, and people were present to be without conflict or contestation. The experimental structures imposed as part of the intervention which sought to merge and increase coherence amongst security, development, and political actors in this complex landscape. Ironically, however, they often had the opposite effect. Instead boundaries were reinforced and hierarchies were created that influenced the interactions amongst these diverse groups of actors. Additionally, the chapter peeled away the layers within these structures and highlighted the ways in which the everyday practices of people even within the same organisation, network, and even guesthouse could diverge significantly and tensions sometimes occurred as a result. The nuanced nature of these realities are explored through stories which highlighted subjectivities that are often left out of academic and policy texts, like that of Sarah, and those which examined mundane activities such as dinner invitations and conversations and social practices, in the cases of Jeffery and Jonathan. These everyday stories, however, reflected global politics. Ultimately, chaos seemed to abound as struggles within structures, across organisations, between groups, and at an individual level were the norm not the exception.

The hierarchies that were created between groups and agencies drew upon discursive and material practices to justify their ordering system. For those working within integrated structures, such as the PRTs and the UN, attempts to force a unified approach and goals led to efforts to create an even greater distance between the various different intervening actors.

Accordingly, boundaries were developed amongst civilian organisations whereby an organisation's identity was often constructed in relation and/or opposition to other actors, and was also based on the organisation's ideological position. Ideals of transparency, participation, and accountability – key to the Code of Conduct created by NGOs – were commonly used to discuss the actors' self-identity, the positions of various agencies within the hierarchy, and how they related to others. From these constructed identities emerged various subjectivities, defined by the way the organisation was constructed and their ability to work in the Afghan environment. The construction of this discourse was evident as the very means by which these subjects claimed their independence from others; yet this was often contradicted in their practice. The principled discourse, however, was sometimes met with contradictory practices. An important theme that runs through the chapter is the multiple ways in which actors view and interpret their environment and their actions. The relationships between actors were influenced by official policy discourse, guidelines, and structures. However, discourses were adopted and adapted by actors depending on the context and how they preferred to see themselves and their practices.

Within agencies, there was an internal disconnect. Coordination and coherence within the PRTs was complicated by the need to respond to international, and domestic directives in addition to challenging inter-group dynamics and individual personalities. The example of the UN in Afghanistan illustrated how different understandings of mandates, and divergent interpretations of practices and guidelines can exist amongst various subordinate groups within one structure. Acts of resistance to the chaos arose that characterised the complicated matrix of relationships and structures explored in this chapter and to consequences that the constant disconnects and fighting between and amongst agencies and individuals produced. At several points within the chapter interveners reach a breaking point where they cannot continue to be part of the organisation that employed them or to be in Afghanistan. Miguel moved between agencies trying to find a space to do 'better work' but was frustrated by the dynamics in both the UN and the aid sector. For the UN humanitarian adviser who resigned, the inconsistencies in the practices of UN staff were deliberate acts of disengagement, attributed to an unacceptable lack of knowledge about and disregard for the politics of the intervention and the impact of civilian causalities and violent attacks on the communities. His final words suggested improving the training of UN employees on humanitarian law and principles. Beyond those recommendations, however, the act of sending a letter which was shared publicly to the senior official, before the adviser left, rather than having a closed-door meeting, was an attempt to force the UN to account for the derelict actions and potential damage caused by their staff. The adviser, as well as several other interveners in this book, was demanding that the UN do better, and his act of resistance was flight.

The context of violence was a crucial factor in how identities and boundaries were constructed and the types of practices which reinforced those divisions. An examination of the distinctions made by civilian aid workers between themselves and civilian PRT and Embassy staff, and the categorisation of aid agencies reflect the means through which aid workers navigated a frightening space. The aid workers who came to dine late because they wanted to avoid being seen associating with interveners who travelled with armed protection and in militarised vehicles were creating distance between themselves and those they saw as a threat. The hierarchy of development agencies represented a means of protection for some signatories of the Code. NGO officials who carried the Code while travelling in the field did so in an effort to distinguish actors from one another and to maintain their safety. Reinforcing their identity in these ways allowed organisations to feel a sense of control in an environment entrenched in conflict. Therefore, the constant reaffirmation of boundaries and the need to devise ways to separate agencies became a matter of principle, but also of promoting a sense of security in the context of increasing violence.

This is the final chapter to focus mainly on the interveners. The following two chapters present the stories of Qarabagh and Behsud Districts, and provide a closer look at the experiences of local communities, and the interactions between district residents, local government, international and national security forces, UN officials and aid workers.

Notes

1 For a more recent critique see Sopko, 2018. *Prepared Remarks of John F. Sopko Special Inspector General for Afghanistan Reconstruction "Fighting Fraud in Afghanistan Reconstruction."* Targeting Fraud – Safeguarding Integrity Conference. Ohio: State of Ohio Office of Inspector General. 1 November 2018.

2 Joined-up government is the term used by the UK government referring to inter-agency governance.

3 The Comprehensive Approach is the terminology used mainly in NATO documents, which encourages a unified strategic approach between civilian and military actors.

4 The Afghanistan Civil–Military Working Group was co-chaired by the DSRSG and ACBAR. The Group ha[d] the participation of senior military officials serving with

the International Security Assistance Force, including the ISAF HQ Chief of CJ9, OEF and a range of humanitarian actors working in humanitarian and development spheres in Afghanistan.

5 See the OCHA Afghanistan Program webpage.

6 The term humanitarian space can be used to refer to respect for IHL, physical parameters or operations. For a further breakdown of different uses of the term see Brassard-Boudreau and Hubert, 2010. Shrinking humanitarian space? trends and prospects on security and access. *The Journal of Humanitarian Assistance*. Available at: https://sites.tufts.edu/jha/archives/863.

7 ANCB was founded in 1991 and aimed to coordinate the activities of Afghan NGOs with the Afghan government, the UN, international organisations and donor agencies. ANCB membership is for Afghan NGOs only. In 2014, it had 190 members.

8 SWABAC is an Afghan NGO coordinating organisation. In 2014, it had over 80 members that operated development and humanitarian programmes in mainly Pashtun areas in the south, southwest and eastern provinces of Afghanistan.

9 ACSFO was established in 2001 as a partnership between Afghan civil society actors and Swisspeace, a private Swiss foundation for the promotion of peace.

10 AWN, founded in 1995, is one of the largest networks of women's organisations in the country.

11 It was unclear to me from our interview why this occurred.

12 Figures collected from the Aid Workers Security Database: Afghanistan Report 1997–2018.

References

Abbaszadeh, N., Crow, M., El-Khoury, M., Gandomi, J., Kuwayama, D., Macpherson, C., Nutting, M., Parker, N., and Weiss, T. 2008. *Provincial Reconstruction Teams: Lessons and Recommendations*. Princeton, NJ: Woodrow Wilson School of Public and International Affairs.

ACBAR. 2005. *Code of Conduct For NGOs Engaged In Afghanistan*. Kabul: ACBAR.

ACBAR 2010. *Report on Private Security Companies*. Kabul: ACBAR.

Afghanistan. 2008. *Letter to the Emergency Co-ordinator, John Holmes*. Kabul: Norwegian Refugee Committee (NRC).

Baitenmann, H. 1990. NGOs and the Afghan War: The politicisation of humanitarian aid. *Third World Quarterly*, 12(1), 62–85.

BBC. 2011. *UN Staff Killed During Protest in Northern Afghanistan*. 1 April 2011. Available at: www.bbc.co.uk/news/world-south-asia-12940014

Brassard-Boudreau, C. and Hubert, D. 2010. Shrinking humanitarian space? Trends and prospects on security and access. *The Journal of Humanitarian Assistance*.

CMWG. 2008. *Guidelines for the Interaction and Coordination of Humanitarian Actors and Military Actors in Afghanistan*. Kabul: CMWG.

Donini, A. 2011. Between a rock and a hard place: Integration or independence of humanitarian action? *International Review of the Red Cross*. Geneva: International Committee of the Red Cross.

Fishstein, P. and Wilder, A. 2011. *Winning Hearts and Minds? Examining the Relationship between Aid and Security in Afghanistan*. Medford, MA: Feinstein International Center.

Gheciu, A. 2011. Divided partners: The challenges of NATO-NGO cooperation in peacebuilding operations. *Global Governance*, 95–113.

Glad, M. 2011. *A Partnership At Risk: The UN–NGO Relationship In Light of UN Integration*. Oslo: NRC.

Haysom, S. and Jackson, A. 2013. 'You don't need to love us': Civil–Military Relations in Afghanistan, 2002–13. *Stability: International Journal of Security and Development*, 2(2).

Hyrchuck, H. 2009. Combating the security development nexus? Lessons learned from Afghanistan. *International Journal*, 64(3), 825–842.

IRIN. 2010. Q+A-How are private security firms and Afghan aid linked. *Reliefweb*. Available at: https://reliefweb.int/report/afghanistan/qa-how-are-private-security-firms-and-afghan-aid-linked

Khalilzad, Z. How to nation-build. *National Interest*, 80(2005), 19–27.

McNerny, M. 2006. Stabilization and reconstruction in Afghanistan: Are PRTs a model or a muddle? *Parameters*, Winter 2006, 32–46.

Michaels, J. 2011. Laying a firm foundation for withdrawal? Rethinking approaches to Afghan military education. *Defence Studies*, 11, 594–614.

Olson, L. and Gregorian, H. 2007. Civil–military coordination: Challenges and opportunities in Afghanistan and beyond. *Journal of Military and Strategic Studies*, Fall 2007, 10(1), 1–12.

Ratnam, G. 2015. *Poor Planning, Coordination Cited in Afghan Intervention: U.S., German Officials Note Lessons from 15-Year War*. Washington, DC: USIP.

UN. 2011. *Decisions of the Secretary-General – Follow-up to the 16 December Meeting of the Policy Committee (4 May Meeting of the Policy Committee). Decision N0. 2011/10 – Integration*. New York, NY: United Nations. 4 May 2011.

UNAMA. 2009. Afghanistan: *Annual Report on Protection of Civilians in Armed Conflict, 2008*. Kabul: UNAMA Human Rights Unit.

UNOCHA. 2009. *OCHA's Structural Relationships Within An Integrated UN Presence*. New York, NY: United Nations Office for the Coordination of Humanitarian Affairs.

UNOCHA. 2011b. *Humanitarian Access Strategy. Discussion Paper – Version 2*. Kabul: United Nations Office for Co-ordination of Humanitarian Affairs.

UNSC. 2000. *Report of the Panel on United Nations Peace Operations*. New York, NY: United Nations Security Council.

UNSC. 2011. UN Resolution 1974. New York, NY: United Nations Security Council. 22 March 2011.

UNSG. 2011. *Statement on The Attack Against the UNAMA Compound in Mazar-i-Sharif, Afghanistan*. Ban Ki-moon. 1 April 2011. New York, NY: United Nations.

4 Qarabagh stories

Qarabagh is not far from Kabul City, the largest urban centre in Afghanistan, but in many ways, Qarabagh is a different world. The district is a mix of peri-urban and rural communities. The land is fertile, as evidenced by the small orchards in the yards of the roadside houses that one encounters on the travelling there from Kabul City. The district also shows signs of decades of conflict and destruction. Much of the infrastructure and housing was damaged during the 1990s in fighting between *Mujahidin* elements. *En route* to Qarabagh from Kabul, Abdul, a member of the research team who grew up in Qarabagh, pointed out the main landmarks along the road. The conversation moved back and forth between Abdul's youth and his life as a man in his 40s at the time of this research. Abdul explained what was important to notice now, what used to be there when he was younger, and what happened during the war. Though he was clearly very proud of the beautiful landscape that still existed despite the conflict, he felt it paled in comparison to what was there before. A statue of a hand holding a large globe sits at the roundabout located at the entrance to Qarabagh. When I asked Abdul what this statue signified, he seemed to think that it had no significance. It was just a statue, something to mark the marketplace and the entrance to the district. Similar edifices could be found at the centre of traffic stops throughout the country. The irony of this roundabout struck me on each trip to Qarabagh: in many ways, this district was tucked away from much of the rest of Afghanistan, and indeed the world; yet the town was marked by this global symbol of interconnectedness.

Embracing this contradiction, this chapter will examine everyday realities through the lenses of district residents, local government officials, community leaders, and external actors that lived and worked in Qarabagh District. Few foreigners lived in the district itself. Therefore, the district stories emerge mainly from the perspectives of Afghan residents, while also considering the perspectives of the external actors who worked on projects in the district, travelled through the district, and liaised with community leaders. These narratives challenge often taken-for-granted, generalised notions about voice and communication found in Western scholarship on Afghanistan. This brief story of Qarabagh revolves around three principal themes. First, it explores local perceptions and experiences of security and development. The chapter highlights the various ways in which security and development were rarely connected in the district, however, did those linkages reflect the story told in international policy discourse. Second, the chapter illuminates the multifarious picture that emerges from the relationship and distinction between violence and security within the district. Indeed, the story of Qarabagh as it unfolds here provides insight into the complexity of the everyday violence of intervention and conflict. Last, the chapter interrogates local governance practices and hybridity. In Qarabagh, the dilemmas and the complicated relationships created as a consequence of the attempts to implement hybrid structures by external actors and elites in the central government come into focus. Throughout this chapter actors utilise a variety of tactics to navigate the dynamics and challenges of the district and to survive.

The district

Qarabagh lies 50 kilometres from Kabul City and 20 kilometres east of Bagram Airbase, the largest US military base in the country (Williams, 2018). It borders Guldara, Farza, and Istalif districts (southwest), Deh Sabz and Kalakan districts (south), and Parwan province (north). For many years, Qarabagh was the scene of intense violence, particularly during the Taliban era, when it was almost completely destroyed. The district is north of Kabul City, and nestled adjacent to Charikar District in Parwan, which was at the frontline of the battle between, Ahmad Shah Masoud and the Northern Alliance and the Taliban forces. Thus, in the 1990s Qarabagh was at the intersection of major warring factions. Many of the residents of the district, including many of Pashtun origin, sided with Masoud, pitting them directly against the Taliban. The area was still heavily marked by the war and by years of persistent drought and seasonal flooding. Nonetheless, it had been a major focus of return and resettlement by the Government of Afghanistan (GoIRA) (Saltmarshe and Medhi, 2010). According to official government reports, however, Qarabagh was considered a 'secure' district. Indeed, in 2010, the district was awarded a Medal of Achievement of Peace by the Ministry of Rural Rehabilitation and Development (MRRD).

The demographics of Qarabagh were similar to many of the other districts in Kabul Province: a national census had not been carried out for several decades; however, for the purposes of this research the population statistics are taken from the Central Statistics Office the official government agency responsible for maintaining this population and household data, which listed Qarabagh as having 73,000 residents (Afghanistan, 2012a). The district is ethnically mixed and its population was approximated as 40 to 60 per cent Pashtun, 40 to 55 per cent Tajik, with only a small number of Hazaras and other tribes (Afghanistan, 2006). The district also has a high percentage of returnees and IDPs, populations which are sometimes hard to capture statistically. Official estimates place the returnee population at approximately half of the total population (Sarkesian, 1975; Afghanistan, 2012a).

Qarabagh houses, Barikap and Alasghan, two of the 26 Land Allocation Schemes (LAS) which are plots of land specifically earmarked by the Afghan Ministry of Refugees and Repatriation for landless returnees and IDPs, in Afghanistan. The scheme was developed by the Afghan government in 2005, through President Decree 104, as part of the Afghan National Development Strategy (ANDS) (2008–2013) was supposed to address the problem of landless returnees and IDPs by allotting them land that was intact but uncultivated (Macdonald, 2011). Barikap and Alasghan were established in 2007, as part of the roll-out of the scheme. Both communities have struggled to become sustainable, challenged by the remoteness of the scheme locations, a lack of potable water, health and education services, basic infra-structural necessities, far distances from labour markets and livelihood opportunities, and an absence of basic services (Afghanistan, 2013, p. 46; Majidi, 2013). In addition, families trying to settle have faced attempts at land grabbing by powerful figures, government corruption, and host community disputes over land rights.

The district capital, where the globe that greeted me on visits to the area sits, is the town of Qarabagh. A few metres away from the roundabout the district market runs along a paved road for about 100 metres. The District Administration Office (DAO), the bureaucratic centre of the district, was located about 400 metres off the main road and not too far from the main marketplace in Qarabagh District. It shared a yard with the police station and the district court. The DAO represented the central government in the area. Beyond that there were several types of *shuras*.[1] Some of which were organic groups of community elders, while others were formalised structures, created through government programmes such as the National Solidarity Programme (NSP). The NSP *shuras*, known as the Community Development Councils (CDC) was a locally elected body. One CDC represents a cluster of families or villages, depending on the population demographics of the area. There were also local *shuras* that dealt with conflict resolution and justice composed of non-elected elders, respected community members and religious leaders. At the district level there was the DDA, an association of representatives from the CDCs. Across the district, these structures varied in number and composition, as well as the power they held.

Qarabagh is vulnerable to extreme weather shocks, such as floods. Access to social services, such as schools, clinics, and electricity, was limited. Civil society groups usually composed of the various village *shuras*. Detailed and accurate figures on the area's development profile, however, as was the case with many other districts in Afghanistan, were difficult to verify.

The statistics in Table 4.1 derive from the District Development Plan that was jointly developed by the GoIRA and the District Development Assemblies (DDA), who fall under the MRRD. In addition, ten aid organisations were listed in 2011 as operating in Qarabagh (one national and seven international NGOs, and two UN agencies), though the figures reported in the government data were highly disputed by community residents, NGOs working in the area, and some government officials that I spoke with.

Table 4.1 Qarabagh District Profile

Health and Nutrition	Basic Health Centres	6
	Hospitals	1
	Health Posts	18
Infrastructure and Natural Resources	% of families that have access to electricity	5
	% of roads that are open to traffic in all seasons	8
Education, Culture, Media, and Sports	Primary Schools	25
	Secondary Schools	11
	Senior High Schools	8

Source: Ministry of Rural Rehabilitation and Development, 2011.

Villagers in Qarabagh were engaged in a variety of economic activities. Approximately 80 per cent of district residents relied on agriculture for an income (Afghanistan, 2006, 2011), though some, like Abdul, also had other jobs. The district produced 9 per cent of the raisins in Afghanistan, and many residents owned large vineyards use for the cultivation of raisins and sultanas, a local speciality (Afghanistan, 2012b). Many residents had been refugees outside the area at one point during the Soviet invasion in the 1970s. These absences contributed to the collapse of agriculture and infrastructure, particularly the irrigation systems. Now local people were undertaking repair and reconstruction work in their villages.

Abdul

Abdul's family had maintained a large vineyard in his village before conflict broke out. He had stayed to protect the land as long as he could but eventually sought refuge in Pakistan in the mid-1990s. Even while in Pakistan he had tried to come back to the district a few times. His family's vineyard, however, was destroyed. After 9/11 he moved back home and secured work in Kabul. He was revitalising the vineyard and had a small garden too. The area lacked electricity and water, however, so he registered for an NGO project which gave solar-powered panelling to district residents to operate water pumps. On our first visit to the district, we went to his house and he proudly showed me the vineyard, the garden and the equipment he had been given by the NGO. A few months later, we went back to his home. The equipment had broken and there was no response from the NGO regarding how or when it could be fixed. He said it was disappointing for him, but he was just going to continue with his plans for expanded the workable areas of the land and hope something else came along or the NGO sent someone to fix the solar panel. Otherwise he would just sell them.

The unavailability and high cost of transportation hindered local people's access to services and employment. Few people in the villages owned cars and taxis were rare. Given the economic situation of the people living in rural communities, even travelling from the villages to the district centre for medical treatment or administrative services was not always possible. The cost of transportation was problematic for men who depended on daily-waged labour in Kabul City, such as IDPs and returnees living on the LASs. A taxi from Qarabagh to Kabul costs approximately 1,000 Afghanis or US$12, whereas the daily wage for labourers is between 500 to 1,000 Afghanis. Men in the LAS discussed the problems they faced in commuting to Kabul for waged labour, sometimes not finding work and being unable to afford to return home.

Most of my time was spent in villages scattered around the district, including Ashrafkhalil, Betaniyar, Baghalam, Denarkhalil, Dawoodzai, Qal'eh-ye Baz, Qal'eh-ye-Bibi, and two LASs, Alasghan and Barikap though, several interviews were conducted in the district capital and Kabul. The pattern of villages in Qarabagh is similar to that of many rural areas in the rest of the country. Most districts have a district centre, a few subdistricts composed of a large village with connections to smaller villages, and then a few houses and farms extending out from the small villages. Between the subdistricts, there is usually a boundary of some kind, usually a road or open space. For a visitor, it is not always clear where one area ends and another begins: even for Abdul, demarcating this boundary involved some guesswork.

Securing the district

There was a consensus between the official statistics, local residents, local *shuras*, government officials, and aid agency staff implementing aid projects in the district that Qarabagh was secure. At the time, the province of Kabul was considered to be under government control, but several districts within the province were identified as volatile. Qarabagh, however, was not listed as one of them. Qarabagh represented only 2 per cent of the total population of Kabul province in 2012 (Afghanistan, 2012a) but witnessed even fewer (1 per cent) of the total security incidents in the province from 2009–2011. Statistics, collected from various sources, recorded only 74 security incidents in Qarabagh District during the period 2009–2012. These statistics use a wide definition of 'security incidents', ranging from criminal acts, such as assault, theft, and murder, to AOG and ISAF-related clashes or causalities. In 2009, there were 16 security incidents in the district. This number increased slightly to 24 in 2010, then began to drop in 2011, with 19 incidents and 18 in 2012. The widespread agreement that the district was secure was complicated by different perspectives regarding the sources of insecurity and different experiences across the district with violence.

Security was often linked to the absence of fighting between armed groups and related violence. Belligerents included the AOG, Afghan army, and international military forces. Many residents, however, saw the Afghan army and ISAF as being the lesser of two sources of insecurity. This is partly because the memory of the conflict with the Taliban was still very strong not only in people's memories but also in their physical surroundings. *Shura* members across the district shared their memories and anger at past injustices. In a group discussion in

Qal'eh-ye-Bibi, *shura* members explained how the conflict with the Taliban in the 1990s had impacted on the lives of village residents:

> Security is good in the area now. The Taliban destroyed the area. They cut all of the trees and destroyed the houses. The Taliban killed many of our people. Many people have family members that died or are now disabled. During the Taliban, the village was forced to move to Panjshir Province.
>
> (F23, Mixed, Qal'eh-ye-Bibi)

The legacy of the conflict lay not only in the pain that comes with the loss of life, but also in the anger felt because of the destruction of the land. The destruction of the land by the Taliban was regarded as an attempt to destroy the life of the community. Members in the group displayed strong emotions when communicating the sense of loss attached to the destruction of their fields. People in the area depended on the land for their livelihoods and family security. *Zameen*, 'land', is significant in Afghan culture and, as in many other parts of the world, it signals wealth. Even more so, though it represented a family's continuity and future potential as well as being a marker of their history and foundations. The village experienced mass displacement during that time, and while Panjshir is not far from Qarabagh, it was not their home. An elder from Alar, another local village, described the destruction and his experience of return:

> When we first came back to our area after the time of the Taliban, our houses were all gone, and all of the trees had been burned by them ... now we are starting our lives from the beginning again. It will take time to get back to the place before the Taliban ... 20 years ago, but at least we are home again.
>
> (I85, Qarabagh Shar)

Gathered together after Friday prayers, a group of local male residents agreed that, overall, they did not have a problem with ISAF occasionally patrolling because they did not have good memories of the Taliban (F27, Male, Baghalam). Ultimately, however, they felt that the patrols through this area had little impact on their lives. Aa a shopkeeper explained: 'Sometimes the French ISAF come to the villages and give some gifts like biscuits and other things to the children' (I82, Baghalam). In another village they argued that ISAF had brought some positive changes to the area and that they were happy that ISAF had come to Afghanistan and removed the Taliban (F24, Qal'eh-ye Baz). These two villages had little interaction with the international military forces, in other areas, however, it was a different story.

ISAF and the National Army were also viewed as a source of insecurity. Villages had a range of different experiences with these groups and while some accepted their presence in Afghanistan might be necessary, they did not want them in their local spaces. A mixed group of NSP and local *shura* members explained that they accepted ISAF presence in Afghanistan for now but did not want them to come into their villages; the deputy head of the shura, who had reflected earlier on his negative memories of the Taliban in the 1990s, explained 'ISAF helped us stop the fighting with Taliban but we do not want them here in our area. They disrespect us. They should stay outside' (F23, Qal'eh-ye-Bibi). In two of the villages, night raids had been a common occurrence. Similar sentiments were shared in Denarkhalil, where a shopkeeper stated: 'They are bombarding our villages without reason. No one here likes them [ISAF], according to our Islamic views and beliefs' (F28, Denarkhalil). In Qal'eh-ye-Bibi, the village that had been displaced to Panjshir, village leaders had recently threatened violence and upheaval if the raids continued. The head of the *shura* explained, 'Previously, ISAF was conducting searches and night raids in our area. We told the DA we would fight the ISAF forces if they came back during the night, so as to protect our families' (F23, Qal'eh-ye-Bibi). Indeed, in 2010, the members of the *shuras* and other men from the village had gone to the district capital en-masse in protest and demanded that ISAF never return to their village. 'Since then, ISAF had not been back for one year' (F23, Qal'eh-ye-Bibi).

The residents in Ashrafkhalil adopted a different approach to those in Qal'eh-ye-Bibi. More than many of the other villages, Ashrafkhalil had witnessed the conflict between pro- and anti-government forces. Residents of the village – located close to Baghram US Air Base – spoke of the regular sound of aircraft overhead, rockets and explosions coming from the nearby base and the road leading to the base. There were regular ANA patrols in the area and military forces had patrolled the village until just a few weeks before I arrived. Residents seemed to accept these occurrences as part of their everyday reality: 'We all try our best to do more for security in the village. We do not allow outsiders we do not know and we do not bother ISAF and ANSF when they come here. Sometimes [they] patrol in the villages' (F26, Ashrafkhalil). A young man from the area added, 'Sometimes the ANA are coming to arrest people in the village, and taking bribes' (F25, Ashrafkhalil). The village was not the site of fighting on a daily basis but its proximity to the US military base and the potential risks and disruption posed by regular national and international military patrols meant the threat of violence was constant. Violence, however, was not normalised by the residents. In the recounting of their experiences it was clear that these were unpleasant and frightening events. Violence had, however, become intertwined with the expectations and activities of everyday life. Residents recognised the danger these occurrences but still described their village as 'secure'. Perhaps in Ashrafkhalil, survival was resistance.

Mohammad

The complex relationship that residents had towards the international military forces was highlighted in Mohammad's story. We met him, he was 24 at the time, in a discussion group which took place in one of the villages near the district centre in late 2011. Later that day as we sat eating lunch, he came to join us to talk further. Mohammad had grown up in Pakistan as a refugee. He learned

English there and had taken additional language classes when his family returned to Afghanistan in 2004, after the presidential elections. A few years later he tried to get work with an international organisation. There were many jobs for young Afghans who speak advanced English with the UN, INGOs, for-profit organisations. The international military forces, however, also recruit local Afghans as translators and other positions. Mohammad had worked with the coalition forces for three years as a translator and guide. Qarabagh had little AOG activity, but he kept his work secret from most people outside of his family. As the international forces began to wind down many of the people who had held positions like Mohammad found themselves out of work.

Several months later he was still looking for work. That was less of a worry, however, than the fact that he had started being harassed by people in the area whenever he went to the district centre. Afghans who worked with certain coalition nations had been given the option of applying for a visa to live in that country in certain situations, including if they felt their life was at risk due to the nature of their employment. After a few weeks, Mohammad had gone back to the base where he worked previously and asked to apply for a visa, but he was told that programme was no longer available. He began to get scared and now rarely left the area around his house. He came into town the day we spoke with him to help his father with purchasing goods. He told me he was not sure what he was going to do. He might leave Qarabagh and try to get a job in Kabul or maybe go back to Pakistan. He felt anger at the coalition forces, but more generally at foreigners in Afghanistan (C14, Qarabagh).

Mohammad did not support the AOGs, but he also had no strong allegiance to ISAF, though he thought some of the work the NGOs and UN were doing was making positive changes in the country. Like most young people he took the interpreting job because it paid well, and he might have an opportunity to go to America with his family. Circumstances had changed, however; now he was unemployed, afraid, and facing an uncertain future. Many of the youths I encountered had come of age in post-9/11 Afghanistan. They were often less cautious about engaging with international actors than their parents or elders. The intervention provided economic opportunities, but also opportunities to improve their language skills, and for cultural exchange. They felt that the removal of the Taliban also provided a chance for change in Afghanistan. As the international narrative shifted, however, and the process of exit began young men and women who had worked with not only the military and also aid agencies and the UN were left in peril. The practices in pursuit of global security as a justification for intervention was constantly reiterated in the US, NATO, and UN policy and programme documents, but it created *insecurity* for individuals like Mohammad. Furthermore, over the two years in which the research for this book was conducted, the significant impact of growing violence in Afghanistan on the youths that I spoke to was apparent. A few studies have shown that the frustration of youths with an uncertain future ahead of them, poverty, and the consequences ongoing conflict, have contributed to increased depression, drug use, and migration (Sataruddin, 2018). During one of my last visits to Qarabagh, as we drove nearby Mohammad's village, we asked Abdul if he had heard from Mohammad. He said he had seen Mohammad's father in the district market a few weekends ago. Mohammad had gone back to Pakistan to look for work.

In Qarabagh, there was a distinct security architecture which involved local officials, local *shuras*, and community patrols, in addition to the military forces. The role of local officials was limited but complex. The district administrator, the main GoIRA representative in the area, felt that he had only a minor role in maintaining security. He attributed responsibility for security to community members, not the government or international military forces: 'The government cannot control security. It is up to the people to do this' (I72, Qarabagh). According to the local government officials, there were only 60 police assigned to the district (I76, Qarabagh Shar). The police said they tried to respond to calls from community residents for assistance but, because of their limited numbers, the onus fell on communities to police themselves. Though the police said that they had little to do with combatting insurgent groups, they also explained that security in the area had been improved recently since the new Chief of Police (CoP) who was originally from outside the province and therefore had no tribal or political allegiances within the province had arrived.

Amongst the villagers, local officials had a reputation for corruption and disinterest in addressing the issues concerning local residents. During a visit to Denarkhalil, I sat in on a community discussion on the issue. Residents were deciding whether they should protest the government if the corruption and lack of actions continued. A resident said, 'It's all because of the government. They have lost the trust of the people' (I84, Denarkhalil). Most residents at the meeting, however, felt this was a bad plan and decided to complain to the provincial officials about their situation instead hoping that they could make changes at the district level. A village *Malik* proclaimed, 'Security is because of the community. They control the area. If strangers come, they stop them and call the police. Even though they sometimes do nothing' (I79, Dawoodzai). Even though officials were not trusted by the community, efforts were made to coordinate and communicate with them. During the interviews, participants were clear that government coordination and patronage were important elements of how security was perceived and maintained in the district. There were powerful personalities in the area that people aligned themselves with, but it was the politics and life in the village mattered most in Qarabagh. In other words, carving out a peaceful existence was possible, but it could mean the acceptance of various forms of coercion and violence.

Some of the villages in Qarabagh are miles away from a paved road. The paved road gives way to a dirt road, which gives way to a hard mud path or clearing until it reaches the village. While travelling, it was easy to wonder what anyone without a purpose would be doing on these roads. Community patrols were a sign to outsiders – and also to those inside the village – that any disruption of village life would have consequences. Local patrols were implemented in several areas to ensure that outsiders – seen as troublemakers – stayed outside the village boundaries. These outsiders took various forms. They could be national or international, security or development actors, and even villagers from other parts of the district.

Local *shuras* and community patrols were key components of the security structure for district and community cohesion. *Shura* members saw themselves as essential for maintaining this cohesion; therefore, when issues arose, people were encouraged to go through the *shura* system before approaching the government. Community patrols were the centrepiece of the security structure. The patrols were tasked with maintaining security within the village by watching over crime and theft in the village and, more importantly, by stopping outsiders from entering the village. As one DDA member explained: 'We have good security and no one has any concern about security … the cause of this is that no one [allows] any strangers in the village for any kind of interruption or violence against the security' (I85, Qarabagh Shar). The strengthening of internal community structures and cohesion was a means of preventing external disruptions to community life. Consequently, the division between 'us and them' was determined within a narrow parameter.

Developing the district

Just as, despite the violence, there appeared to be a consensus that the district was 'secure', local actors agreed that there was a lack of development across the district. In interviews and discussions on what development meant responses were two-fold: physical infrastructure and the provision of social services in the area. These responses were not very different from those given by the external actors in Chapter 2; however, residents offered a unique perspective on the purpose of development in the area and the way they envisioned the process of development.

If development was perceived as physical infrastructure, district residents stated that the district had low levels of development. However, not all areas of the district suffered from poor physical infrastructure. Villages in Qarabagh varied in terms of the infrastructure, facilities, and overall economic position. Ashrafkhalil was the least developed village in the field study, in terms of the built environment. The poverty of the village was evident not just from the lack of facilities and infrastructure, including a lack of roads, health services, and schools, and only a small informal marketplace, but also from physical signs of poverty amongst the community residents that were not apparent in any of the other areas.

Local *shura* members at the DDA meeting from other villages commented that some assets had been built in their villages, such as bridges, but there had been no other major construction projects (I86, and F37, Qarabagh Shar). 'We have some development in our village', said one member. He continued, 'We have a school and, at first, after the Taliban, CARE helped us by building our houses and giving things such as doors and windows' (F30, Denarkhalil).

In Qarabagh, where so much of the built infrastructure had been destroyed during the conflicts in the 1990s, this was unsurprising. Physical infrastructure, such as roads, water canals, and electricity systems would assist with farming, schooling, household activities. Road projects were valued because they increased the ability of residents to travel and engage in commerce in all weathers, as well as providing an opportunity for the community to access services and increase their employment options. *Shura* members commented that this accessibility was particularly important for young people, as many had returned from Iran and Pakistan addicted to drugs. They felt that the lack of employment in the district made them depressed and led to drug dependency (F30, Denarkhalil). This physical development, therefore, was perceived as a potential pathway to other opportunities.

In some areas, residents agreed that there was little in terms of physical infrastructure in their respective villages, but argued that development could also be viewed in other ways, such as education and training. A resident of Dawoodzai suggested: 'We can see some development in our village. Before, no one sent their children to school, but now they try their best to send them there. This is also a kind of development' (F21, Dawoodzai). Similarly, a taxi driver from Denarkhalil commented, 'Before, we did not have any educated [people][2] in the village, but now we have one' (F29, Denarkhalil). Women in particular mentioned training in women's rights and hygiene as a source of development in the district. They commented that this kind of training allowed residents to improve their everyday quality of life by strengthening community and household relationships.

The desire for development was accompanied by a causal acceptance of the involvement of external actors, like the UN, NGOs, ISAF, and GoIRA – who tended to be considered as development actors. Some communities had initiated small-scale infrastructure projects but, according to the CoP, these were limited in their impact:

> The community has done some work, but they cannot, for example, complete an entire road themselves. They need assistance from the government, but the government is waiting for the PRT, the PRT is waiting for the government, and the NGOs are doing nothing.
>
> (I75, Qarabagh Shar)

A point of vigorous debate amongst the military, UN agencies, and INGO community is the need to distinguish themselves from each other in the eyes of Afghan communities, since community residents saw little difference between external agencies outside the community. Qarabagh's DA defined NGOs as private organisations that implemented small projects and the UN as an international organisation that implemented larger projects. According to his understanding, ISAF had two parts, security and development. A farmer from Denarkhalil stated, 'NGOs are part of ISAF, and what they bring from other countries in the name of help and aid they [take] back sometimes' (I83, Denarkhalil). A resident of Baghalam commented: 'We just know that they are foreign, but also there are some NGOs that are Afghan' (F27, Baghalam). Similarly, a man in Ashrafkhalil remarked, 'We don't know much about them [the UN and NGOs] we just know sometimes they are helping people' (F26, Ashrafkhalil). Other residents gave more detailed reflections. A young woman from central Qarabagh suggested that when she saw NGOs, she thought they were on the side of the government, so the government and NGOs were the same (F20, Dawoodzai). During a focus group in another village, a young man of a similar age said, 'They are all private organisations. They don't take care of poor people … just themselves' (F29, Denarkhalil).

Community residents also showed little preference for who carried out development work in their area. In Dawoodzai, one community member said: 'It does not matter who does development here. We all need work. The international community is all the same – as long as they give aid, it is fine' (F19, Dawoodzai). The CoP took this point further, arguing that people did not know the difference between the UN, NGOs, or even government programmes. 'It does not matter to them who does what; they just want improvement and security in the area' (I75, Qarabagh Shar). The small number of organisations and external actors in the area may have contributed to the lack of knowledge about different intervening bodies. The differences between the group that were present in the district were not always clear, nor necessarily important for residents.

While this does not negate the important debates about humanitarian space and the politicisation of aid, it does, however, raise interesting questions about the gap between the way aid agencies see themselves, and the way local residents may perceive them. In addition, several Western aid and political actors, in previous chapters, discussed development as a social and economic phenomenon, that is, as an act of social transformation whereby society is re-engineered to accept new, more modern ways of doing things. By contrast, for those local residents, development was not a process of special re-engineering but an investment in the community. There was no reason for them to change their life, they did, however, desire resources to improve the conditions in the area. The intervention, however, created conditions whereby that desire required negotiation with external forces, interveners, and otherwise.

The land allocation schemes

The journeys to the LASs differed from trips to other areas of the district: Abdul took different routes to show me how the LASs were connected to, but also separate from, the rest of the district. The first route began along a paved road, which ended about 30 minutes outside Kabul City. After the road ended, our Toyota Corolla pushed its way through the desert sand for 45 minutes until we reached another paved road that took us to Barikap. The area along this last stretch of road to Barikap was vastly different from what we had seen from the roads we had been taking over the previous month on the other side of the district. The familiar road was lined with farms, small holdings, some cleared land, small marketplaces, and shops that would pop up periodically with food and drink vendors and small refectories. On that road the occasional sheep crossing stopped traffic at random junctures. By contrast, on the final road to the LASs, which ran through a flat dusty valley and broke at the edge of a mountain range, there was nothing: no shops, no farms, and very few animals and people. The second route we took to the LASs, much longer than the first, was on the other side of Qarabagh District. We drove from Kabul to the centre of Qarabagh and then turned off the main road into the villages. We continued weaving our way through the villages into the interior of the district until we came out on the other side near Alasghan.

The two LASs almost face each other on opposite sides of a road, positioned near the end of Qarabagh District, not far from the Baghram Air Base. Most of the communities in the other parts of the district have histories that can be traced back for hundreds of years to a particular piece of land or village, whereas the communities of Barikap and Alasghan were only created a few years ago. LAS residents were mainly returnees from Pakistan or Iran, or IDPs from other parts of central Afghanistan[3] and other scattered areas of the country. While these residents live in Qarabagh, their histories are to be found in other parts of Afghanistan. This reality made the establishment of a group of community elders and the development of community trust a more complex task than in other parts of the district. Land conflicts were also an issue with the residents in Alasghan. Residents of other villages disputed some of the land assigned to the LASs by the Ministry of Refugees and Reparations. Residents of Qarabagh, from large areas like Dawoodzai, argued that the land in Barikap and Alasghan actually belonged to families within their communities. However, the claims had not been taken to court, as only one man in the Dawoodzai area was old enough to remember land ownership titles, and all of the land tenure documents had been destroyed during the conflict.

The LASs are located in spaces where the terrain is arid: the sites are areas where people had previously chosen not to settle because natural resources, infrastructure, or linkages to other areas and communities are few. Both Barikap and Alasghan have no electricity and only a limited water supply and farmable land. There were, for example, only two wells with several water pumps in Barikap and most of the water was brought in tanks from Kabul because the wells are often dry. Therefore, residents suggested that development was the process of constructing a reliable water supply for the schemes, providing transport links to the urban trade centres, and building up the physical surroundings of the village, particularly boundary walls.

The LASs lacked the physical structures to keep the community space private and separate from the outside world. Without infrastructure, such as pathways and boundary walls within and around the community to protect them, residents felt more vulnerable to outsiders, who were a source of insecurity because they disturbed village life. The accessibility of their land to outsiders threatened community security. A *shura* member explained: ‘Anyone can pass through our lands, military people and foreigners[4] and make insecurity … even animals are taking our children from the hills’ (F32, Barikap).

Alasghan

The LASs, Alasghan[5] in particular, had been the source of international attention.[6] In June 2007, a US$10 million project was funded by the Australian Government, managed by the United Nations Development Program, in collaboration with UNHCR and UN-Habitat and several Afghan ministries including the MoRR, aimed at providing 1,525 families Afghans running water, shelter materials, infrastructure, and community training and awareness workshops to support the establishment of Alasghan was inaugurated (UN News, 2007). Several INGOs were implementing partners on the project (Australia, 2013; UN News, 2007). Four years later, in 2011, during my visits to the area many of the homes lay empty, and amongst those that were inhabited a significant number were falling apart. Estimates have suggested an occupancy rate as low as 25 per cent (Australia, 2013). The poor quality of the materials used for the project meant that some of the planned homes could not be constructed. Alasghan is made up of deep rows of small brick and mud two-room houses that are closely spaced together. Many of the shelters were constructed disregarding cultural norms and lacked the boundary walls needed to shield women and children from outsiders. Therefore, making it difficult for families to occupy the homes. The school in Alasghan was built without toilets because they were not specified in the contractor's terms of reference (Callinan, 2012). Instead pit latrines were dug by the community a safe distance from the school itself. The only solid and vibrant structures in the area were the women's centres, which were built with donations from an Afghan diaspora from Europe.

The staggering problems in Alasghan were compounded by local conflicts over land and water. Since the creation of Alasghan its residents had been in a long-standing dispute with the neighbouring villages for access to their water source. Still unresolved in 2011, this meant the residents of Alasghan had to rely on water tinkering provided by government officials and aid agencies which was inconsistent at best. Qarabagh residents have also questioned the Alasghan returnee's rights to the land. The failures and staggering challenges in Alasghan resulted in a debate between the donor government, the UN agencies, and the Afghan government regarding whether to continue to work in the area. The UN and some aid agencies wanted to 'close the door' on the project arguing the Afghan government had not carried out its role to stem corruption and resolve the local water and land disputes. The government disagreed, and the donor was advocating for continued investment in the area but also admitted that they were unsure if a needs assessment had preceded the project start-up.[7]

In the meeting with community leaders, it was clear that they knew external actors, including the GoIRA, could provide assistance, but the residents mistrusted them due to years of poor interventions, unacknowledged complaints, and a lack of transparency. In fact, in conversations it seemed the local community had been given very little information about any aspects of the project. For example, a bus was given to the community to transport workers and residents to Kabul. The bus had been allocated to the area through a project run by the government in partnership with an INGO. Soon after the bus was given to the community it was repossessed by a Ministry representative from Kabul who told the residents the bus had been allocated to another community. They were told another bus would be sent in its place within a few weeks. No further transportation vehicle ever materialised. The INGO staff managing the project was informed by the *shura* members they enquired at the Ministry, but no one seemed to know what happened to the bus and no further actions were taken.

As one *shura* member commented, 'We do not co-ordinate with the government. We co-ordinate with each other. We prefer to work by our own hand' (F35, Alasghan). At one point the frustration of the community residents had boiled over and they had chased aid workers from the area throwing rocks and threatening violence if they returned. As a result of the repeated failures the community had grown more distrustful of outside officials and aid organisations. The irony was the development that the community wanted would facilitate their connection to other parts of the district and the country, but also provide security by protecting them from outsiders, including the organisations that were supposed to bring development to the area.

Hybridity, co-option, and local governance

The establishment of new hybrid structures to organise and control community life was a common feature of intervention in Afghanistan. The initiatives attempted to harness the authority vested in traditional structures in service of national government and international objectives. One such programme was the National Solidarity Program. The NSP programme, one of the National Priority Programmes (NPPs), was designed in 2002 and launched in 2003 by the MRRD. The programme was funded in the amount of US$2.7 billion, through the World Bank and the Afghanistan Reconstruction Trust Fund (ARTF), a multi-donor trust fund. In 2011, the programme was in its third and final phase, which was meant to run from 2011–2015.[8] The aim of the programme was to build local governance by setting up CDCs that would become effective institutions for local governance and social-economic development' (Afghanistan, 2015). The complex dynamics of this hybrid structure and the local *shuras* were important to understanding the intersection of security and development at the local level with national and international objectives in Qarabagh.

The NSP structure was quite simple. NGOs, both international and local, and UN agencies referred to as facilitating partners, were hired by the international donors to implement the program in the rural areas of the country. The facilitating partners' role is to raise awareness and train the community on the NSP process, to assist with the elections, and provide support to the CDCs and the communities to select development projects. They also trained the CDC members in proposal writing, and technical skills such as accounting and logistics.

The CDCs were elected by the community, which could consist of 25 to 2,000 families. Once elected, council members elect a management team, including a president, deputy, secretary, and treasurer. The CDC membership could take several forms. Some were only male while others were mixed; additionally, in some areas, there were separate CDCs for men, women, and youths. In the villages in Qarabagh where I conducted research, there were several female but no mixed CDCs. One aim of the NSP was to encourage women's participation in community affairs, but this had not translated into practice in many areas in spite of the creation of female CDCs.

The CDCs were a response to the identification of priorities, which was supposed to be an inclusive community-driven process, of which the end result is a Community Development Plan (CDP). The CDC chose the top CDP priorities and submit a project proposal through the facilitating NGO or UN agency to an Oversight Team, hired by the international donors. A condition of each proposal was the inclusion of an in-kind contribution by the community which could be cash, labour, land, or materials. Upon approval of the proposal the MRRD sent money to the CDC bank account, set up after the election to implement the projects, which are monitored and reported on by the CDC and the NGO, back to the MRRD. At the village level, the NSP operated through the CDC. By 2010, a total of 22,490 CDCs were set up in 35,200 villages across Afghanistan (Miakhel, 2010).

The NSP was heralded by government, international organisations, and scholars as a successful programme that had modernised local structures to organise, govern, and develop communities. Indeed, it was assumed that widespread agreement existed that 'the NSP was now recognized both by the people of Afghanistan and the international community as the central policy instrument for Afghan state building and development' (Barakat, 2006). The programme was conceptualised as a hybrid initiative that would alter but not dismantle traditional governance and conflict resolution systems and help rebuild communities. According to the MRRD:

> The introduction of democratically elected community decision-making bodies as a viable alternative to the traditional local governance structure has provided a vehicle to re-build the social fabric and relationships at grassroots level.... Through the promotion of good local governance, the NSP works to empower rural communities.... Empowered rural communities collectively contribute to increased human security.
>
> (Afghanistan, 2015)

The NSP represented a jointly held vision, by the central government and international actors, that would offer an alternative to traditional governance practices at the village level. The CDCs were considered 'modern' because their representatives were elected and not appointed through familial ties or other patronage networks, as was often the case with customary *shuras*. The hybrid function of the NSP was its makeover of the traditional *shura* as a democratically elected body that linked local communities with the Afghan government and international actors operating in Afghanistan. The program was framed by the MRRD, in this instance, as offering communities a chance to 'be empowered' and achieve 'human security'. The implication however is that these goals are dependent upon modernisation, submitting to central government control, and further aid dependency. Villages were able to use the CDC as a tool for community consultation and negotiation with aid agencies and government to achieve what they saw as better conditions in their areas. The programme was also characterised by conflict, little accountability, and attempts at co-option.

Qarabagh's *shura* structures and dynamics were complex and the governance structures of each village differed in number and composition. In addition to the NSP *shuras* or CDCs, there were also what people referred to as local *shuras*, composed of non-elected elders, respected community members, and religious leaders. While some villages had four or five different kinds of *shura*, others only had one or two. In Alar, there were four *shuras:* the CDC, the local *shura*, the tribal *shura*, and the peace *shura*. In Burgharaq, there were three *shuras*: the CDC, the local *shura*, and a co-operative *shura* for agricultural issues. Qal'eh-ye-Bibi, Langar, and Denarkhalil each had two *shuras*: a CDC and a local *shura*. The expansion of *shuras* in the district was attributed to the combination of the existing customary structures in addition to the new groups that were sponsored by different Afghan ministries, and international donors. Agencies contracted to be facilitating partners conducted community awareness and training on the NSP in the initial stages of the programme community residents, but often did not understand the new *shura* systems. Ironically, some CDC members themselves were unsure why the new structures had been created. At the DDA meeting a CDC member from Alar village, where several *shuras* were in place explained:

> We have many *shuras*. The last one was created a while ago by one of the NGOs, I forget the name. We had a 40-day workshop in the district centre and then we created a shura for each village for peace and at the district level too.
>
> (I85, Qarabagh Shar)

The purpose of the various *shuras* was not always clear to the Qarabagh residents, aid agencies, or *shuras* members themselves; however, they were a new source of power and so for the village elite it was necessary to participate in or control these structures. The NSP adopted and, in some cases, absorbed the local elders and powerholders into the elected structure. Often the same people sat on more than one *shura*. In Baghalam, some of the *shura* members sat on both the CDC and the local *shura*, while in Qal'eh-ye-Baz, the community had integrated all the *shuras* into one structure. In areas where the pre-existing elite were not members of the CDC conflicts and suspicions sometimes arose between the local *shura* and the CDC members: there was conflict between the CDCs and other powerholders in the community.

During the DDA meeting I spoke to Jan Mohammad, who was a CDC member from one of the smaller villages in the district: he had been elected as the Deputy Head of the CDC in his area. His family was not part of the local *shura* in his area whose members were decided by familial ties or inheritance. He had been educated in Pakistan, was a business owner, and had a reputation for being fair to his neighbours. According to Jan he was chosen for the CDCs because the villagers felt he would know about development projects and be a good liaison to the aid agencies. In his area, the local *shura* did not have a good reputation with the people and only a few of them had been elected to the CDC. He said this had caused problems and the district administrator had come to the area and told the people that they had to have another election. The community refused and now their applications for projects were being delayed. He said 'the local *shuras* are supported by the DAO in our area. It is a way to maintain a kind of feudalism and control over the area' (F37, Qarabagh Shar). *Shura* members are usually the first point of contact and the focal point for maintaining relationships with officials or organisations outside of the area. Accordingly, the first visit Abdul, Wais, and I would make once we arrived in an area was always to see a member of the *shura*. Anyone wanting to speak with the community or to implement projects there usually had to go through them. Jan Mohammad's CDC had disrupted this practice because now vital information and resources had to flow through them.

The CDCs were seen as a positive force in several villages including Baghalam where the villagers trusted the CDC members. As one resident explained,

> The CDC co-ordinates with the district about development and we have got some projects. Also, the local *shura* co-ordinates with the government and the CoP is taking meetings on security and stability in the district and its villages. Sometimes they are dealing with ISAF and NGOs to bring development.
>
> (F27, Baghalam)

Currently one project was being implemented through the NSP, and the residents felt the CDC had been able to negotiate with a variety of actors within the government, aid agencies, and others to the benefit of the community.

Conversely, the community in Denerkhalil was struggling. In 2002, the village was close to the frontlines of the fighting between the US forces and the armed groups. The village was bombed and the residents had fled. Ten years later, in 2012, most of the families had returned, but unexploded devices had endangered villagers and slowed the economic recovery, particularly farming activities (Human Rights Watch, 2002). The levels of literacy were low and most people of working age were unemployed. In addition, Denarkhalil was one of the villages where night raids by Afghan and international security forces still took place. The community residents in the village were displeased with the CDC and felt the lack of development in the area was caused by the local leadership. Mohamed, a local resident, who was not working at the time we met, said, 'We don't have any development in our village because we don't have the best elders to help us' (F28, Denarkhalil). His opinion was shared by Fatima, a young teacher at the only girls' school in the area, who said, 'We don't know the cause of this no development. I think it might be our elders are taking things for themselves' (F31, Denarkhalil).

The head of the *shura* and the CDC in the area said that they had sent proposals to the NGO for approval, but the process was taking a long time and previously the proposal had been sent back. Since the people in the village had become suspicious of him, and he did not know what else he could do to show them he was not corrupt. It was impossible for me to be certain whether the head of the *shura* was indeed impeding the allocation of resources to his community through the NSP, or telling the truth, or both. The CDC members were accountable to the community but also expected to represent the village priorities to aid agencies and international donors. Those layers of accountability were complicated by confusion over the programme procedures amongst the community and CDC members, and a lack of communication from the aid agencies implementing the programmes. As a result, suspicion of CDC members and the NSP was not only apparent in Denarkhalil. At times, however, CDCs members, as was the case with other *shuras*, did abuse their power.

The funding the communities received was not without conditions. Attempts to use the *shura* system to implement the larger social, development, and governance projects carried out by international agencies and the Afghan government were not as empowering as was proposed in government official policy (Nixon and Ponzio, 2007). At the district level sat the District Development Assembly, an association of representatives from the CDCs across the district. The DDA had its own elected governance structure and met weekly with local officials in Qarabagh at the District Administration Office. DDAs were part of MRRD's National Area-Based Development Program (NABDP), and were supposed to coordinate the activities of CDCs in the district. The head of the CDC and local *shura* in Barikap was a member of the DDA. He only attended the DDA meetings occasionally in order not to be bound by decisions taken at the district level. This tactic allowed him to benefit from his membership in the DDA, as he was seen as being compliant with the NSP rules and coordinating with local government. At the same time, he was able to maintain control over the situation in his village. He was were aware of the risk of co-option through the DDAs, but he also understood the benefits, including the access to the block grant and materials, of participation.

The hybrid NSP structures in Qarabagh reaped some positive gains for several communities but were also mechanisms of control used by the government and international bodies to try and manage the district. The infrastructure projects, in principle, did contribute, on some level, to what many community residents saw as their development needs. Where community members were unhappy with the *shura*, little was done to challenge the *shura's* authority, or the slow response to complaints and snail-paced bureaucratic processes of the donors, government officials, and aid agencies. These practices in turn created mistrust and resentment, feeding into villagers' perceptions that the *shuras*, government officials, and agencies were corrupt. Although *shura* members expressed suspicion of the government and external actors, they willingly participated in and co-opted these new hybrid structures which reinforced their power within the community and provided access to the government and resources simultaneously; in some areas the CDC members facilitated development in their villages. The activities were not mutually exclusive: the NSP emerged in an environment characterised by uncertainty, violence, and foreign intervention. Community survival, therefore, was therefore dependent on the ability of more well-established practices to endure. The attempt to incorporate the *shura* system into a larger state-building programme, aid, and counterinsurgency plan underestimated the resilience of the customary institution and the personalised and patronage-based networks which connect communities.

Community development, counterinsurgency, and dissonance

There were few aid programmes in Qarabagh, with one noticeable exception: the Qarabagh Development Programme (QDP),[9] which was a US$60 million project implemented by an NGO, that had extensive countrywide programming, from March 2009 to September 2011. The project sought to create short-term employment opportunities such as rehabilitation or reconstruction of a critical community infrastructure, such as irrigation systems, rural farm-to-market and feeder roads, public buildings, and drainage systems, for 46,272 food-insecure households throughout the province (USAID, 2011).

At the village level, the QDP worked through local governance structures. For, example, the local *shura* determined who benefited from the development resources of the QDP project. Because LAS residents were internally displaced refugees from different areas, therefore the village leadership was created as opposed to being organic. Barikap had three *shuras*: the local *shura*, the CDC, and the female *shura*. The same person was the head of both male *shuras*, the local and CDC. His wife was the head of the female *shura*. This meant the male head of the local and CDC *shuras* was able to push forward decisions in the community and wielded a great deal of power). Though most community members said it was important for the NGO to work with the *shuras*, several men from the area acknowledged that, at times, the *shuras* wielded power to increase inequality. Certain groups benefited from their personal and familial relationships with *shura* members, either through receiving extra resources or by gaining employment opportunities offered by aid programmes being implemented in the area (F34, Barikap).

The project focused mainly on cash-for-work (C4W) projects,[10] which operated on a rotating basis amongst households in the scheme. Barikap *shura* members often interrupted the rotation system amongst the families so one group of workers stayed on for two or three shifts, while other groups had to wait. Several of the workers challenged this dynamic and complained to both the

NGO and local district officials about the project. This disregard of hierarchy was risky – the *shura* argued with locals if they took complaints outside of the community. The district government officials confirmed that there was a problem and tensions had arisen between Barikap residents and *shura* members regarding the project (I73, Qarabagh Shar). Similarly, NGO staff commented that they were aware that *shura* members might be allocating programme resources based on patronage but felt that it was not their responsibility to interfere at this level. As one staff member commented:

> Part of the programme is to strengthen development and local-governance structures, so challenging the [shuras'] authority would undermine that objective.... Also, we work with local solutions, so at some point, we have to let the community work things out themselves.
>
> (C5, Kabul)

Despite their efforts, residents expressed frustration that no actions were taken by the NGOs or district officials to address their complaints. Therefore, families became increasingly dependent on the *shuras* for their access to resources. Ultimately, rather than engaging with the local dynamics to better understand the implications of their intervention, the NGO staff and local government official chose to step away from the situation. Ironically, they also struggled with the broad implications of their practices.

QDP was part of the USAID stabilisation programming, which was established in 2010 'to coordinate all USAID activities with the military – both the US military and ISAF – and the Afghan government, and in particular the MRRD and Independent Directorate of Local Governance (IDLG)' (Glick, 2016, pp. 1–2). The principal objective of stabilisation programming was 'to enhance stability by supporting the military-led counterinsurgency strategy' (ibid). In late 2012, as the transition process began to transfer responsibility for security to the Afghan security forces, the stabilisation goals also shifted. Though the substance of the programming remained consistent the objective was now focused on reinforcing the legitimacy of the government and improving community resilience to malign, anti-government actors. The QDP was part of the community-focused stabilisation initiatives, which aimed

> to support [the government] peace efforts by linking government officials to local populations and support counterinsurgency efforts in kinetic areas through the short-term employment of community labourers working on prized local infrastructure....
>
> (USAID, 2012)

Therefore, the purpose of the QDP activities was to leverage community development for counterinsurgency aims, and government support.

By contrast, at a workshop that took place in June 2011, with the NGO implementing the QDP, dissimilar perspectives were shared regarding their practices. Mixed views were shared by the staff members working on the project in Afghanistan on the outcomes and purpose of their QDP activities and the ambivalent position of the NGO. There were two dominant views arose. The first acknowledged that there was a contradiction in using counterinsurgency money for development programming, from an agency that also contributed significantly to debates on the shrinking humanitarian space. However, they felt that they needed to accept USAID money to survive as an organisation. As one senior staff member commented,

> We receive almost 80 per cent of our funding from USAID. It would be impossible for us to refuse funding from them. It would mean the end of our operations, not just those programmes.
>
> (W3, Kabul)

The second group moved away from the financial implications, and suggested it was a means of co-opting the existing limitations within which they were working, and framed what the QDP as a human security-focused project. As one staff member explained,

> The area was secure, but because of the lack of resources and poverty of the population, it is vulnerable. It is hard to attract funding for these areas, so even though USAID thinks we are supporting counterinsurgency, we don't. We are a development and humanitarian agency.... These areas need assistance. We can still meet the aims of the development part of the programme without being a counterinsurgency project.
>
> (I53, Kabul)

Another participant added that what distinguished their work from counterinsurgency projects like QIP was the use of participatory approaches to provide local solutions similar to those advocated by alternative development scholars, such as Chambers (1994) and the post-development school, and their respect for local authorities and structures (W3, Kabul). The purpose and techniques of the project were agreed upon by the donor and the organisation: a level of cognitive dissonance, however, seem to play a role in allowing these contradictions to stand.

The NGO staff demonstrated, 'a willingness to improve' (Li, 2007), but there was a refusal to interrogate and acknowledge the implications of their practices both on Barikap and as part of the broader landscape of the intervention. A lack of action to address the community residents' complaints about the *shura* was rationalised as being sensitive to local structures. The agency did not work directly with the military as part of their daily practice, and they used human security language to discuss their activities. Therefore, the linkages between what they were doing and the counterinsurgency campaign was not explicit in their minds. The evidence of their contradictory practices, however, were all around, in the stated objectives of the programme, the SU, and the funder, and in the experiences of the communities. In the absence of accountability structures, beyond the loss of funding, there was no impetus for the NGO to adjust their practices.

Reflections on Qarabagh

This chapter discussed how security and development are perceived, put into practice and challenged by actors within Qarabagh District. Over the period of the study security slightly improved in the district while low levels of physical and social development persisted. The community conceptualisations of security were much more complex than the *us* and *them* mentality of international actors. The international military and national security forces also brought violence, corruption, and fear into the community. Therefore, the distrust of one group did not translate into support for the other when neither group was desirable. Likewise, with development the perspectives communicated by the residents were not completely divergent from the perspectives put forth by interveners in Chapter 2 by although there were some clear differences. Notably, for many external actors, development was a process of transformation or *modernisation*, as understood in Western/Global North terms – for example 'developing' local *shuras* from a kinship-based to a democratically elected model. However, according to many in the district, development meant *aid investment* in the community, not a process of fundamentally transforming their way of life or value systems. Finally, security and development were connected in various ways within the district, but rarely did those linkages reflect the story articulated within international policy discourse.

In Qarabagh it became apparent that, though distinctions were sometimes made, the local community residents did not view external actors from the same perspective assumed by the intervening actors themselves. A significant theme in the previous chapter was the way that security and development discourses were used by aid, military, and intervening political actors to construct and distinguish themselves from each other. Distancing attempts were deemed necessary by certain actors to preserve their reputation and communication with local communities. Most district residents, however, did not focus on the difference between civilian actors, but grouped them together, only distinguishing at times between the military and aid actors. This suggests that perhaps the way actors in previous chapters constructed themselves may have had very little to do with the realities and perceptions of local communities. Rather *the local* community perspective was fashioned by external actors in relation to how interveners wanted to perceive *the intervening self*.

Relatedly, 'human security', has been framed as an emancipatory challenge to traditional mainstream security and development approaches, both theoretically and in practice. As Wheeler suggests, human security 'places suffering humanity at the centre of its theoretical project' and puts the 'powerless and disposed at the heart of theory and emancipatory practice' (Wheeler and Harmer, 2006, pp. 126–128). In the district, however, a different picture emerged. Reliance on the human security discourse allowed the agency implementing the project to ignore the fact that the programme was part of the counterinsurgency project. Despite explicit linkages in their contractual documents it would have been unthinkable for the INGO to use the language of counterinsurgency to describe what they were doing. The language of human security and practices deemed *culturally sensitive*, which resulted in a lack of accountability, provided a safe retreat for the INGO. In addition, the belief that human security was the right approach to the development of legitimised project activities and reinforced their self-perception as the 'right' type of developers. Accordingly, human security was an abstract discourse that suggested symbiotic goals between the community and the aid agency. Ultimately, however, it served the interests of the INGO more than and even to the detriment of the district residents. The dissonance displayed by the aid workers was interwoven with the emptiness of human security.

The distinction drawn between *violence* and *security* is an important theme that emerged throughout the chapter: an area can be deemed *secure* even though that security is predicated upon violence, or the potential for violence. Even though the district was considered 'secure', different types of violence did occur there: the wider context of violence and the conflict shaped relationships and interactions between all actors. The local patrols maintained security through tight control over what happened and who entered the village. Violence against outsiders was justified if it protected those inside the village. In Denerkhalil and the LASs communities turned inwardly to protect what they had. The possibility of violence, as an 'everyday' experience in conflict zones, was manipulated by residents to resist interventions from aid and military actors. Indeed, in Qarabagh the suggestion of mutual goals and shared interests between the intervening nations and the Afghan people found in the many international policies, declarations, and statements on Afghanistan produced since 9/11 begins to fall apart. Consequently, the communities in the district protected and distanced themselves from the forces of intervention rather than engaged with them.

The dynamics of the NSP and range of constructed hybrid shuras in Qarabagh challenge arguments that cast hybrid peacebuilding in a positive and emancipatory light. As discussed earlier, as a result of the local turn in peace and conflict studies, hybrid structures of security, peace, and governance have begun to receive more attention. Scholars have suggested that hybrid peace can collapse the distance between the local and the liberal international (Richmond, 2011) providing the potential for 'a politics of liberation for subaltern constituencies' (Prabau, 2007, p. iv cited in Suthaharan and Rampton, 2015). Indeed, the international and government statements on the NSP projected the programme in this light. The discourse of empowerment, freedom, and tradition were all deployed in relation to the CDCs by the Afghan government. The programme was marketed as a way to both conserve traditional structures and improve them through the incorporation of democratic processes and aid dividends. The promotion of hybridity as emancipatory, however, can serve to ignore the politics of the intervention and the complex matrices of power that exist between different actors.

The newly constructed shuras in Qarabagh reaped some positive gains for several communities, but also produced discord, disruption, and conflict. Government officials and external actors had different perspectives on the goals of the NSP for example, but ultimately the programmes were employed as a technique of control and oversight by the government and international bodies to manage security and development in the district. For national elites that designed the NSP, it was a way to diminish the autonomy of local communities, and incorporate them into the central government state-building project. For the civilian ISAF contractors working in the ministries the NSP and other hybrid *shuras* were a key element to the counterinsurgency campaign, and being embedded in the government allowed the contractors to have oversight on the government officials as well. The purpose of the new structures, therefore, was to reorganise and control communities not empower them.

Attempts to transform local structures through external-driven impetus are often met with forms of resistance that contest the legitimacy of configurations that are framed as emancipatory but operate as tools of domination. In Qarabagh the residents, leadership, officials, and those that worked in the district employed different tactics to try and control their environment and counter the disconnect between these structures and their reality. *Shura* members, though expressing disillusionment with the government and external actors, willingly participated in, subverted, and manipulated these structures which gave them power within the community and also access to the government. They were aware of 'the rules of the game' and in this sense, these structures became a site of resistance (Marriage, 2006), but also disempowerment. Therefore, recognition of the differentiated power relations is key to understanding the district story.

Collective systems of accountability and responsibility were already part of, not external to, the organisational logics of local governance structures in Qarabagh. Many district residents, however, wanted more accountability from the CDCs, in fact this was a common theme in both Qarabagh and Behsud. Local leaders were provided access to additional resources which, at times, were used to the benefit of the community but could also be used to discriminate against community members and enhance personal networks simultaneously, in villages where the community sought a platform to contest the actions of the CDCs, they were hindered by the lack of accountability of the government officials, the aid agencies and the donors, and the looming structures of intervention and violence in which they were implicit. In Jan Mohammad's village the dereliction of responsibility by the NSP implementing bodies compromised the ability of CDC leadership to provide answers to their constituencies leading to tension in the village. Failing to acknowledge the impact of their actions, external actors dismissed instances of corruption by CDC members as part of customary practice and tradition. Ultimately, reproducing a narrative which constructs local culture as backwards and in need of external solutions. Consequently, in many villages the programme disrupted, not strengthened, systems of accountability and responsibility.

The multiple realities of the residents, officials, community leaders, and aid actors all collide within the district. These realities are shaped by the beliefs that actors hold, the nexus discourse and policies, and by the context and experience of conflict, violence, and intervention. This chapter has sought to illustrate how the perspectives and experiences of community residents in Qarabagh interacted with the ideas expressed by interveners and in policy discourse. Chapter 5 will explore the dynamics in Behsud, a district in the eastern region of Afghanistan.

Notes

1 *Shura* is an Arabic word for consultation.
2 Here the interviewee is referring to an Islamic scholar.
3 According to the administrative divisions of the country, the central region consists of Kabul, Parwan, Panjshir, Wardak, Logar, and Kapisa provinces.
4 The term 'foreigner' refers to actors from outside Afghanistan. This includes Western actors, civilian and military, but also Pakistanis, Chinese and Arabs. In this instance, the elder is referring to the latter.
5 AlasGhan is also referred to as AliceGhan in literature. The area was named after Afghan camel drivers who worked in central Australia in the 18th century and worked on the construction of the Alice Springs rail link by carting equipment, material and supplies.
6 See Kelly, J. 2015. Afghan project failing in a town called AliceGhan. *The Australian*, 15 June 2015.
7 This was also confirmed by a DANIDA report (2012) *Evaluation of Danida Support to the Education Sector in Afghanistan*, where the authors stated they were unable to find an initial assessment or any evaluation of the project at all. For further.
8 The NSP was designed to be rolled out in three phases. The first phase took place from 2002–2007 and the second phase ran from 2007–2011.
9 The name of the program has been changed to respect the anonymity of the organisation staff.
10 Cash-for-work projects employ local residents to work as manual labour on physical infrastructure projects in exchange for cash payments.

References

Afghanistan. 2006. *Summary of District Development Plan, Qarabagh District, Kabul Province*. Kabul: Ministry of Rural Rehabilitation and Development.

Afghanistan. 2011. *Summary of the District Development Plan: Qarabagh District. Kabul Province*. Kabul: Ministry of Rural Rehabilitation and Development Kabul.

Afghanistan. 2012a. *Afghanistan CSO Population Data – 1390 (2011–2012)*. Kabul: Afghanistan Central Statistics Office (CSO).

Afghanistan. 2012b. *District Plan Qarabagh*. Kabul: Provincial Governor's Office. Available at: www.kabul.gov.af/en/page/2264

Afghanistan. 2015. *National Solidarity Programme Phase Three (NSP III)*. Kabul: Ministry of Rural Rehabilitation and Development.

Australia. 2013. AliceGhan. Chapter 9: *Case studies. Australia's Overseas Development Programs in Afghanistan Australia's Overseas Development Programs in Afghanistan.*

Canberra: Ministry of Foreign Affairs and Defense. 16 May 2013. Available at: www.aph.gov.au/Parliamentary_Business/Committees/Senate/Foreign_Affairs_Defence_and_Trade/Completed_inquiries/2010-13/afghanistan/report/c09

Barakat, S. 2006. *Mid-term Evaluation Report of the National Solidarity Programme (NSP). Afghanistan*. Kabul: Islamic Republic of Afghanistan Ministry of Rural Rehabilitation and Development.

Callinan, R. 2012. We can't abandon refugees, says architect. *Sydney Morning Herald*, 8 February. Available at: www.smh.com.au/national/we-cant-abandon-refugees-says-architect-20120207-1r5k8.html#ixzz1vJMMtF8Q

Chambers, R. 1994. The origins and practice of participatory rural appraisal. *World Development*, 22, 953–969.

DANIDA. 2012. *Evaluation of Danida Support to the Education Sector in Afghanistan*. Copenhagen: DANIDA.

Glick, D. E. A. P. 2016. *Assessing the Stabilizing Effects of Development Programming: A Review of USAID's Evaluation Efforts in Afghanistan*. Working Paper. California: RAND.

Human Rights Watch. 2002. *Fatally Flawed: Cluster Bombs and Their Use by the United States in Afghanistan*. New York, NY: HRW. 18 December 2002. Available at: www.hrw.org/report/2002/12/18/fatally-flawed/cluster-bombs-and-their-use-united-states-afghanistan.

Li, T. M. 2007. *The Will to Improve: Governmentality, Development and the Practice of Politics*. Durham and London: Duke University Press.

Macdonald, I. 2011. *Landlessness and Insecurity: Obstacles to Reintegration in Afghanistan*. Washington, DC: Middle East Institue-Fondation Pour La Recherche Stratgique.

Majidi, N. 2013. Home sweet home! Repatriation, reintegration and land allocation in Afghanistan. *Revue Des Mondes Musulmans Et De La Mediterrane*, 133, 207–225.

Marriage, Z. 2006. *Not Breaking the Rules Not Playing the Game*. London: Hurst and Company.

Miakhel, S. 2010. *Many Shuras Do Not a Government Make: International Community Engagement with Local Councils in Afghanistan. Peace Brief*. Washington, DC: United States Institute of Peace.

Nixon, H. and Ponzio, R. 2007. Building democracy in Afghanistan: The statebuilding agenda and international engagement. *International Peacekeeping*, 14, 26–40.

Paiman M. A. 2017. Suicide and deliberate self-harm in Afghanistan. *Asian Journal of Psychiatry*, 26, 29–31.

Prabhu, A. 2007. Preface. *Hybridity: Limits, Transformations, Prospects*. New York, NY: State University of New York Press, pp. ix–xvi.

Richmond, O. 2011. *A Post-Liberal Peace*. London, Routledge.

Saltmarshe, D. D. and Medhi, A. 2010. Local governance in Afghanistan a view from the ground. In: Lough, O. (ed.) *Synthesis Paper*. Kabul: AREU.

Sarkesian, S. C. 1975. *The Professional Army Officer in a Changing Society*. Michigan: Nelson-Hall Co.

Sataruddin, S. C. 2018. The impact of addiction on Afghan youths. *Intervention: Journal for Mental Health and Psychosocial Support in Conflict-Affected Areas*, 16, 283–286.

Suthaharan, N. and Rampton, D. 2015. The limits of hybridity and the crisis of liberal peace. *Review of International Studies*, 41(1), 49–72.

UN News. 2007. Afghanistan: UN-assisted mine clearance enables 1,000 families to return home. *UN News*, 21 June 2007. Available at: https://news.un.org/en/story/2007/06/223132-afghanistan-un-assisted-mine-clearance-enables-1000-families-return-home

USAID 2011. *Stabilization Unit Portfolio*. Kabul: USAID Afghanistan.
USAID 2012. *Fact Sheet*. Kabul: USAID Afghanistan.
Williams, H. G. 2018. *Mission Accomplished. Killing for Power and Profit: Remembering the Victims*. Bloomington, IN: Archway Publishing.
Wheeler, V. and Harmer, A. (2006) *Resetting the Rules of Engagement: Trends and Issues in Military–Humanitarian Relations*. London: Overseas Development Institute.

5 Behsud stories

Significant changes occurred in Behsud between 2005 and 2010. The first time I visited the area in 2005, there were only a few paved roads. The rest were well-travelled, but very uneven paths of neatly moulded together rocks and mud. The market stalls lining the road into the district stocked mainly basic goods. The buildings which lined the main road were often bombed out, half-constructed, and slowly disintegrating with each strong wind or sandstorm. Yet there was a vibrant energy that encompassed the markets and public areas. People were doing business, arguing, sitting down for meals, and praying. However, by 2010, not only Behsud, but much of Jalalabad, the neighbouring district, and provincial capital, had undergone major changes. There was a new main road and several other paved secondary roads. Markets were still bustling, but now much more extensive and well-stocked with a variety of goods of various quality, including fruit, household items, cloth – indeed anything travellers or local residents might desire could be found there. Newly built schools and public buildings appeared sturdy and were adorned with large signposts listing the Western agencies and governments that had funded and constructed them, a practice that began to change by 2012. Schools for both boys and girls, with high boundary walls for the latter, were present in many of the areas far from Jalalabad City. I had done the drive from Kabul to Behsud many times during the years I lived in Afghanistan. It was one of my favourites roads to travel because although the road itself was often rough, bumpy, and winding the changing landscape was beautiful. The journey by road took approximately eight hours in 2006. My first trip to Behsud in 2010 was also a road trip, but it took less than four hours and almost the entire road was paved. In preparing for my trip, however, before leaving Kabul I met extensive opposition from my intervener friends and some cautious looks from the Afghan research staff, although the latter were less worried I would be attacked than that I would get lost. The drive was fine and I enjoyed it as I had before, but the changing landscape in Behsud would become much clearer over the course my trips there over the next 12 months.

Thus, this chapter presents stories that emerged from Behsud District. As in the previous chapter, we begin with an exploration of the perspectives of the different stories of security and development in the district. Behsud, like Qarabagh, challenges the established security–development nexus logic: the increasing levels of development ran alongside rising levels of violence and fear. In Behsud, however, the number of external actors was much greater than in Qarabagh. Therefore, the interactions between district residents, international, and national aid workers, UN staff, international, and national security forces, government officials, and community leaders, came more sharply into focus. This chapter explores three main themes. First, the chapter explores the simplistic constructions of 'the Other' in contrast the complexity and fluidity of movement between different positions that individuals in the district adopted. Second, the chapter outlines the friction that occurs between different groups of actors in the district, and the practices and strategies that are used to negotiate their competing realities. Insights are also provided into the underpinning ideologies and assumptions that fuel these fractious relationships. To do this, the chapter will further explore the Eurocentric and racialised mindsets held by interveners discussed in the first three chapters of the book, and the cognitive dissonance that emerged in Qarabagh discussed in the last chapter.

The district

The perimeter of Behsud is situated five kilometres outside Jalalabad City. Indeed, until 2004, it was part of Jalalabad District. Now Behsud surrounds Jalalabad City and District, the urban centre of the province, like a giant 'U'. It is bordered by Surkhrod, Chaparhar, and Rodat Districts (to the south), Kama District (to the east), Kuz Kunar District (to the north), and Laghman Province (to the West). Behsud was the location of several important gateways to and from Nangarhar Province. The provincial airport, which also housed an American military base on the compound, is located in the district. The Behsud Bridge is an important gateway for transportation and commerce, linking the eastern region provinces with Kabul. Daily hundreds of Afghans coming from different parts of the country take the road that runs through the southern part of Behsud on their way to the Torkham border crossing[1] into Pakistan.

In 2011, the population of Behsud was 108,700 (Afghanistan, 2012), spread out across 40 villages, making it one of the larger districts in the country.[2] National government statistics stated that Behsud District was 100 per cent ethnically Pashtun, but local sources[3] and research studies conducted in the area suggest the population was more diverse, including Afghan Arabs, and smaller groups of Kuchi nomads and Pashai (TLO, 2014). Returnees constitute approximately 13.5 per cent of the population (Afghanistan, 2007).[4]

The district-level governance structure was similar to Qarabagh, with the governor's office, administration, police, and courts located in close proximity to each other. The DDA had 30 members. In addition, national government records listed 47 active administrative staff based in the district, of which 14 belonged to the Ministry of Education (Afghanistan, 2010a). Much like Qarabagh, each community in Behsud had several *shuras*, including local *shuras*, and CDCs.

The local *shuras* were mainly responsible for liaising with government officials, and conflict resolution. Between 2006, when the NSP started in the district, and 2011 100 CDCs had been established in the district (Afghanistan, 2010a), facilitated by BRAC, UN-Habitat, and several other INGOs. Although the eastern region is known for being conservative in their approach to women's mobility and gender norms, many of the villages had female shuras and several areas also had youth associations.

Behsud is economically diverse, with employment and livelihood opportunities in agriculture, manufacturing, and several other industries. The economic vibrancy of the district is closely related to its location as the hub of several important gateways to and from Nangarhar Province. The majority of district residents engage in agricultural and livestock rearing. Many of the residents maintain farms and cattle while working outside the home as well. The accessibility of the roads throughout the year due to the district's warm weather and proximity to Jalalabad City means residents can maintain small businesses in the city and commute daily. The district had a sugar refinery and a textile-processing factory, both supported by external aid funding (USAID, 2010).

The provision of services in Behsud differed from Qarabagh (See Table 5.1 Behsud District Profile). The availability of water and sanitation facilities was much higher in Behsud than Qarabagh. Even though Qarabagh is reported as having a few more schools than Behsud, this is offset because many of the students in Behsud attend schools in Jalalabad, including pursuing university degrees at Nangarhar University, one of the largest higher education institutions in the country. While the number of health facilities in the district is limited, residents near the Jalalabad border could also access hospitals and clinics in the city. At the time of the study, 23 organisations were recorded operating in Behsud: 11 international agencies, eight national agencies, and four UN bodies (Muzik, 2013). The UNAMA Eastern regional office, was headquartered in

Table 5.1: Behsud District Profile

Health and Nutrition	Basic Health Centres	5
	Comprehensive Health Centres	1
	Health Posts	23
Infrastructure and Natural Resources	% of families with access to safe drinking water sources and traditional latrines	90%
	% of families that have access to electricity	8% public, 3% private
	% of roads that are open to traffic in all seasons	100%
Education, Culture, Media and Sports	Primary Schools	29
	Secondary Schools	14
	High Schools	8

Source: Ministry of Rural Rehabilitation and Development 2007; Independant Directorate of Local Governance 2010.

Jalalabad City, along with several other UN agencies including UNICEF, IOM, UN-HABITAT, and WFP. The main areas of activity for aid agencies in the district were employment, market development, agriculture, health, education, and legal aid. Most basic services in the area, such as health and education, were provided by local and international NGOs (Afghanistan, 2010a).

Behsud has an interesting mix of urban and rural life. While one corner of the district surrounds Jalalabad City, to reach the opposite side means travelling past many smaller villages and farmlands. The communities were the research took place – Walayti, Balandghar, Samarkhalil, Hada, Qasimabad, and Taghar – were located in a mixture of rural, peri-urban, and urban settings. The villages in Behsud resembled those of Qarabagh closely in terms of the style of housing and layout of the villages themselves. Behsud also had a high number of returnees, former IDPs, in the villages, as was the case in Qarabagh. Since Behsud is less than three hours' drive to Pakistan, migration between the two points was frequent and circular. Many people lived in the district, but regularly travelled to Pakistan for work, medical care and family events.

Throughout the eastern region of Afghanistan there was a large presence of international and national security forces. The region's shared border with Pakistan and mountainous terrain had made the area the main theatre of combat since the 9/11 intervention. The Americans had a military base at Jalalabad Airport, one of the largest in Afghanistan. The provincial PRT in Nangarhar Province, also American-led, was separately located just kilometres away. The road to Behsud runs north of Jalalabad City and continues on to Kunar Province, which experienced some of Afghanistan's highest levels of armed conflict involving international and national security forces, and armed opposition groups (Clark, 2013; UN, 2016). The collateral effects from the regular armed conflict in Kunar impacted the residents of Behsud and those that travelled the winding roads through the district. In addition, Behsud itself sometimes experienced conflict between international military forces, residents, and armed opposition groups. The district's role as a hub for transporting people and goods through the region made it a prime location for kinetic activity and ambush. The Afghan army maintained a routine presence in the area; although the number of police was low they still patrolled some areas. There were six main checkpoints in the district run by national security forces. Also, nightly patrols by armed groups made up of men and youths from the villages occurred regularly. Thus, there were multiple lines of conflict, opposition, and allegiance drawn between these various groups and the dynamics shifted, depending on the time and location.

Insecurity and fear

The official statistics on Behsud come from a variety of sources. The heavy presence of international and national military forces made access to information on security-related topics a challenge, not only because of the political concerns of the nations involved, but also because several different military units were operating in the district without necessarily knowing each other's activities. Therefore, in many of reports I had access to, (in)security often only related to AOG activities. Several other reports, (Lee, 2011; UNAMA, 2011, 2012; USAID, 2012) included incidents such as criminal activity, international and national military raids, and attacks that led to civilian causalities or the harassment of NGO workers. The district experienced a 114 per cent increase in security incidents from 2009 to 2012. Behsud accounted for 15 per cent of the total security incidents in Jalalabad between 2010 and 2012. This is disproportionately high, given the population of Behsud was only approximately 8 per cent of the population of Nangarhar Province (Afghanistan, 2012). In contrast to Qarabagh, the official statistics deemed Behsud a district with rising and regular insecurity.

Whereas the available statistics described Behsud as an area of frequent and violent incidents, insecurity was sometimes measured in relation to other places rather than from an objective starting point. For example, in Walayti, a resident said, 'I think in our district security is not too much bad. I think it's good because we have other places in Nangarhar where their security situation is worse than our district' (F3, Walayti). Others focused just on security in their area: some villages were considered to be more secure than others. In addition, the community leaders tended to comment that security was better than the community residents believed. Differing opinions occurred between areas, between focus groups and even within focus groups that I conducted. In conversations with community residents and external actors, however, it became clear that violence and armed conflict was more a part of their daily life than in Qarabagh.

In Behsud the international and national security forces accounted for much of the violence. An official in the District Office of Behsud claimed that people in the district were unhappy with ISAF, especially due to the arbitrary detention of local people and night raids and searches in the villages (I11, Behsud Centre). In Hada, this perception was reinforced by accounts from both local residents and shura members; these spoke of the international military forces the main cause of insecurity in the area. The youth shura in Balandghar discussed the frequent problems caused by the ISAF in the area, such as road closures lasting for hours which prevented them from attending university classes; the bombing of houses in the village and traffic accidents that resulted in the death and injury of civilians. A young man summarised the feeling of the group; 'We didn't see any profit from ISAF without damage and miscarriage. All the time they are bombarding people and they have killed many civilians' (F3, Walayti). The prevalence of night raids in the area and arrests of residents added to the perception that ISAF was a driver of insecurity (I12, Behsud Shar). Such operations contributed to the perception that, as one elder said, 'The ISAF are bringers of both security and damage' (F6, Balandghar). In Walayati there was a recognition that ISAF had done some good for the community; however, it was still thought that they were outsiders and therefore should leave. One participant said, 'According to our Islamic principles the ISAF can never be our friends, but because of ISAF we have some peace' (F2, Walayti).

In my conversations with the international military in the district it was evident that for them, security was tied to counterinsurgency and the Taliban. The district had been referred to as a centre for Taliban and al-Qaeda activity in Nangarhar Province (Roggio, 2011). Rooting out and eliminating the insurgency was a key priority for the international military as the means through which security would be achieved at the international level. Frequent raids and operations took place in the district but the military officials I spoke to were hesitant to discuss these issues in detail. They did, however, mention security sector reform as a prime focus, with particular focus on the training of ANSF and rule-of-law capacity building with local elites. Effective training in these areas was perceived by the international security officials as being means of achieving counterinsurgency aims and winning hearts and minds.

Within the communities, the national military forces were also seen as a cause of insecurity for several reasons. First, hostility from the community due to the ongoing military operations was directed at the national as well as the international military because many of the night raids in the district were joint operations between international and national forces (I12, Behsud Shar). Second, the local community held in low esteem the Afghan security forces, both the police and the army. In several areas people commented that the problem was with those who joined the security forces. An elder in Samarkhalil explained that many Afghan security personnel were jobless men or youths that had been turned out by their families. He also commented that many of the local security forces were politically affiliated to various warlords and commanders:

> Eighty per cent of the army is related to political groups. If the commander or power person in that group orders them to resign from the army they will resign and switch sides. How can we trust them to keep our security?
>
> (I19, Samarkhalil)

Thus, the ANSF are viewed as an arm of the state, partners of the international forces, and tools of local power brokers at the same time. Their actions therefore served to support the aims and goals of these various groups, which were often not supported local communities.

Another source of violence in the district were local-based conflicts: Behsud has figured prominently in reports on land disputes and violent intra-community clashes regarding land rights (Foshini, 2012). Qasimabad, an area close to Jalalabad City, became a prime settling ground for the many returnees coming back from Pakistan after 2002. Local commanders controlled the land and sold it off to supporters, family, and for profit from those that could pay. The government, though unable to prevent the sale of land by the warlords, also began selling the land with ‘municipal revenues from the sale of public land in Qasimabad amounting to 33 million Afghanis’ (US 700,000) (Giovacchini, 2011). According to reports, conflict amongst residents of Qasimabad for control of more space has caused the death of several people and many injuries (Mumtaz, 2011). There was, however, a clear divide between the comments of the local leadership and the residents on the issue of local conflicts. The *shura* members rarely cited local conflicts as a security concern, but attributed problems to the national government and its lack of capacity to monitor land distribution. The local residents explained that *shura* members were often involved in land disputes, and benefited from the sale of land.

The perception that the government did not have the ability to protect the Afghan population and what resources they did have were squandered for personal gain, making the district residents lack confidence in the government officials. As a result, the departure of the international military forces from Afghanistan was a topic that received mixed responses and caused considerable concern. An interesting dynamic therefore existed in that while many of residents criticised the international military for being a destructive force, when asked about their feelings about the transition they also said that they did not support the international military leaving Afghanistan immediately. One reason for this was that many people felt the ANA had neither the human nor material resources necessary to maintain Afghan security on its own (F10, Taghar; F8, Samarkhalil; F11, Qasimabad). The conversations regarding local officials, ANSF, and the ISAF forces reflected the wide range of opinions amongst community residents and the complex ways both local and external actors are sometimes viewed.

While the drivers of insecurity were multiple in Behsud, for the locals a common definition of security was the predictability of everyday life in the community. Predictability was not always related to an absence of conflict within the wider community, but rather a sense of knowing what to expect and a system of rules by which people abided. For example, in a focus group discussion it was agreed that a sign of security in the area was that people could leave their tools in the fields at night and they would still be there in the morning (F5, Balandghar); women spoke of previous regimes, for example the Muhjiddeen era and communist rule, as times when security was not good and their houses had been destroyed (F1, Walayti). At that time, various groups were vying for power and the local populations were uncertain from one day to the next what would occur. The female *shura* members said that during the Taliban they were able to predict events (F4, Balandghar). The group went on to say that, in spite of this, they did not want the Taliban to come back because the Taliban allowed the abuse of women and did little for the economy.

Security was also understood as the protection of one's honour or *namus*,[5] often rooted in unwritten codes of conduct.[6] A man's honour requires him to protect the dignity of his family members, property, and land. The inability to protect one's dignity was considered a type of insecurity. Damage to someone's honour challenges not only the individual's perception of self, but also the family and the community's feeling of security and regard for that individual. Thus, a young man from Walayti observed:

> ISAF has no behaviour with villagers. One day they came by my house and made a lot of noise. They scared our women and they killed my dog. Why

> did they have to kill the dog? They invaded the privacy of my home, with their searches. We are not safe.
>
> (F3, Walayti)

The feeling of fear can linger much longer than the backlash from physical violence. Discussions of honour and security tended to focus on international military activities such as night raids and house searches (I11, Behsud Centre) though it also figured prominently in neighbourhood conflicts. Some suggested that honour violations by the international forces created greater ill will towards perpetrators and Western actors than civilian casualties did (Azarbaijani-Moghaddam *et al.*, 2008). There was little evidence in my field research to support this claim. The diverse understandings of security shared by the district resident inform a more nuanced understanding of the drivers of insecurity, what feeling secure means, and the positioning of actors within the district; such understandings are all too often absent from international policy on Afghanistan, in which the binary of 'us and them' figures prominently.

Development and insecurity

Three main understandings of development throughout the district were communicated by interviewees: physical infrastructure, social and basic needs, and community cohesion. Development as physical infrastructure was commonly spoken of in the communities. Physical development referred to roads, buildings, and irrigations systems. An elder from Balandghar said, '[The PRT] built a Bridge and some other roads for us, we have a school and health centres in our village which means development in our view' (I18, Balandghar). The proximity to the urban centre and the position of Behsud meant that the infrastructure of the district had received significant attention over the past 10 years. One participant explained:

> A lot has been done in the last 10 years, especially in terms of school buildings and clinics. We also have high schools in most places and teacher training colleges.
>
> (W1, Jalalabad)

Others commented:

> There is no doubt things have changed in the last ten years in our area. Before there were no vaccines now people can go to the clinic. There are many more roads. It only takes a short time to get to Torkham now, before it was a long drive on poor roads.
>
> (W1, Jalalabad)

Behsud had been the recipient of many Quick Impact Projects, small-scale, low-cost projects, planned and implemented within a short timeframe; examples of

QIPs include wells, school construction, or building refurbishment,[7] often conducted by the international military forces and civilian agencies. An official from the PRT commented on the changes in the district saying,

> We have done a lot to develop this area. A lot has been done to build up the area in terms of construction and infrastructure development. Compared to the majority of the districts, Behsud is far ahead. We have done a lot but there are still many issues. The government has to step in and do something to support the structures we have built … we cannot do everything. That is not sustainable.
>
> (I6, PRT/USAID, Telephone)

However, development as a social phenomenon most commonly appeared in the narratives told by interviewees. The majority of participants were pleased with the physical development projects in the area, but pointed out more was needed for actual development in their communities. For example, in Balandghar there are schools and health centres but a lack of qualified staff (F4, Balandghar). Frustration due to the lack of human resources within the health and education facilities in the area had led to conflict. In Balandghar, lack of access to a health centre resulted in the staff being assaulted,[8] though incidents of this nature did not seem to be commonplace. Development was therefore not just a matter of having infrastructure, such as school buildings and hospitals, but also the social and human infrastructure and human resources to maintain it.

An important part of such development was community cohesion. The community's ability to work together was viewed as an important foundation for other aspects of everyday life. In discussions in Balandghar, an interviewee described what this meant:

> We have good development here in all sections. I can see all of this development depends upon community unity and co-ordination and understandings between villagers. This is good here. This is a kind of development for us as well. Development to make all the other sections develop.
>
> (F6, Balandghar)

Development in this sense is a process of social understanding between community members that facilitates other activities. Cohesion at community level facilitated discussions around what type of development the area needed and its maintenance. This participant linked community peace with development at a very local level.

In conversations with the district officials, the Qasimabad area was highlighted as development success in the district. The leader of the District Youth Association described Qasimabad:

> If we take Qasimabad as an example, it was a desert just a few years ago but now it is a government scheme town which has over 8,000 families. It has a

> school, health centres, and new roads constructed by the government. Also, the community structures are in place. There are some problems with the villagers sometimes but not too many.
>
> (I1, Jalalabad City)

A UN official explained what she saw as the complexity in understanding development in the area:

> The district, particularly that one, has been developed because it is close to the city. They have schools, clinics and everything. What they don't have they can access in the city.... But the development is uneven so those in the far areas might have a problem with access.
>
> (I2, UN, Jalalabad)

There were several sources of development within the district. The international military forces, local and international NGOs, the Afghan government, and local community structures were all seen as development actors. As with security, the *shura* structures were seen as playing an important role in development in the area. In Hada, participants mentioned the village school, an Islamic school, and health centre in their area as proof of development and attributed development to the villagers and the *shura* (F13, Hada). The presence of many development actors working in the district implied that a much more substantial level of aid money was disbursed here than in Qarabagh. Ultimately, communities noted the political nature of any assistance they received and the temporary nature of international interest in Afghanistan. Therefore, while external actors were providing aid to the area it was the everyday contributions and efforts of the community that allowed the sustainability of the development projects. Their efforts however were increasingly challenged by the insecurity and violence in the area.

In Behsud, rising levels of development and insecurity accompanied each other. A common remark was that the district was perceived as 'too secure', and so it had not received enough attention from the international community for its development. Some argued that international attention had prioritised insecure southern provinces like Helmand and Kandahar to try and get them developed as a means of increasing security and opening the way for further development. Statistics on overall aid distribution in Afghanistan as a whole seem to confirm the validity of the focus group's observations. (See Figure 5.1: Top Ten Provincial Aid Recipients, 2002–2010).

From 2002–2010, however, Nangarhar received US$1.051 billion in aid assistance, making it the fourth-largest recipient of aid in Afghanistan (Afghanistan, 2010c). Qarabagh had not received much aid assistance, while maintaining a relatively low number of security incidents. This was evidenced by the small number of agencies operating in the area, the lack of government presence, and aid from other sources. Comparatively, Behsud had received significant amounts of aid assistance, with numerous aid agencies and government offices present and

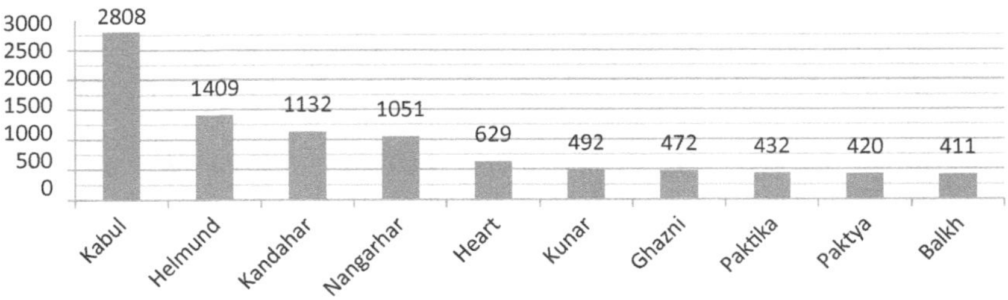

Figure 5.1 Top ten provincial aid recipients, 2002–2010 (in US$ millions).

implementing programming, as the district became increasingly insecure. Thus, it is likely that rising insecurity contributed to the sustained aid investment in the area. Security and development are linked through international policy and practices rather than as a necessary process of explicably linked causality. The dynamics in Behsud were much more complex than the simplistic policy logic suggests.

Constructing the other

Behsud, unlike Qarabagh, was a frequent meeting ground for many different groups, including the international and national military, local government, Afghan civil society organisations, the INGO, the UN development corporations, and so forth. Interaction with each other happened in coordination meetings and social settings, and everyday activities in Jalalabad City. Proximity to each other, however, did not always translate into a deeper understanding of each other. People used their own logics to justify their positionality and to construct their Others.

Charlie and Joe

On a trip to the PRT I met two young American soldiers: Charlie and Joe. I engaged them in conversation about their backgrounds, jobs, and perceptions of the situation in the area. The soldiers, both in their 20s, hailed from different parts of the United States. Their main job was guarding the entrance to the PRT and conducting physical searches. Both young men were shocked that I travelled in the city and villages on my own, doing research and speaking to local people. Beyond the PRT and related tasks they had very little interaction with local people. When asked about the security situation in the district, Charlie responded: 'It's dangerous, of course it's dangerous. This is Afghanistan, the whole place is dangerous. It's full of terrorists and Muslims. It doesn't get more dangerous than that' (C1, Behsud). Joe agreed, nodding his head and added:

> I remember watching the Twin Towers on 9/11 when I was a kid in elementary school and I thought it was really scary. I am glad I can be part of the effort that makes sure these people don't ever do that to us again.
>
> (C1, Behsud)

The racialised stereotypes they repeated are rooted in the Global War on Terror policy discourse. The international intervention in Afghanistan has been heavily criticised for relying on a simplistic formula of for us or against us when approaching the politics and positions of Afghans. For these soldiers, the difference between the Taliban and Afghans was that the former were armed insurgents, the latter a potential threat. These generalisations made (mis)understanding their place situation easier for them. They had a clear enemy, a clear task, and they saw Afghans through this lens. Their fight was for their own national security, part of a liberal Western project, in which the society they found themselves was a constant threat. Even though both men were now based in Afghanistan, their perceptions of Afghan people were filtered through GWOT lens; this was pre-determined long before their arrival in the country, and continued to colour their perceptions of the Afghan realities that surrounded them. However, it would be a mistake to assume that it was only the military that expressed these stereotypical views.

Comments were commonly uttered at social gatherings of mainly expatriate staff, or made in casual conversations. These remarks rarely used the explicitly racialised language of Charlie and Joe, but rather focused on the 'barbaric' nature of the communities, a discriminatory trope that has been used to describe Afghans society by colonial administrators since the 1800s[9] and Western officials in the post 9/11 invasion.[10] During a social event one evening a UN staff member that had been in the region for two years said:

> Anyone that thinks they are going to change this society is kidding themselves. Their culture is backwards. That's just it. That is how they are. They live a tough and primitive life. In all of the places I have been, this is the most backward place I have ever seen. If ever you can understand Hobbes, it is here … where life is nasty, brutish and cold.
>
> (C10, UN, Kabul)

An aid worker based in Kabul who travelled regularly to the eastern region described Afghan society similarly:

> If you take away the cars, you could be back in biblical times, and that is how they live here and that is how you feel when you speak to them. They still have not learned how to communicate without beating one another up and that is why this is a violent society and always will be.
>
> (C8, INGO Worker, Kabul)

Of course, not all UN staff and aid workers or even military officials held these views. Many aid workers had been in the region or the country for several years and had knowledge of the local communities and expressed a commitment to learning more about the local context.

Hannah

Hannah, arrived in Afghanistan in 2004, having previously been posted to East Timor, where she had been working with the UN. She had left Afghan the region after three years, but had returned in 2010. Hannah did not speak Pashto so her interactions were mainly with her Afghan colleagues at work, but she had also maintained friendships with the staff she met over the years. When she first arrived in the region expatriates could travel to all the districts in the province by car. Some districts were more accessible by car than others, and tribal disputes often over land or family matters, which could be quite violent and had to be avoided. When we read the rules governing movement for UN staff and many aid workers, they had changed and movement was drastically reduced to a select number of districts in the province, including Behsud. She explained:

> Movement is so restricted so people coming here now only see a small part of the region and everything else is insecure. I think that reinforces the idea that Afghans are dangerous. But yeah, you do hear really inappropriate comments but it is more about the way people are speaking to each other and treat each other. An uneven dynamic exists with internationals, regardless of who they are, coming here and thinking they are better than Afghans, Afghans resent internationals seeing them as symbols of all that is going wrong and we both fear each other. Other people are just racist. There's no check for that on job applications.
>
> (C26, UN, Jalalabad)

Thus, working in the provincial or regional offices outside of Kabul offered expatriate aid workers an opportunity to engage with the population outside of the built-up security architecture of the largest urban centre in the country. Movement in the central districts of Nangarhar Province, which included Behsud was easier than navigating around Kabul in terms of the shorter distance one had to travel, and the location of many aid agency compounds within proximity to Afghan neighbourhoods. The opportunity for a more intimate engagement of the people and their country, however, did not always translate into a deeper understanding of each other, nor of ways in which, as Hannah intimated, the mutual experience of intervention influenced their engagement with each other.

Navigating the agencies

While distinctions between the different foreign entities are important for clarity in policy, they tell us little about local perceptions and understandings regarding these actors. In Behsud District residents used their own set of categories to differentiate between the different local and international groups with whom they frequently came into contact. Local distinctions between the international military forces and other groups were pronounced, yet their perceptions of differences between civilian actors were often ambiguous. Categorisations were dependent on material but also temporal factors and the position of residents in the district themselves.

First, there was little conflation between the military forces with the UN or aid agencies. While residents in two villages considered both groups into the category of 'foreign interveners', they did acknowledge that they operated differently. The daily presence of the military forces in and around the district facilitated the separation of international military forces from other foreign actors. In Hada and Samarkhalil, areas where regular military patrols took place, some residents dismissed any knowledge of ISAF. Comments were: 'I don't know anything about ISAF. They come here but I know nothing about them'; 'Our people are not interested in ISAF'; 'Our people don't know anything about ISAF and so I cannot tell you about them' (F8, Samarkhalil; F13, Hada). However, many of the same interviewees went on to explain what they thought of ISAF in greater detail. The initial dismal of ISAF perhaps more a sign of disdain than ignorance.

Interestingly, one of the perceived local distinctions between these broad groups rested on having arms as opposed to using them. In Qasimabad, for example, residents suggested that security forces came with weapons whereas other public agencies, referring to aid agencies and the UN did not (F11, Qasimabad). There were several civilian organisations, however, who also carried weapons. Organisations like DAI and ARD used armoured vehicles and were accompanied by private armed close protection when travelling or residing in the district. In 2010, estimates of Private Security Companies fell between 140–170, of which only 50 were registered with the Afghan government (Alexander, 2010).[11] Officially, very few aid organisations had armed guards or staff members; unofficially, depending on the organisation, this was not the case, depending on the location of the project – drivers, for example, often travelled with small arms. In a country in the midst of conflict, the proliferation of weapons cannot be understated. The security practices of these few aid actors were recognised by the community residents, however, these securitised development actors were not, however, conflated with the international military.

A second, significant marker of difference for residents was their understanding of what various organisations gained from their interactions with the community. The residents of Balandghar, a village located on the road leading to Kunar Province, distinguished between the UN and NGOs, for example, in terms of the revenue derived for their activities. NGOs were described as private organisations similar to private sector companies, whereas the UN was considered a public organisation. Thus, NGOs were regarded as for-profit businesses rather than charitable agencies. During an early morning discussion group male community members suggested that they were not sure about the UN, but said NGOs were private organisations and that they were taking the projects from the donors and dividing the profit (F2, Wayalati). Similar sentiments were expressed in Samarkhalil and Hada villages.

This framing was exacerbated by several factors. First, several agencies, such as DAI and the Association for Rural Development (ARD), who were working on large-scale economic development projects *were* for-profit entities. The political economy of aid organisations figured prominently as a structuring factor in the hierarchy of aid agencies discussed in Chapter 3. For-profit development corporations such as DAI and ARD were located towards the bottom of the scale because their development interventions were money-generating activities. Second, it was not uncommon for local NGOs to be private businesses. They had benefited from the proliferation of cash-for-work and QIPs that focused on infrastructure development and construction. In June 2005, the Afghan government had tried to curb this trend with the introduction of the Law on Non-Governmental Organizations (Afghanistan, 2005), which required all NGOs in the country to register with the government (Article 4) and prohibits NGOs from participation in construction projects and contracts (Article 8). Registration alone, however, was of little significance as many organisations that registered with the government were local contractors or 'for-profit' firms. While communities rarely commented on the specific financial structure of the different aid agencies, this categorisation implied an understanding of the political economy and a perception of the intervention as an extractive practice where both security, and development actors took from the communities for their own benefit.

Third, residents associated organisations with the type of work they did. NGOs were seen to work predominantly for shelter, water, and human rights, while the UN sometimes worked in schools and with refugees. The UN was also known for proving humanitarian aid to the district. For example, in Waylati, the village had experienced earthquakes and floods during the past five years. In the aftermath of these natural disasters, the UN had also provided emergency non-food items and other materials to the village (I15, Walylati). The PRT and government were also mentioned providing development to the communities in terms of bridges, schools, and irrigation projects. Lastly, the position of the resident in the village also determined how much they knew about the mosaic of local and international actors operating in the district. they were more informed about the mosaic of local and international actors operating in the district. For instance, members of the local and the youth *shuras* were as a linkage between the villages and the outside world in Balandghar, Samarkhalil, and Qasimabad. They often distinguished between different types of actors and their activities. A *shura* member from Qasimabad explained 'that local people could make the differen[ce] between the army and public but little beyond that' (I21, Qasimabad). This was sometimes the case.

Behsud residents utilised a variety of filters to order the various local and foreign aid organisations that operated in the district. Perceptions of these different actors were tied to their practices in the communities, the nature of their interactions with the community, and what they left behind. However, comments from the community also place different actors into generalised categories, which reflected the district residents' broader understanding of the purpose of the intervention. Therefore, local residents were not unaware of the differences between actors, but had a particular lens through which they chose to view them that allowed them to make sense of the web of agencies and organisations moving through their district.

Negotiating realities and spaces

The politicisation of aid, which is a strategy that has been used by donors in Afghanistan for decades, suggests that aid assistance can be used as an incentive to mould the behaviour of states and communities to be in line with the objectives of external forces. The underlying logic, that loyalty and behavioural change can be produced by aid interventions, however, did not seem to be reflected amongst the communities in Behsud. Rather, a more complex narrative emerged in which the dynamics within local communities could shift from one day to the next, and individuals negotiated between different positionalities. Both the communities and the local aid workers struggled with the insecurity and development that characterised the district.

A USAID-funded civilian-assistance programme which was implemented in the district by an inter-governmental agency aimed 'to support stabilisation initiatives, leverage resources and strengthen civilian-military collaboration'; the goal of the programme was to 'provide assistance for Afghan families and communities that have suffered losses as a result of international military operations' (Ahmadi, 2010, pp. 9–10). The programme also provided assistance on a 'no-blame-basis', meaning assistance was given regardless of whether the loss was incurred due to international forces targeting anti-government elements or due to anti-government elements targeting international forces. Therefore, the provision of assistance was not to be confused with the international forces taking responsibility for the losses incurred by the community, families, or individual. The nationwide programme was most active in the south, southeast and eastern regions of the country where military operations were the highest number of civilian causalities occurred. The implementing partner for the project was a large international organisation, headquartered in Kabul.

Since most of the programme activity took place in areas deemed insecure by the organisation's security division, project staff were sub-contracted and put on special contracts, similar to Sarah's in Chapter 3, which removed responsibility for the inter-governmental agency in the case of death or injury. The majority of people hired were national staff, but a number of interveners were also employed and based in the provinces. The social ordering of risk and life-chance divide that is created through such practices was striking. Literature on remote management and bunkerisation of aid workers (Duffield, 2012) often focuses on the shifting of responsibility and risk to local staff, but rarely does it consider the hierarchies amongst interveners that are created by international organisations through such contracting practices.

A few months previously several houses in the village had been damaged by mortars fired at the nearby military base: residents in one household had been killed. Accordingly, the programme provided new housing materials and financial compensation to the residents with damaged property. Several focus group participants had been given assistance by the project or were aware of other members of the community that had. One of the males in the group explained his perspective on the programme: 'Yes, there was damage to the community, but they provided us with materials to rebuild our houses. For this, we were content' (F8, Samarkhalil). During the conversation it was clear that this assistance did not affect residents' perceptions of the military or the insurgents. The most senior member of the discussion group stated: 'It is right that they gave us shelter material, but we don't like ISAF because of that. And we have no power to control the Taliban, so this will happen again. We are just here living our lives' (F8, Samarkhalil).[12] They were also unsure of, or unconcerned with, which actor had actually provided the assistance, whether it was ISAF, the PRT, the UN, or a local or international NGO. Resources provided in the context of violent conflict could assist with the physical repair of the area, but this kind of aid but did not negate the impact of the violence on the residents or shift their loyalties, which invariably were to their families and the community.

At an individual level, aid workers also negotiated different spaces. In the summer of 2011, I held a series of workshops with Afghan aid workers in Jalalabad, although the topic of the workshop was health and education, we talked about the specific realities between which they moved. A local staff member of an INGO, who had been working with development and humanitarian agencies since the 1980s explained the complex dynamics of the province:

> Many of the areas have schools and clinics now. In some areas, the insurgents are bombing the schools or sending night letters[13] to the community and teachers so that they do not send their children to school. But in some other areas, it is the shuras and the religious leaders that are creating conflicts with the families that send their children to school … particularly the girls. In other areas, the insurgents are encouraging people to go to school because they realise education will be good for the community so they allow it, but this does not mean that they will stop attacking the foreign forces or Afghan forces.
>
> (W1, Jalalabad City)

Navigating the shifting landscape within the districts was difficult and sometimes dangerous for the local staff and to do so required some independence from the organisations who employed them. Of the 19 NGOs that worked in Behsud, eight were Afghan NGOs. In addition, most of the international NGOs were intended to have only 2–5 expatriate staff working with every 100 Afghan colleagues. Therefore, local aid workers performed the bulk of aid work and community interactions in the district. In a small group conversation after the workshop, aid workers described different strategies they used to adapt activities to better suit the community dynamics, as understood by the NGO staff. The poor monitoring habits of some local aid agencies, and the limited ability of expatriate staff to travel into the districts or rural areas, created space for corruption and nepotism, but also gave local staff some flexibility in how they worked with the communities. As intermediaries between Western actors and the local communities, the Afghan aid workers felt they could use their positions to negotiate the different worlds with which they interacted.

Meetings in the district

Unlike Qarabagh, in Behsud there was a space for regular interaction between local residents, UN staff, for-profit development employees, private security contractors, local and international NGO staff, international military forces, ANSF, and government officials. The nature of these interactions included UN meetings with government officials, military community patrols, coordination meetings, consultations over aid projects, and so forth. Each of these interactions had its own set of practices informed by the tactics of different groups in their engagements with each other.

Outside of community patrols and active military operations, international military forces, and tribal and village leaders met regularly in two main forums. First, large gatherings were held every month at the PRT with key local groups and community leaders. Second, military officials and soldiers would travel into the districts occasionally to meet with residents in their villages. Their arrival to the meetings in villages usually took place using armoured military convoys and military personnel who were always armed. Discussion could take place inside or outside, with a small group of officials and community leaders using an interpreter, while remaining members of the convoy stayed at a distance. Meetings were often held with village elders to begin with, but could also be held with other groups, such as women and teachers.[14] In addition to military personnel, the community-based meetings would often also include civilian PRT staff and local government officials.

As a representative from the international military base in Behsud explained,

> During these visits we always tried to bring local Afghan government officials so that people could see the presence of the government and our association with them. This gave the perception of a unified front to some extent. The civilian staff were also important. They were able to observe and speak to some of the social dynamics that we might miss.
>
> (I65, Former ISAF PRT Military, Kabul)

The topic of discussion varied and sometimes the military would also bring things for the community. In Taghar, according to the community, ISAF – or ‘the foreigner army’ as locals referred to it – had passed through the village previously and had sometimes asked questions, mainly about village security

(F10, Taghar). In Balandghar, the ISAF had come to the area and enquired about the villagers' problems and the security situation. Villagers said they also brought stationery for the students and other helpful household items for the residents (F7, Balandghar). Reflecting on the meetings they had attended a senior military official remarked:

> I recognise that the visits were manufactured to an extent because of the guns on the large armoured vehicles, but there was no way to move around this and it was not safe. It is not only the international military forces that travel like this. Afghan VIPs also arm themselves. The power of the gun is respected in Afghan society after years of war. I was more respected by the communities than the governor.
>
> (I65, Former ISAF PRT Military, Kabul)

The approach to these meetings could vary but generally, the way the outsiders came, whom they brought, and what they left was consistent.

The UN political affairs official mentioned above who doubted much could be done to change Afghan society, explained how these games figured into his meetings with local leaders:

> They rarely tell you the truth. You can be sitting there with someone who you know is obviously lying to your face and you just have to smile. Half the people I meet with are warlords and they kill or have killed people. If you think about it, it's terrible but we have to engage with them. So, when you deal with them, you play their game, listen to their demands, engage in negotiations, and drink a lot of tea, but ultimately you are just marking time and hoping to keep the situation manageable until it is time to move on.
>
> (I3, Jalalabad City)

Local residents had their own set of tactics to manage such interactions. Villagers tended to provide a mixture of truths and untruths regarding the needs of the community and the security situation, the resulting ambiguities allowing space the elders to maintain some control over their environment. For example, local leadership could repeat what they thought others wanted to hear in order to mould the image of the village to their benefit (F13, Hada; F2, Walayti). People understood the prime purpose of the meetings was for the international military to obtain information about the area. Even discussions focused on the development needs of the village were viewed with suspicion. Community needs were sometimes exaggerated, portraying village residents as desperate, or villagers asserted requests for assistance simply to encourage investment in their area, whether through short-term projects or longer-term interventions. Community gatekeepers could not prevent the security forces from coming into the village, with or without violent intentions, but they could withhold information and construct a particular image of the area. Posturing and withholding of knowledge were a set of practices which were common to a variety of meetings that went on in the district.

Women, peace, and security

Women in Behsud mentioned numerous challenges, including access to education, justice, and public spaces and the ability to make personal choices. Growing insecurity in the area, night raids, insurgent activity, and criminality had led to increasing restrictions on their freedom of movement, which in many of the villages was already limited to the household and community boundaries. Even though most civilian causalities and persons involved in various different types of conflict were men, the fear of increasing violence and impunity led to further reluctance of families to allow their female members to travel and work away from home.

Women-focused aid programmes in the district were a popular component of military and civilian programming. The majority of the projects focused on small business development, attached to skills training in skills such as tailoring, gardening, craft-making, and literacy improvement. The projects had employed a significant number of the local female aid workers in the area. During a workshop with local aid workers, when the discussion turned to women's development, participants said that women's freedom and education was under attack by many sources in the eastern region, and not only by the Taliban. Rahela, who had been working on women's empowerment programme for several INGOs in the area for the past five years, stressed that opposition to their work on women's rights, intimidation and threats, came not only from insurgent groups but also from the women's own colleagues, family members, community residents, and local power holders, including government officials. International agencies have also sometimes failed to provide support to local women.

Shafika

I met Shafika for the first time in 2005. At that time, I was working for an international organisation and had just been sent to work at the regional office for several months, and she was working as a programme officer, for an INGO based in Jalalabad, on a women's empowerment programme. We would see each other occasionally at coordination meetings convened by the Ministry of Women's Affairs, which were usually held bi-weekly though sometimes monthly, to bring together agencies working on women's issues. After I left the region in 2007, we kept in occasional contact. When I returned to Afghanistan, in 2010 and 2011, to do research, we saw each other in Kabul and Nangarhar several times. Over the course of those two years her story unfolded.

In 2010, Shafika was working as the project manager of a women's shelter and empowerment programme in Nangarhar Province. The names and origins of the women the shelter housed were confidential, but women from Behsud had sought assistance from the programme. The shelter also dealt with elopement cases from other regions in the country. The women were provided with a place to stay, counselling, exercise time, and different skills training programmes. The shelters were in undisclosed locations, to prevent family members from seeking out the women and forcing them to return home. Some provincially based government authorities, however, were aware of a few of the locations, and female police officers were assigned to act as internal guards. The setting up of the shelter programme in the eastern region had been an ongoing discussion between the MOWA, UNAMA, and women's organisations for several years.

At lunch one day, Shafika described a situation that had developed at one of the shelters; this was of growing concern for her. In the evenings, a senior police official had been trying to gain access to one of the shelters. The female guards at the time had refused to allow him in, and had called Shafika the next day. After two more attempts, including one where Shafika had spoken to the official herself, the visits stopped. In the meantime, Shafika had reported the incident to the regional and Kabul-based UN agency implementing the project. Soon afterwards, she began to receive threats, and her children were harassed on the way to school one day. The situation deteriorated over several months: her daughters had stopped attending school and her son began to suffer from depression. I mentioned the situation to an international staff member of the agency running the program in Kabul, they snickered and shrugged their shoulders, saying

> That project has been doing very well. Shafika is not easy. She also gets in trouble sometimes. The national staff have their disputes. It's better not to get involved. I am sure things will be fine, and anyway that's not my programme so I can't say much.
>
> (C27, UN, Kabul)

As Shafika's insecurity grew, she made repeated visits to the Kabul office to ask for assistance. On one occasion, she sat in the HQ office building, waiting to speak to someone, but to no avail. In a follow-up conversation with the expatriate staff member I had spoken to earlier about Shafika's case, they mentioned they heard she had left, but were not sure what had really happened. Apparently, the agency did make some enquiries but did not think the details would ever be clear. Indeed, Shafika stopped working for the project soon after her visit to see me in Kabul; the harassment of her family, however, continued, and by the end of the year she and her daughters had moved out of the province (C28, Various).

The shelter program provided refuge and skills training approximately 400 women from Behsud, other districts across the region, and from other regions. In a society with high levels of violence against women, where domestic violence is considered to fall within the jurisdiction of the family and sometimes the community, shelter programmes providing options for women outside of local institutions are inevitability controversial. Such programmes are also a target for conservative elements in the government; these tend to associate advocacy for women's rights with a Western-backed liberal feminist agenda contrary to traditional Afghan values (Wimpelmann, 2015). In 2011, unsurprisingly, civil society organisations spoke out against an initiative of the national Ministry of

Women's Affairs to take over the management of women's shelters in the country (Williams, 2011). Of the approximately dozen shelters that were registered with the government at the time, the majority were run by NGOs, and UN agencies, whereas only one shelter was government-run. Women's organisations expressed concern that uniformly government-run shelters would be far more susceptible to corruption, intimidation, and pressure by families and communities to return abused women (Williams, 2011). Shafika's story also illustrates the ways in which the practices of international agencies, committed in principle to advancing women's rights, jeopardised the individual security of the local Afghan staff.

The international aid agency failed to grapple with some of the fallout of intervention on the lives of the women in the shelter and the Afghan women involved in implementing the project. The physical separation of the UN HQ in Kabul from the project sites in Nangarhar meant the office could distance itself from the unforeseen consequences of the project. An underlying distrust of local staff, coupled with the cultural barriers that existed between Afghan and expatriate staff were both factors that rationalised the excuse to not engage with the difficult dynamics that emerged around the project, and the insecurity caused by what was generally framed as a 'successful' development intervention.

Reflecting on Behsud

In Behsud, however, the number of external actors was much greater than in Qarabagh. Therefore, the interactions between district residents, international and national aid workers, UN staff, international and national security forces, government officials, and community leaders, came more sharply into focus. This chapter explores three main themes. First, the simplistic constructions of 'the Other' in contrast the complexity and fluidity of movement between different positions that individuals in the district adopted. Second, the chapter outlines the friction that occurs between different groups of actors in the district, and the practices and strategies that are used to negotiate their competing realities. Insights are also provided into the underpinning ideologies and assumptions that fuel these fractious relationships. To do this, the chapter will further explore the Eurocentric and racialised mindsets held by interveners discussed in the first three chapters of the book, and the cognitive dissonance that emerged in Qarabagh discussed in the last chapter.

The stories from Behsud suggest a way towards a much more nuanced understanding of security and development, and of the actors involved. While Behsud was able to benefit from the increased aid spent in Nangarhar, this aid did not lead to a reduction in the level of insecurity in the district. Rather, levels of violence increased alongside the increase in development. The interdependence of security and development is thus deconstructed through examining the experiences and perspectives of the various actors living and working in the district, who had a much more nuanced view of their environment. In addition to this diverse range of understandings, there was a sense amongst those in the district that they were being forced to respond to an externally defined framework, even if this did not correspond to the realities that locals observed in their everyday lives. Understanding the way development and security were conceived in the district was not solely about defining terms, but also about understanding the different lenses through which participants viewed the situation. For example, both local leaders, international military and anti-government forces were all sources of insecurity, as well as providers of security and aid assistance. Security and development are indeed linked in several ways in Behsud, but the relationships do not reflect the logics of liberal frameworks which have shaped the intervention in Afghanistan.

The main theme that recurs in the district is the multiple roles actors can hold, and the fluidity of movement between different spaces and positions. In addition, members of the community, and local aid workers negotiated and renegotiated their positions regularly, shifting between different worlds at various moments. This fluidity challenged the ‘us vs. them’ binary of the GWOT discourse and the logics of strategies that attempt to use aid as a political tool or to garner support to certain stakeholders. In the context of violence and intervention communities were not swayed by the resources offered by external actors. Even if residents accepted the presence of outsiders they were aware of the extractive nature of intervener practices. Consequently, residents cautiously approached the variety of actors engaged in the district, reflecting on their objectives, methods, and usefulness to the community. Community members, and local aid workers navigated their environment by adopting different positions in their efforts to survive and to mitigate the damage of the conflict and the intervention.

Violence is abundant in the story of Behsud, where there was frequent fighting between belligerents in the villages, military operations, civilian causalities, and violence within the community. The impact of such conflict on the community was stark not only in its physical manifestations of structural damage, but also in the legacy of violence on the wellbeing of the community members and their ability to trust each other, the ubiquitous fear, restricted movement for women, and increased rates of depression. It also permeated the relationships between the interveners and locals, producing distance and distrust in a context where physical proximity to each other and daily interactions could have worked against those tendencies. This was mediated by constructions of the Other that were rooted in Eurocentric and racist discourse and material practices that were embraced by some like Joe and Charlie and the UN sand aid staff members, and problematised by others like Hannah. The combination of fear and loathing was consistently present in the perceptions, interactions and relationships between interveners and Afghans in Behsud.

In Behsud, each set of actors can be viewed as engaging in a variety of games with the other. These interactions reinforced the constructions that actors already had of their Other, producing what Lowenhaupt Tsing (2005) calls the ‘friction’ of international intervention. While Tsing’s research focuses on the way international actors perceive local actors, clearly the dynamics in Behsud run both ways. Comments from local actors often demonstrated the very specific way they had chosen to view external actors, and dismiss the difference amongst them. In addition, local leadership tended to bestow credit for development activities on actors, while negating the roles of others, essentialising the Other, and attempting to control interactions. Clearly, the geopolitical power dynamics which frame the intervention cannot be ignored. Yet in Behsud different sets of actors asserted their power through various means: the community controlled information; the senior military officer brought to the meetings those props she perceived as locally symbolic of power, particularly weapons and armoured vehicles; and the UN staffers received the local leadership with tea and politeness in meetings, while holding their culture in contempt. All the individuals involved in these interactions attempted to construct a reality which they wanted others to accept and that might offer them a means to maintain control over the situation.

Finally, a common strategy of the protagonists of intervention to increase their legitimacy is the promotion of activities relating to norms and values that hold some resonance to their publics. As such, the myth of 'rescuing' Afghan women from the violence of their own society has been a central and reoccurring trope in international justifications of the US-led post-9/11 intervention in Afghanistan. In addition, women, peace and security, and empowerment programmes implemented by the UN and international aid agencies have regularly invoked similar images of oppressed Afghan women and girls in need of 'saving' (Cooke, 2002; Abu-Lughod, 2013). The influx of donor money and attention to women's issues in Afghanistan presented an opportunity for change furthered by the social and political mobilisations and efforts of Afghan women at the national and sub-national levels. However, as Shafika's story shows, the deleterious effects of military intervention and the practices of that international aid community have also exacerbated the situations of insecurity many women were already facing. In the end, in Behsud, achievements in women's security were tangled in a complex web of violence in which many everyday experiences remain invisible.

Notes

1 Torkham refers to the Torkham border. One of the main crossing points on the Afghanistan–Pakistan border.

2 Other sources however provide different population figures. The District Development Plan suggests the population is approximately 165,000 (Afghanistan, 2007). District Development Plan, Behsud District, Nangarhar Province. Kabul. Local research organisation put the figure at 500,000 people across 60 villages (TLO, 2014), This likely includes parts of Jalalabad City.

3 These latter figures were provided by *shura* members and district officials in Behsud. Official statistics of the ethnic breakdown of the district's population differ slightly and include other groups such as Sikhs, Hindus, and Pashies.

4 Since no census has been conducted for decades all figures are approximate.

5 *Namus* is an Arabic word that means honour, respect or virtue. In Afghanistan the term has been broadened. Pashtun men are required to protect the honour of their: zan,

zar, and zamin (women, gold, and land). In general, land refers not only to the household and nearby area but also the tribal lands and even the country of Afghanistan (see Rubin, 2002).

6 Afghaniyat and Pashtunwali are traditional unwritten codes of conduct used in Afghanistan. The simplest translation would be a sense of Afghanness. Islamiyat is another code that refers to Islamic codes of conduct. These codes are supposed to guide the conduct of Afghans; however, interpretations vary.

7 For further details see small-scale, low-cost projects, funded by our missions, that are planned and implemented within a short timeframe.

8 This was recorded in the official list of security incidents in the district on 12 December 2012.

9 For historical reference see Wylly, H. C. 1998. *The Borderland: The Country of the Pathans, Safdar Mehdi, Karachi*, (originally published 1912), p. 5. Mr Temple, Secretary to the Chief Commissioner of the Punjab in 1855, as 'savages, – noble savages perhaps – and not without some tincture of virtue and generosity, but still absolutely barbarians nevertheless'.

10 Both American and Canadian officials have described Afghans as barbarians in public statements following 9/11. See statements by Canadian Mayor Regis Labeaume on CTV News, 27 February 2009 and Dick Cheney's remarks on Meet the Press 16 September 2011.

11 In March 2011 President Karzai disbanded all but 25 PSCs. These companies were reinvented and are now commonly referred to as Risk Management Companies (RMC).

12 These members of the focus group were not from Samarkhalil but a nearby area.

13 Night letters are written threats.

14 Meetings with women in the villages and military were not common. This would only be allowed to take place if the military personnel were also female.

References

Abu-Lughod, L. 2013. *Do Muslim Women Need Saving?* Cambridge: MA: Harvard University Press.

Afghanistan. 2005. *Law on Non-Governmental Organisations. Official Gazette no. 857.* Kabul: Ministry of Economy.

Afghanistan. 2007. *District Development Plan, Behsud District, Nangarhar Province.* Kabul: Ministry of Rural Rehabilitation and Development.

Afghanistan. 2010a. *District Assessment Report, Beshood District, Nangarhar Province.* Kabul: Independent Directorate of Local Governance.

Afghanistan. 2010b. *National Education Strategic Plan for Afghanistan 2010–2014.* Kabul: Ministry of Education.

Afghanistan. 2010c. *Development Co-operation Report 2010.* Kabul: Ministry of Finance.

Afghanistan. 2012. *Afghanistan CSO Population Data – 1390 (2011–12).* Kabul: Central Statistics Office.

Alexander, D. 2010. Firms Halting Afghan Projects Over Security Ban. *Reuters*, 21 October 2010.

Ahmadi, B. 2010. *Final Project Evaluation Report for the Afghan Civilian Assistance Program (ACAP).* Kabul: Cheechi Consulting.

Azarbaijani-Moghaddam, S., Wardak, M., Zaman, I., and Annabel Taylor. 2008. *Afghan Hearts, Afghan Minds Exploring Afghan Perceptions of Civil–Military Relations.* Kabul: European Network of NGOs in Afghanistan (ENNA) and British Agencies for Afghanistan Group (BAAG).

Clark, K. 2013. *What exactly is the CIA doing in Afghanistan? Proxy militias and two airstrikes in Kunar*. Kabul: Afghanistan Analysts Network.
Cooke, M. 2002. Saving brown women. *Signs: Journal of Women in Culture and Society*, 28(1), 468–470.
Duffield, M. 2012. Challenging environments: Danger, resilience and the aid industry. *Security Dialogue*, 43(5), 475–492.
Foshini, F. 2012. *Land Grabs in Afghanistan(1): Nangahar, the Disputed O-Rangeland. Land Grabs in Afghanistan*. Kabul: Afghanistan Analysts Network (AAN).
Giovacchini, T. 2011. *Governance and Representation in the Afghan Urban Transition*. Working Paper. Kabul: AREU.
Lee, N. 2011. *ANSO Quarterly Data Report and Annual Summation (Q.4 and 2011)*. 1 January 2011 to 31 December 2011: Kabul, ANSO.
Lowenhaupt Tsing, A. 2005. *Friction: An Ethnography of Global Connection*. Princeton, NJ: Princeton University Press.
Mumtaz, W. 2011. *Jalalabad's 'Grab-Town' a Difficult Case of Illegal Settlement and Land Dispute*. Research and Reflection from Afghanistan. Kabul: AREU.
Muzik, T. 2013. *ANSO Quarterly Data Report and Annual Summation (Q.4 and 2012)*. 1 January 2012 to 31 December 2012. Kabul, ANSO.
Roggio, B. 2011. ISAF targets 'al Qaeda affiliated' Taliban leader in Nangarhar. *Blog of the Long War Journal*. Available at: www.longwarjournal.org/threat-matrix/archives/2011/05/isaf_targets_al_qaeda_affiliat.php#ixzz2ZxXh8VdQ 2012.
TLO. 2014. *Justice & Security. Practices, Perceptions, and Problems in Kabul and Nangarhar*. Kabul: TLO. May 2014.
UN. 2012. *Consolidated Appeal Process* (CAP). Kabul: Multi-agency.
UN. 2016. *Education and Healthcare at Risk*. Kabul, United Nations.
UNAMA. 2011. *Annual Report on the Protection of Civilians*. Kabul: UNAMA.
UNAMA. 2012. *Annual Report on the Protection of Civilians*. Kabul: UNAMA.
USAID. 2010. *Facility Improves Local Textile Quality. USAID Telling Our Story*. Washington, DC: USAID.
USAID. 2012. *Overview of observed security incidents resulting in civilian casualties* (January 2008 to September 2011). Kabul: USAID.
Williams, M. J. 2011. Empire lite revisited: NATO, the comprehensive approach and state-building in Afghanistan. *International Peacekeeping*, 18(1), 64–78.
Wimpelmann, T. 2015. One step forward and many to the side: Combating gender violence in Afghanistan, 2001–2014. *Women's Studies International Forum*, 51, 101–109.

Conclusion

This chapter concludes this volume by bringing together its findings and contributions. This book has sought to investigate the everyday realities of the international intervention in Afghanistan that occurred at a moment in history which offered an opportunity to test the relationship between aid, conflict, and security. The stories presented in the preceding chapters have explored this experiment. This final chapter brings to an end the everyday stories of intervention that I collected, observed, and participated in during the research for this book. These stories presented seemingly mundane, simple, repeated, and interconnected practices, which came together to provide a nuanced yet deeply troubling picture of security, development, and violence ten years into the intervention in Afghanistan. They tease out the complexity of the relationships, and power hierarchies that shape everyday interactions and the related struggles and acts of resistance that emerge in amongst and between the interveners and Afghans. Beyond that, however, they have provided clues into the ways in which global politics are played out in everyday spaces. In fact, the everyday stories in this book are global stories. The chapter is divided into three sections. First, it maps the analytical pathway that the book has taken. The second section outlines six themes that run throughout the book and addresses the book's contributions to peace and conflict studies and development studies. The last section provides a few concluding remarks on the legacies of the stories since 2014, when this research was completed.

The pathway

In this book I analysed the experience and representation of an intervention that presupposed that development and security issues were mutually reinforcing. Drawing on post- and decolonial ad critical peace and conflict studies literature the book locates the security-development nexus and the liberal peacebuilding agenda within a colonial framework that reinforces hegemonic power relationships and hierarchies. Using an ethnographic and reflective approach to fieldwork, I then proceeded to explore the everyday narratives and practices of security, development, and violence that emerge within Afghanistan as both interveners and Afghans struggle with the chaos and conflict of the international intervention. The findings here are based on 14 months of extensive field research and informed by years of professional experience in Afghanistan, involving committed engagement with both the interveners and Afghans. The *everyday* of international intervention described in the chapters of this book are explained through diverse subject lenses which are connected and dynamic. Each chapter in the book focused on a different set of actors and their stories. The purpose of this configuration was to give deeper insight into specific scenes and different perspectives in the wider context of the intervention. The story frame highlighted the plurality of and connections between experiences, the shifting conflict and political dynamics, and the prevalence of uneven and differentiated power hierarchies in everyday intervention. Using this approach, the book has sought to contribute to prevailing scholarship in development, peace, and conflict studies on intervention and peacebuilding, by deepening our understanding of the lived everyday experiences and consequences of a violent intervention in Afghanistan.

Deconstructing intervention through everyday stories

This book used the exploration of everyday stories to deconstruct and give insight to the broader context of the intervention in Afghanistan, and intervention as a global practice. It suggests that an analytical lens focused on everyday practices, relationships, and experiences allows us to understand the realities of intervention and conflict, and the struggles of the people who exist within these spaces in ways that are often missing from scholarship focused on policy discourse or structure. The everyday stories that form the bulk of the book attempt to demonstrate how global discourses and policies are experienced, reproduced and enacted in the everyday lives of Afghans and interveners and the ways in which everyday practices are reflected and translated into global discourses. There are several overarching themes that emerge across the chapters, namely: empire and intervention; contesting security and development; connected subjectivities; everyday violence; tactics and resistance; and affect and dissonance. Each theme reflects a unique empirical contribution of the book to critical peace and conflict and development studies.

Empire and intervention

As much as the emergence of the security-development nexus in the post-9/11 era marked a shift in international approaches to conflict, it was also a continuation of the colonial discourse and approaches of the past. Indeed, in a certain respect it resembled a return to the paternalist High Empire discourses of the colonial past. Each chapter of this book reflects the contemporary reproduction of these strategies of neo-empire in Afghanistan. The narratives speak to the multiple policy approaches, structures, and shifting discourses that were put in place to support the intervention and promote coordination and synergy of security and development. Chapters 2 and 4 detailed policy approaches adopted by NATO interveners in their efforts to address so-called 'fragile states', the numerous civil–military coordination forums that were established then failed, and the internal and external contestation to the integrated mission structure; Chapter 5 detailed the implementation of the NSP highlighting the contradiction in hybrid governance institutions. These multiple yet disparate structures rarely addressed the needs of the local communities, or in some cases the needs of the interveners themselves; rather, they arose from an unrelenting logic which presupposed the superiority of Western knowledge and policy prescriptions.

Power-laden assumptions about global hierarchies of life were built into the justification for and practices of the international intervention discourse in Afghanistan. The moral responsibility to save local people, particularly women, by bringing security and development to Afghanistan was part of the justification of the intervention by both the UN and the US. The discourse of mission failure began to dominate in 2010, as the transition agenda unfolded, and drew heavily upon a constructed notion of Afghanistan as backwards and untameable – the construction used to fuel the intervention in the first place. While organisations were debating where to attribute blame, they simultaneously engaged in practices which demonstrated their lack of accountability and responsibility to local communities. In fact, the political economy of the intervention and lack of accountability of interveners and local officials to communities facilitated the flourishing of corruption. As the perspectives shared in the two chapters which focused on the districts, and the stories of Mohammad and Shafika, show, however, local lives often became 'collateral damage' wrought by the liberal project in Afghanistan. It would be myopic, however, to view this only as an Afghan–intervener dynamic. Maria's story of her life at Green Village, Nigel's existence in the UN compound, and the hiring practices of private companies revealed the different ways in which intervention projects are fuelled by and reflect global inequalities and hierarchies of life.

The privileging of Western knowledge and representations of *the Self* and *the Other* within binary systems of power and domination were central to an international project in Afghanistan that justified violence to achieve peace. Strikingly, many of the interveners in Chapters 5 and 6 spoke of Afghans and Afghanistan as barbaric and primitive as if these racist and colonial perceptions were objective truth. The assumed superiority of external actors and the solutions they brought became their reality even as they simultaneously acknowledged having little knowledge about the context in which they found themselves. In addition, some of the interveners, like Hannah, Kamini, Jeffery, and Susan, did not go unscathed by the violence and contradictions of the intervention. Paradoxically, the discourse and practice of liberal intervention in Afghanistan engendered the same problems it claimed to be addressing.

Contesting security and development

Recognition of the diverse understandings of security and development presented here are commonly absent from international policy and discourse on

Afghanistan. My research contributes to these critiques by considering the impacts of intervention policy and practice, and the different ways in which local communities understand security and development and the relationship between them. At times, the perspectives of locals on the meaning of security and development did not completely diverge from those put forward by political, military, and aid actors, although there were some clear differences. For many external actors, development tended to be perceived as a process of transformation or modernisation. According to most of the community residents in both Qarabagh and Behsud, development was equated with investment in the area, not a process of fundamentally transforming their way of life or value systems. In this regard, very little development was actually being achieved by the intervention. The district residents' elucidations of security were much more complex than the *us vs. them* rhetoric of the GWOT and that characterised the international policy discourse and public statements made at the outset of the intervention. A variety of understandings amongst a diverse group of actors transcended organisational affiliations and local-vs.-international binaries. While security and development were connected in various ways throughout the book, rarely did those linkages reflect the presupposed logic of the security–development nexus and liberal peacebuilding projects. As a result, many felt forced to operate within the frameworks even that did not respond to the realities they observed in their everyday lives.

One of the ongoing struggles documented in this book is a conflation of humanitarian, development, and military agendas. This is complicated by the practices of agencies who are doing multiple types of projects work without acknowledging the contradictions. In fact, several aid agencies discussed in Chapters 3 and 5 were contractually tied to the counterinsurgency agenda and were undertaking development projects while also sitting on forums advocating for the protection of humanitarian space and independence. The claim to uphold humanitarian values also allowed some agencies to side-step central government officials and regulations, thus reducing an already low level of accountability to Afghan actors. These practices cannot just be attributed to dissonance, but spoke to a level of intellectual dishonesty which few participants acknowledged. Recently, discussions on the development–humanitarian nexus have attempted to frame the explicit association of the two as necessary and desirable. It is difficult not to hear echoes of the security–development nexus debates outlined in this book. One must wonder how likely it is that the problems highlighted in the stories here – poor communication with communities, negation of local experiences, dishonesty, and the lack of accountability of agencies that were double-dipping, and violence – will characterise, and even be intensified, in the explicit merging of humanitarianism and development in other conflict-affected spaces. Indeed, a repeat of the short-term amnesia and revisionist history of the donor governments, international organisations, and aid agencies that has characterised much of their engagement with Afghanistan is unlikely to increase the potential for peace and better quality of life. This is an area where further and future research is needed and could make an important contribution.

Connected subjectivities

The everyday space of intervention that this volume presents is one in which interests and practices are connected but can also diverge, where the realms of reason and realities collide, and in which rationalisation and policy representations frequently seeks to conceal the messiness of practice and the damaging consequences of technologies of control, paths of resistance, and moments of silence. It is important to note that the subjectivities in the book were on one level often oppositional, but on another were connected to each other, and speak to the positionalities, linkages, and commonalities between actors. This relational montage of perception and practice is demonstrated in various ways in the book. First, the thinking of different actors sometimes converged in surprising ways. For example, in Chapter 6, the military and community residents shared a more intimate understanding of the everyday violence than the civilian NGO staff did. This shared outlook can be explained by the two sets of actors' previous conflict experiences, in addition to the fact that violence, direct and implied, also underscored many of their contemporary interactions with each other. Second, the circulation of knowledge amongst *thought communities* demonstrated the intersubjectivity of experiences apparent at times in understanding of the everyday context. The interviews with embassy and UN officials in Chapter 2 highlighted the ways in which knowledge was circulated. Most expatriates had very little first-hand experience with Afghan people outside of work situations. This was due to several factors, including the restricted movement of foreign actors outside of urban areas, the frequent dismissal of local knowledge, and learning about the environment, and the physical and cultural resistance of Afghans to external forces. As a result, certain ideas became validated as they were circulated and reproduced within groups of people sharing the same spaces. Examples included above were numerous and included not only how interveners perceived local actors, but the community residents and local aid workers views of interveners expressed in Chapter 2 and 6.

Third, the logic through which subjects understood themselves was connected to the practices and logics of others. Numerous examples are given in the book, such as the avoidance of the NGO guesthouse by aid workers because of the presence of military personnel in Chapter 4, the attendance of local *shura* members at local government meetings in Chapter 5, and the meeting practices described in Chapter 6. Discursive representations of the environment were paired with everyday practices which served to create and reinforce boundaries between groups. Chapter 3, for example, detailed the process through which civilian and military actors defined themselves in relation to each other. The aid agencies positioned on the high echelons of the hierarchy also claimed to have a deeper knowledge of the environment and the right to a moral imperative, symbolised through the Code of Conduct. These divisions revealed the dynamics at play between different groups whereby the act of distancing was meant to legitimise certain organisations, and in so doing these practices represented claims to power.

Everyday violence

The analysis and the stories in this book bring everyday violence to the forefront. One of the main contributions of the research is its presentation of the nuanced yet pervasive nature of everyday violence in Afghanistan, which impacted everyone in this book, myself included, and their relationships with each other. In the stories presented there are multiple layers of violence within one space that were interlinked and fuelled each other in different ways. Death, distrust, and a loss of control and loss of honour are part of the everyday life of all actors: the violence of social engineering, the destruction and displacement of communities, violence against women, military operations, attacks against aid workers, street fights, civilian casualties, criminal activity, conflicts between community members and communities, community riots, night raids on NGO offices, and the effects of improvised explosive devices on bodies and minds are all present. These are not one-off events, but are part of the environment of conflict and intervention. Very few actors discussed in the book understood violence as a 'new normal' (Woodward, 2009), a commonly used concept in conflict research. Even though no one in the book denied the existence of violence was part of their everyday life, the impact of it was not neutralised. Rather the pervasive everyday violence was inescapable, disruptive, frightening and difficult to process. Indeed, the research furthers our understanding not only of the typologies of violence in conflict-affected spaces, but of everyday violence and its impact of the lives and relationships of the people who occupy the spaces subjected to intervention.

Tactics and resistance

A key contribution of this volume is its nuanced exploration the everyday tactics of resistance employed by subjects within Afghanistan. The site of the intervention is a negotiated space where the different strategies, discourses, and practices of authority are met, absorbed, and resisted. The tactics that are at play speak to the different types of relationships that are forged amongst the actors, the tools they have at their disposal, and the diverse circulation of power. Chapters 4, 5, and 6 highlight various tactics, spanning from co-option and manipulation to subversion, used by groups and individuals in response to the structures of the intervention, the programmes that were implemented, and other actors. One of the main tactics used was to try to control and manipulate the information that was shared. This was apparent in the interactions between civilian and military actors in Kabul and the PRTs, between Afghan NGO staff and the expatriate management, and between district residents and the military. By constraining knowledge, actors sought to maintain power and to prevent even well-meaning actors from interfering in their everyday. The stories in Qarabagh and Behsud explored how residents attempted to co-opt programmes, such as the so-called 'hybrid' NSP and the ACAP. Unsurprisingly, in a situation marked by increasing violence. Some residents chose to use violence or the threat of violence as a means of resistance to further destruction in their area. This was a constantly negotiated process, whereby the discourse and tools of the intervention weighed heavily on the reality of actors but were also contested by them.

Our understanding of community resistance must heed two other important findings. First, resistance was not only apparent against the products and structures of the Western-driven intervention. Residents spoke of their efforts to confront armed opposition groups, corrupt government officials, and local power holders in their areas and others. Qarabagh residents, for example, created their own patrols to keep the village safe from all outsiders, including Afghan ones; while in Behsud, they contested the decisions of local government officials. The communities faced challenges from numerous violent and extractive forces, including aid agencies, security forces, and government officials, which produced frustration and anger and different forms of defiance. Second, resistance did not always take an active form. As Jabri (2013, p. 13) points out, even 'the claim to resist … itself is a political act, 'in which the subject constitutes itself as a force to be reckoned with'. In Qarabagh, for example, residents had decided they would not leave their homes again, as they had done several times before. They planned to stay in the area despite the disruption to community life from the nearby military operations and the high employment and lack of government investment in the area. For those residents and many other Afghans, resistance is everyday survival.

Lastly, studies have called into question the exclusive lifestyle of interveners in post-conflict missions (Austerre, 2010, 2014). The analysis tends to link such behaviour to Western entitlement and deems it as reflective of the boundaries that are created between the interveners and locals. In Afghanistan, there was indeed an expatriate 'bubble' which was inaccessible to most Afghans. There was also, however, concerted efforts by Afghans to prevent outsiders, interveners in particular, from coming into their private spaces. This book offers numerous examples of the distancing tactics used by Afghan NGO staff and community residents to defend Afghan communities from violent intrusions, to curb the practices of expatriate NGO and UN staff and management, and to safeguard their way of life and culture. This was not only a question of resisting the occupation. These practices also reflect the values of the communities and residents in the book, which challenges the assumption made by several interveners that Afghans also subscribe to the racial and global hierarchies that they did: that a belief in Western superiority is a shared and neutral truth rather than historically based and contextually constructed. These local distancing practices are rarely discussed in academic texts, which focus on the intervening groups – civilian and military staff in the diplomatic, administrative, private and aid sector – and conceptualise power as uni-directional.

Moreover, local leadership mistrusted many of the interveners that came to the communities, military and civilian. In Chapter 6 the *shuras* used hidden tactics by framing information to encourage further assistance to their area. As the local NGO worker said, 'they were always asking for more'. Shura members, however, had a heightened awareness of the self-interested and time-bound nature of whatever material or financial resources interveners brought with them. Therefore, the communities played the same game using means that would maximise their benefit while the interveners were still occupying their country in large numbers. This is something interveners struggled to understand and sometimes served to reinforce perceptions of the local community and leaders as dishonest and corrupt, which characterise many of the negative intervener comments in Chapter 3 and 6. They often failed to acknowledge, however, how the structures they belonged to and their own actions produced the practices they critiqued. Ultimately, the construction of intervention as having emancipatory effects made it difficult to understand the communities' subversion of aid assistance as resistance. Why resist the saviours?

There were many different power relations at play in the book and different motivations for contesting power and authority. Actors were also self-interested and sometimes resisting one actor was a means to consolidate power, often at the expense of others. This is an important insight that is highlighted in several chapters but particularly the district stories in Chapter 4 and 5. Local leadership in both districts used their power to benefit personally from the aid projects in their villages. Indeed, people engaged in practices for personal material advancement. In Qarabagh, for example, families in the LAS were constantly put at a disadvantage because the *shura* control the work rotation system. Residents also tried to gain from the aid that was provided. The political and emotional complexity of individuals, particularly of local actors, and the complex and uneven manifestation of power in everyday spaces is often left uninterrogated by scholars. Not all acts of resistance are in service of emancipatory aims or community survival. To strip actors of the range of desires which they may hold is another act of essentialisation which limits rather than furthers our understanding of the lived experience of conflict and intervention.

Affect and dissonance

An important contribution of this book is its exploration of affect and emotion as everyday practices. To understand the landscape of intervention, the stories in this volume paint a picture that refuses to strip subjects of their political and emotional agency, depth, desires, contradictions, and dynamism. Human interactions are complex, and conflict-affected environments are more complex and intense still. Therefore, the challenge is to unravel the material, discursive, and emotional intricacies, while being cautious of dismissing complexity for the sake of making easy theoretical claims. This does not mean that one cannot talk about the violence of the intervention, global hierarchies, or colonial legacies. Indeed, these are recurrent themes in the book and reflect the manifestation of grand strategy level power in everyday relationships. Rather it meant recognising the complex interplay of emotional practices that underpin hierarchies of power across this diverse social and political landscape. While many of the emotional expressions in the book were troubling or negative even hateful there were also strong friendships and family bonds formed in several of the chapters. These practices were essential to the survival of individuals and communities.

A further theme throughout the book is the internal conflicts *within* individuals themselves. The frustration displayed by some aid actors reflects the disconnect that occurred whereby actors were engaged in practices that they recognised as contradictory to what they saw and believed. Dissonance allowed them to continue to engage in these activities. This was significant because, through this process, actors actually reproduced knowledge about the environment in which they worked and reinforced the way that security and development and perceptions of *the Other* had been framed. Therefore, a widening chasm was created between discourse and the everyday experiences of different actors. Consequently, the story of the intervention in Afghanistan was reproduced by a number of people who on some level did not believe in the tale of the liberal peace that they themselves reproduced daily. This dissonance allowed actors to invest in a reality that deemed their everyday practices as necessary, even when those actions had damaging outcomes. But dissonance also served another function.

While dissonance may have provided temporary relief, many of the organisations and people I encountered during the project were struggling with an internal crisis, in which the environment constantly challenged their belief system but they were unwilling to or unable to find an alternative. Contesting their constructed reality was inconceivable for many because it would have required confronting not only their role in a violent intervention, but also their role in global hierarchies of power and domination, which were fundamental to the construction of their identity, careers, and purpose. Their vision of the world was based on the knowledge that maintained the global hierarchies of power and reinforced binary categorisations between those with the right to intervene and those who are the target of intervention. Dissonance and discrimination are used as defensive tools in the face of a stark contradictory reality than the one many of the interveners wanted to invest in. The stories in this book unravel the consequences of these unresolvable internal battles that were reflected in the affective practices of interveners. Anger, frustration, and malaise are sprinkled throughout the book in the responses, stories, and conversations of interveners. As such the book highlights the emotionality of intervention, a topic where much more remains to be said.

A final word

Things have not gone well in Afghanistan. As this book concludes, its opening statement should not seem surprising. Since 2014, Afghanistan has witnessed increasing dependence on aid and a growth in remote management practices by NGOs, has continued to negotiate uncertain terms with a greatly reduced but continuous foreign military forces, and has experienced different iterations of a contested peace process, a brief investigation by the International Criminal

Court with an unclear outcome, and several tumultuous subsequent elections. In 2018, for the first time international and pro-government security forces were responsible for more civilian causalities than anti-government forces (UNAMA, 2019). The country continues to face an increasingly unpredictable future. At present, both Qarabagh and Behsud have witnessed increased levels of insecurity, and armed fighting and are, at least in part, no longer regarded as accessible to many civilian aid agencies and the UN. People, however, continue to build relationships, contest and confront each other, and struggle – perhaps less so under the banner of security and development, but now for survival and some version of peace.

This study began in 2009 when I, a recent former aid worker, pondered how to craft the questions that occurred to me daily over the last few years into a coherent research project which allowed for further investigation of the everyday realities of intervention projects. While at Kabul International Airport waiting for my flight home, I was again struck by how different the airport looked compared to 2005, when I first arrived in Kabul. Though not a fancy airport by any means, back then it was a simple structure without the VIP lounges, cafés, and duty-free shopping kiosks that I walked by this time. A new airport road had also been constructed since then. It was paved, with multiple lanes separated by a concrete median dotted with trees. I suppose for some this was 'development'. The frequent attacks on the road, however, were a sign of increasing insecurity and violence. Development and security were constructed and contested in various ways in this environment, but they were not inextricably linked in the context of a violent intervention.

It was common for expatriates in Afghanistan to know each other from UN missions in Eastern Europe, Africa, or elsewhere in Asia; many of those I spoke to have since moved on to Libya, Iraq, Syria, and Somalia. The significance of the legacy of violence, dissonance, disillusionment, and even tactics of resistance that characterised the intervention in Afghanistan for many of these interveners remains unclear or even forgotten. The documentation of these stories, however, seeks to disrupt the privilege of short-term amnesia often afforded to interveners. This book does not make policy recommendations, to do so would be to simplify the complexity of the stories that I have just shared. Rather it calls for deeper reflection and greater honesty, at the institutional level, but also by individuals about the realities of intervention and the everyday practices of those who work in conflict-affected areas.

The process of carrying out this research and writing up the findings was a difficult one. At times it involved awkward conversations, tough realisations, and constant and testing self-reflection. Aside from this book, the friendships I developed, and the insights I gained about the people, the communities, and the intervention itself which are shared here; I also emerged from this project with a greater understanding of my own positionality, and history in Afghanistan, a deeper commitment to understanding the possibilities for collaboration, and greater appreciation of how difficult these endeavours can be. Some of the questions I had at the outset of the project were answered during the study but many more emerged as I left and in the years since. A number of which may never be resolved. There is a need for scholars, however, to further engage theoretically as well as through grounded methodologies to understand the different types of knowledge, resistance, and power relationships that characterise different interventions and spaces affected by violence. This would require a commitment to research and discussion outside of elite spaces. Research of this sort will allow us to gain a deeper insight into what goes on in the everyday of sites of conflict and intervention, and perhaps enhance our understanding of the possibilities for peace.

References

Autesserre, S. V. 2010. *The Trouble With the Congo: Local Violence and the Failure of International Peacebuilding*. New York, NY: Cambridge University Press.

Autesserre, S. V. 2014. *Peaceland: Conflict Resolution and the Everyday Politics of International Intervention*. New York, NY: Cambridge University Press.

Jabri, V. 2013. *The Postcolonial Subject: Claiming Politics/Governing Others in Late Modernity*. Abingdon: Routledge.

UNAMA. 2019. Afghanistan: *Annual Report on Protection of Civilians in Armed Conflict, 2018*. Kabul: UNAMA Human Rights Unit.

Woodward, S. L. 2009. Shifts in global security policies: Why they matter for the South. In 'Inclusive Peace and Security'. *IDS Bulletin*, 49(1A). Brighton: IDS. April 2018

Appendices

Appendix 1: List of interviews, focus groups, workshops, and sited conversations

Individual interviews (I)

Jalalabad City

1 2011, Youth Association, Jalalabad City
2 2011, UNAMA, Jalalabad
3 2011, UN Staff, Jalalabad
4 2011, Development Corporation, Jalalabad
5 2011, Development Corporation, Jalalabad
6 2011, Telephone, PRT, December
7 2011, Military Officer – PRT, Behsud
8 2011, NGO, Staff member – A Jalalabad City
9 2011, NGO, Staff member – B, Jalalabad City
10 NGO, Staff member, Jalalabad City

Behsud District

11 2011, Local Government, Behsud Centre
12 2011, Local Police, Behsud Centre
13 2011, Female Shura, Walayti
14 2011, Female, Walayti
15 2011, Female, Walayti
16 2011, Malik, Walayti
17 2011, Female, Shura, Balandghar
18 2011, Elder and NSP Shura, Balandghar
19 2011, Elder, Samarkhalil
20 2011, NSP Shura, Taghar
21 2011, NSP Shura, Qasimabad
22 2011, Shura, Ada

Kabul City

23 2010, Inter-Governmental Agency, Staff, Kabul

24 2010, Afghan Government, International Advisor, Kabul
25 2010, Afghan Government, Official, Kabul
26 2010, ISAF Senior Civilian, Staff, Kabul
27 2010, UN, Kabul
28 2010, NGO, Director, Kabul
29 2011, NGO Director, Kabul
30 2010, UN, Senior Staff, Kabul
31 2010, ISAF/DFID, Civilian, Kabul
32 2010, UN Agency, Civil Military Co-ordinator, Kabul
33 2010, DFID, Kabul
34 2010, UN Mission, Senior Representative, Kabul
35 2010, NGO, Director, Kabul
36 2011, Embassy, Political Official, Kabul
37 2011, ISAF Civilian, Kabul
38 2011, UN Agency, Staff, Kabul
39 2011, Embassy, Political Official, Kabul
40 2011, Diplomat, Staff, Kabul
41 2011, ISAF HQ, Kabul
42 2011, Afghan Government, Senior Official, Kabul
43 2011, USAID, Senior Official, Kabul
44 2011, Embassy – Political, Kabul
45 2011, Embassy – Political, Kabul
46 2011, European Commission, Political Official, Kabul
47 2011, Member of Parliament – Female, Kabul
48 2011, Afghan Public Sector Reform Agency, Senior Official, Kabul
49 2011, Embassy, Political Official, Kabul
50 2011, Embassy, Political Official, Kabul
51 2011, ISAF, Kabul
52 2011, NGO, Political Mandate, Kabul
53 2011, NGO, Staff member, Kabul
54 2011, Afghan Women's NGO, Director, Kabul
55 2011, Afghan NGO Co-ordinating Body, Director, Kabul
56 2011, Afghan NGO Network, Director, Kabul
57 2011, NGO, Director, Kabul
58 2011, NGO, Director, Kabul
59 2011, NGO, Staff member, Kabul
60 2011, ISAF Joint Command, Civilian, Kabul
61 2011, Afghan Independent Body, Senior Official, Kabul
62 2011, Afghan Ministry of Justice, Senior Judge, Kabul
63 2011, ISAF, Senior Military Officer, Kabul
64 2011, Turkish PRT, Political Official, Kabul
65 2011, Ex-ISAF PRT, Military, Kabul
66 2011, British Embassy, Political Official, Kabul
67 2011, Doctor, INGO (Former ICRC), Kabul
68 2011, NGO, Mazar-based-Kabul

69 2011, ISAF, Senior Civilian Official, Kabul
70 2011, Afghan Directorate for Local Government, Senior Official, Kabul
71 2011, Development Corporation Senior Manager, Kabul
72 2011, UN Agency, Staff, Kabul

Qarabagh District

73 2011, District Administrator, Qarabagh Shar
74 2011, District Administrator Assistant, Qarabagh Shar
75 2011, Chief of Police, Qarabagh Shar
76 2011, Deputy Chief of Police, Qarabagh Shar
77 2011, District Hospital, Female Doctor, Qarabagh Shar
78 2011, Local Malik, Betaniyar
79 2011, Elder, Dawoodzai
80 2011, NSP Shura, Baghalam
81 2011, CDC Deputy, Baghalam
82 2011, Shopkeeper, Baghalam
83 2011, Farmer, Denarkhalil
84 2011, Religious Leader, Denarkhalil
85 2011, Local Shura – Alar, Qarabagh Shar
86 2011, Local Shura – Baghareq, Qarabagh Shar

North America and Europe

87 2010, INGO, Director, Geneva

Focus groups (F)

Behsud District

1 2011, Female, Walayti
2 2011, Male, Walayti
3 2011, Youth, Walayti
4 2011, Female Shura, Balandghar
5 2011, Local Shura, Balandghar
6 2011, Youth, Balandghar
7 2011, Male, Balandghar
8 2011, Male, Samarkhalil
9 2011, Youth Shura, Samarkhalil
10 2011, Male, Taghar
11 2011, Male, Qasimabad
12 2011, Shura, Ada
13 2011, Male, Ada

Kabul City

14 2011, Afghan Youth Civil Society Network, Kabul

15 2011, Afghan Women Civil Society Network, Kabul
16 2011, Member of Parliament – Male, Kabul

Qarabagh District

17 2011, Female Health Professionals, Group A, Qarabagh Shar
18 2011, Female Health Professionals, Group B, Qarabagh Shar
19 2011, Youth, Dawoodzai
20 2011, Female, Dawoodzai
21 2011, Male, Dawoodzai
22 2011, Female, Qal'eh-ye-Bibi
23 2011, Mixed NSP and Local Shura, Qal'eh-ye-Bibi
24 2011, NSP Shura, Qal'eh-ye Baz
25 2011, Male Group A, Ashrafkhalil
26 2011, Male Group B, Ashrafkhalil
27 2011, Male, Baghalam
28 2011, Male Group A, Denarkhalil
29 2011, Male Group B, Denarkhalil
30 2011, Local Elders, Denarkhalil
31 2011, Youth, Denarkhalil
32 2011, Mixed NSP and Local Shura, Barikap
33 2011, Female Shura, Barikap
34 2011, Mixed Male and Female Youth Group, Barikap
35 2011, Mixed NSP and Local Shura, Alasghan
36 2011, Female Shura, Alasghan
37 2011, Local Shura – Langar and Akhundzada, Qarabagh Shar

Workshops (W)

Jalalabad City

1 2011, NGO Group A, Jalalabad, 9 September
2 2011, Local NGO Group B, Jalalabad, September

Kabul City

3 2011, NGO Kabul-based, with staff from several offices in Europe in attendance, Kabul, 9 June

North America and Europe

4 2010, Mixed Group Practitioners and Academics, 20th Academic Council on the United Nations System ACUNS) Summer Workshop: Civil–Military Relations in Peace Missions, Geneva, 26 July
5 2009, NATO Stabilisation Workshop, Norfolk, August

Conversations and meeting specifically cited (C)[1]

Jalalabad City

6 2011, Military, Behsud, July
7 2011, Aid Worker, Jalalabad, July

Kabul City

8 2010, European Commission, Kabul, November and December
9 2011, International Organisation, Researcher, March
10 2011, Meeting, NGO Co-ordination, Kabul, March
11 2011, NGO, Staff member, Kabul, June
12 2011, Former Head of UN agency, Kabul, July and November
13 2011, NGO, Staff Member, Jalalabad, September
14 2011, Intergovernmental Organisation, Staff, Kabul
15 2010, UN Mission Staff, Kabul, November
16 2010, NGO Staff member, Kabul, November
17 2010, International Organisation, Researcher, Kabul, February
18 2010 and 2011, NGO Worker, Qarabagh and Kabul – Divya
19 2011, Youth Male, Qarabagh and Qal'eh-ye Baz – Mohammed
20 2011, Aid Worker and Contractor, Various and Kabul – Sarah
21 2011, UN Staff, Kabul, June – Jeffery
22 2011, UN Staff, Kabul – Neel
23 2011, USAID/PRT Staff, Kabul – Jonathan
24 2011, Multiple, Kabul Dinner, Field Notes and Observations, Kabul, May
25 2010, Communications Consultant, Kabul – Jenny
26 2010 and 2011, UN Staff, Kabul – Nigel
27 2011, Contractor, Kabul – Maria
28 2011, Advisor, Kabul – Kamini
29 2011, International Organisation, Kabul – Suzanne
30 2011, International Organisation, Kabul – Catherine

Note

1 These conversations were directly cited in the text but it should be noted that many conversations with various actors informed this book although they have not been directly cited.

Index

Page numbers in **bold** denote tables, those in *italics* denote figures.

For Product Safety Concerns and Information please contact our EU representative GPSR@taylorandfrancis.com Taylor & Francis Verlag GmbH, Kaufingerstraße 24, 80331 München, Germany